THE CANADIAN LEFT

A Critical Analysis

THE CANADIAN LEFT

A Critical Analysis

WITHDRAWN

Norman Penner

PRENTICE-HALL OF CANADA, LTD. SCARBOROUGH, ONTARIO

To Norma

HX
106
P45

DEC 5 '78

Canadian Cataloguing in Publication Data

Penner, Norman, 1921—
  The Canadian left

Bibliography: p.
Includes index.
ISBN 0-13-113126-5 pa.

1. Socialism in Canada—History. 2. Communism—
Canada—History. I. Title.

HX106.P45   335'.00971   C77-001192-6

Prentice-Hall, Inc., Englewood Cliffs, New Jersey
Prentice-Hall of Australia, Pty., Ltd., Sydney
Prentice-Hall of India Pvt., Ltd., New Delhi
Prentice-Hall International, Inc., London
Prentice-Hall of Japan, Inc., Tokyo
Prentice-Hall of Southeast Asia (PTE.) Ltd., Singapore

Design: Julian Cleva

ISBN 0-13-113126-5

1 2 3 4 5 W 81 80 79 78 77

Printed and bound in Canada by Webcom Limited

CONTENTS

Frequently Used Abbreviations

ACCL All-Canadian Congress of Labour
AFL American Federation of Labor
CC Central Committee of the Communist Party of Canada
CCCL Canadian Catholic Confederation of Labour
CCF Co-operative Commonwealth Federation
CCL Canadian Congress of Labour
CEC Central Executive Committee of the Communist Party of Canada
CI Communist International
CIO Congress of Industrial Organizations
CLC Canadian Labour Congress
CLP Canadian Labour Party
Comintern Communist International
CPC Communist Party of Canada
CPSU Communist Party of the Soviet Union
ECCI Executive Committee of the Communist International
GGG Grain Growers' Guide
ILP Independent Labor Party
IWW Industrial Workers of the World
LPP Labor-Progressive Party
LSR League for Social Reconstruction
NDP New Democratic Party
NPL Non-Partisan League
OBU One Big Union
RILU Red International of Labor Unions
SDPC Social-Democratic Party of Canada
SPC Socialist Party of Canada
SPNA Socialist Party of North America
WUL Workers' Unity League

CHAPTER ONE

INTRODUCTION

When craftsmen from Britain began to pour into Canada at the end of the nineteenth and beginning of the twentieth century they brought more than their industrial skills with them. They brought a trade union consciousness from a country where the labor movement was already highly developed, and many also came with socialist ideas, which they proceeded to implant on Canadian soil. Socialist ideas also came at the same time from the United States, and somewhat later immigrant laborers from Eastern and Central Europe added to the strength of socialism in Canada.

By this time, socialism was a world idea, described by O. D. Skelton in his 1911 work on the subject, as "the most remarkable international political movement in history, commanding the adherence of eight million voters representing every civilized country under the sun."[1]

Modern socialism was an outgrowth of the industrial revolution, which had originated in Britain and then spread to Europe and America. It appeared as an ideology that expressed the aims and concerns of the industrial proletariat, the most distinctive product of this revolution. Yet socialism as a theory was not

---

[1] O. D. Skelton, *Socialism: A Critical Analysis* (Boston, 1911), p. 15.

created by workers but by some of the foremost intellectuals of the nineteenth century. It was the merging of socialist theory with the labor movement that made socialism a powerful political force, comprising mass electoral parties where democracy had begun to develop, and potent underground organizations in countries such as Tsarist Russia where absolutism had not yet been dislodged. From 1864 on, socialist parties formed international links which, while of a consultative nature only, increased the effectiveness and impact of the socialist idea on a world scale. At international congresses and bureau meetings and through publications experiences were regularly exchanged, and lively and heated debates on the application of these ideas were carried on. Socialism was perceived by its adherents as a worldwide phenomenon in which the expressions of internationalism reflected genuine fraternity among the workers of all countries.

Though there were different varieties of socialist thought, they all shared essential assumptions which were noted by Skelton:

Socialism is in the first place an indictment of any and all industrial systems based on private property and competition ... Socialism in the second aspect presents an analysis of capitalism ... From a third view-point socialism presents a substitute for capitalism ... Socialism in this aspect may be defined as the demand for collective ownership and utilization of the means of production and for distribution of the social dividend in accordance with some principle of justice ... Finally, socialism involves a campaign against capitalism ... In each of these—indictment, analysis, panacea, campaign—socialism is intelligible only as the antithesis of the competitive system. [2]

Socialism was thus understood to be a counterculture that challenged the fundamental values of capitalist society and also a political movement that aimed at replacing the capitalist mode of production, distribution, and exchange. Using Skelton's definition as a guide, this book will examine the socialist idea in its origin and genesis in Canadian society, viewing this development as an inseparable compendium of theory, agitation, and organization.

Socialism began to emerge in Canada at a time when the world movement, according to Skelton, was dominated by the

---

[2] *Socialism*, pp. 2-3.

personality and ideas of Karl Marx:

Karl Marx is the greatest name on the roll of socialism. For half a century his theories have been the intellectual backbone of the movement, and whatever modifications and more or less ingenuous reinterpretations they have undergone these later days, it is still his personality which dominates the minds of millions of his fellow men.[3]

This was certainly the case in the Canadian socialist organizations and press until 1921. Marxism was their creed; and although there were many differences within and between the socialist parties, these were not differences about Marx's ideas but about their interpretation and application. It was the Russian Revolution, and Lenin's definition of Marxism, that split the Canadian socialists along fundamental lines. Revolutionary socialism, or Communism, became the outlook of one section of the socialist movement; and following the adoption by the British Labour Party of a socialist platform in 1918, social democratic ideas evolved as the doctrine of those Canadian socialists who could not accept the revolutionary path or the dictates of the Communist International.

Although this split was triggered by international events and both wings appeared to be following external models, it ushered in a period when the socialist movement became more or less Canadian. This development was a result of the attention that socialists began to pay to Canadian conditions, as contrasted to the formative years, certainly up to the First World War, when the socialist movement paid little or no attention to the specific features and history of the society which it was proposing to transform.

The previous neglect was understandable at a time when socialism was new in Canada as were the immigrants who brought it here and who dominated the early socialist movement. These working-class men and women established the early socialist organizations without attracting any elements from the intellectual community, such as had been the case in all other countries. It was not until the First World War that a number of dissenting ministers identified with the socialist cause, and not until the thirties that they were joined by a number of academics. For a considerable period, then, socialist theory, which sub-

---

[3] *Ibid.*, p. 13.

sumed political economy, history, sociology, and philosophy, was propagated by a group of worker-intellectuals, who earned their living at their vocations, and who studied, wrote, and taught Marxism in their spare time. These early socialists were also active in the trade unions and played a substantial role in establishing the organized labor movement, and in leading it in important economic and political battles.

The rise of the socialist and labor movement was paralleled by the growth of the agrarian populist organizations. At first there was little or no connection between them, but gradually a relationship began to develop which ultimately made it possible to establish close organizational and political links between sections of the working class and the left wing of the farmers' movement.

This came about through a recognition that by the very nature of Canadian society and its dominant political culture, the radicalism of these dissident and alienated groups or classes had a common source and, by some ideological compromises, sufficient agreement could be reached in the political arena against what was presumed to be a "common foe".

Though this book is primarily a study of socialist ideas in Canada, attention had to be given to the organizational contexts in which these ideas developed. The interdependence of theory and practice is nowhere more evident than in the development of Canadian socialist thought.

Because the Canadian society into which these ideas were brought differed in important ways from the countries of their origins, it is necessary to say something about the Canadian society and how adaptations came to be made in the imported ideas as a result of their interaction with the specificities of Canadian political culture.

Little is said in most of the book about the development of the socialist idea in French Canada, although quite a bit is said about the attempts of the main socialist organizations in English Canada to come to grips with the nature of French-Canadian society and to win adherents to the socialist idea. All these attempts failed for a number of reasons which can only be briefly sketched for want of a more basic analysis which it is impossible to attempt here.

In contrast to English Canada, into which socialist ideas were imported by immigrants, and in which there was constant cultural contact with the source of their ideas, French Canada was cut off from France prior to the French Revolution and remained so. The victory of clerical absolutism in Quebec made it possible to treat socialism there as a forbidden doctrine, expurgated from universities, colleges, schools, and even from a large segment of the labor movement. All this changed after 1960, and all forms of socialist thought and action are now widely discussed and practiced there.

One of the central objects of this book is to integrate the history of the various socialist movements, to show their continuity as well as their differences. In spite of conflicts between socialists that at times became quite savage, the socialist parties and groups have interacted with each other and have made their respective contributions to the impact of the socialist idea in Canadian political thought.

The socialist idea has been evolving during most of the period since the birth of the modern Canadian state in 1867, and by now can be accurately considered as an indigenous part of the Canadian ideological spectrum. This at least is the contention of this book, and the documentary evidence presented bears this out.

CHAPTER TWO

THE SHAPING OF CANADIAN IDEOLOGY

Socialism appeared in the nineteenth century as a challenge to the prevailing capitalist system and its values. It opposed the whole concept of private property and unlimited appropriation. Against liberal individualism based on private ownership of the means of labor it set collectivism and the idea that the means of labor must belong to society for the social good. It posited a conception of man as a cooperator rather than a competitor. Everywhere socialism appeared it took on more and more the elements of a counterculture, gathering around it the disaffected and alienated members of society.

Yet in spite of the universal features of socialism, there developed differences in every country reflecting varied traditions, culture, political history, and class structure. This was certainly true for Canada. Socialist ideas came to Canada mainly from Britain and the United States, and to some extent from Central and Eastern Europe. They were brought here by working-class immigrants and also through the socialist literature imported from abroad. To explore Canadian socialism one must look at the interaction between socialists in Canada and the institutional and ideological framework already entrenched in Canada by the time socialism began to develop here.

To do this it is necessary to survey the main themes in Canadian political thought in their origin and genesis. It will then be possible to give a detailed treatment of how socialism, communism, and social democracy reacted to and influenced the principal political currents in Canadian society.

The main ideological themes of Canadian society bear the heavy imprint of the confluence of the three great empires that have shaped so much of Canadian development: the French, the British, and the American. Though Canada has drawn its people from all parts of the world, its political thought has been derived almost exclusively from those empires as a result of military, financial, institutional, and a multitude of other tangible as well as intangible connections. It was the British army that established the institutional and ideological framework of Canada in the wake of conquest, and that opened the country to British capital, British merchants, and British landowners, to fashion a political society agreeable to the laws and customs of England. It had to impose this framework on a society which was already in existence and whose values, language, religion, social and economic structure were completely different. Moreover, no sooner had this process begun than the British authorities had to contend with the American Revolution and the consequent emergence of a radical society in North America in revolt against the British system, challenging its ideas and positing a whole set of new ones.

It took a hundred years for the modern Canadian state to take shape out of these contradictory forces and pressures. Their resolution in the British North America Act of 1867 concluded a long period of domestic controversy and conflict in which external circumstances merged with local conditions to produce a political system that was distinctive as well as derivative.

The Predominance of Toryism

The British decision, expressed in the Quebec Act of 1775, to rule their newest acquisition in North America in cooperation with the remnants of the ruling elite of New France powerfully reinforced the Toryism of the British authorities with the clerical absolutism of *l'ancien régime*. This alienated both the English-speaking merchants who had been promised an elective assembly, and the French-speaking habitants who had looked to the British to free them from the onerous exactions of the tithes to the Church and the feudal rents to the seigneurs.

The conservative stance of the colonial rulers brought to the fore elements of resistance and protest among both the new English-speaking and the French-speaking population. The dominant ruling ideology was imperial, Tory, conservative, and the opposition to it was democratic, liberal, and radical. The ruling ideology was reinforced by the immigration of United Empire Loyalists immediately after the American Revolution, by the War of 1812, and by the defeat of the Rebellions of 1837 and 1838. On the other hand, the powerful currents of social upheaval throughout the Western world, and especially the victory of the American Revolution, gave sustenance to the democratic elements in Canadian society. A number of writers stress the impact of the open frontier, with its spirit of localism and independence, on the mentality of the North American settlers including *les habitants*.[1]

Except for the exodus of Loyalists in the period immediately after the American Revolution, most of the immigrants from the United States came not out of rejection of the American values but in search of free land. In the period between 1788 and 1812, the population of Upper Canada grew to 75,000,

... of which number about one fifth were Loyalists and their children, a lesser number British immigrants and their children, and the remainder non-Loyalist Americans. Apart from the Loyalist movement into Upper Canada, after the Revolutionary War, it was chiefly one common westward movement of land seekers which peopled both the British province and the neighbouring American territory.[2]

The presence in the population of two American elements, one Loyalist and the other not, had an important effect on the political culture of Upper Canada (and in the other British North American colonies as well).

The Loyalists tended to reinforce the Tory ideology of British rule. S. D. Clark contends that this aspect of their ideological outlook became even stronger after the War of 1812.

The War gave to the Loyalists a new self-consciousness and a new sense of their importance, which quickly made them a powerful

---

[1] See S. D. Clark, *Movements of Political Protest in Canada 1640-1840* (Toronto, 1959).

[2] Fred Landon, *Western Ontario and the American Frontier* (Toronto, 1967), p. 1.

conservative force in Upper Canadian politics in a way that they had never been before. Through their influence toryism became a much more distinctive creed of the ruling class, in politics, religion, and social life generally.[3]

These forces of conservatism in Canada drew strength not just from the local colonial administration but from its source, Britain, where at this period, "Toryism was very much in the ascendancy" and "the political conservatism of the mother country offered direct support to the political conservatism of the colonial population".[4]

But following the collapse of Tory power in Britain with the victory of the reform movement there, the roles underwent a change. Instead of the local Tory elements acting at the behest of the governors appointed by the British government, these governors began more and more to act as creatures of the local entrenched interest. And when the local Tory power collapsed in the face of the growing popular support for the reform movements in Upper and Lower Canada, the British army had to step in on behalf of local conservatism, which it regarded as the only reliable bastion of British colonial rule.

Thus two tendencies of importance in Canadian history made themselves felt at this time. First, the change in the political culture of Britain did not change the political culture in the colony. Britain, now moving towards democratic liberalism at home, supported the elements that were fighting democratic liberalism in her Canadian colony. Henceforth, Canadian Toryism was to develop as a self-generating ideology, in conflict with the local forces of democracy, and taking on distinctive characteristics in response to local circumstances. Second, the local Tory elite was able to make use of the British colonial connection to bolster its hold on the privileged positions of domestic power. More and more it found it useful, if not vital, to maintain the forms, together with some of the substance, of colonialism as an instrument of self-protection. It extolled the old British values, clung to a Burkean emphasis on constituted authority, was conservative about social change, and upheld hierarchical privilege and tradition.

The democratic elements, on the other hand, drew considerable ideological support from the American and French Revolutions (including the French revolutions of the nineteenth cen-

---

[3] S. D. Clark, *Movements of Political Protest*, p. 247.
[4] *Ibid.*, p. 251.

tury), and from the Chartist movement which was in direct contact with the reformers of Upper and Lower Canada. They included sections of the rising middle class of merchants, artisans, professionals, and farmers. Their numbers were constantly expanding through immigration of dispossessed peasants, skilled and semi-skilled workers from the British Isles, and farmers, traders and merchants from the United States. The bulk of the immigration during the first half of the nineteenth century tended to strengthen the forces of democracy and radicalism in Canada.

An important feature of the immigration from England, Scotland, and the United States was the large numbers among these immigrants who were members of dissentient religious groups and who regarded the established position of the Church of England in Upper Canada as odious.

The concept of political society that the Reform movement epitomized shows a mixture of classical liberalism with the populism of a frontier agrarian society. The reformers wanted small and cheap government, universal suffrage, abolition of non-elected ruling bodies, control over finances by the elected representatives, disestablishment of the Church, public education, elimination of land monopolies and absentee landholding, free trade, local government, good roads, and an end to hereditary titles and ranks.

The democrats in Lower Canada had similar demands, together with resentment over the maintenance of feudal and clerical exactions. The granting of an elected assembly by the Constitutional Act of 1791 provided an arena for the newly emerging *petit-bourgeois* class to become the political leaders of the *Canadien* community. As one writer has put it:

This assembly, elected through a semi-universal male suffrage by a French Canadian electorate which was mainly rural, very quickly opposed itself to an executive on which it was not represented, and which was aimed at establishing bases for British colonization. In a country in which the oligarchy is not even of the same nationality as the majority, the demand for the rights of the majority becomes at the same time a national demand.[5]

It was this group, made up mainly of "the professional bourgeoisie", that, according to another writer, played the principal

---

[5] Jean-Paul Bernard, *Les Rouges, Liberalisme, Nationalisme, et Anti-Clericalisme au mileu du XIX siecle* (Montreal, 1971), p. 11.

role in the period following 1791 of defining the nature of the French-Canadian "collectivity". It made its own demands and conditions the general definition of that society, and

... *in their opposition to the commercial bourgeoisie (who were predominantly British) and to the competitive society, the most radical of the (French-Canadian) bourgeoisie, quickly moved in the direction of radical ideologies.*[6]

It was because of this radicalism that the Roman Catholic clergy soon became the principal adversary of the petit-bourgeoisie.

Before 1837, the opposition of a large fraction of the clergy to democratic tendencies already manifested itself. This can be doubtless explained by the necessity of the Church to constantly demonstrate its loyalty to a colonial government which had maintained its authority in the Society. It was also a long survival among the Priests, of the mentality of the old Regime. But one can also suggest that between the professional class and the clergy, lay a class conflict. Here were two groupings who by the training of its members, their respective roots in the populace, their types of power and prestige, had to oppose each other in a whole manner of means.[7]

Thus the democratic bourgeoisie in its various institutional forms, whether as *les Patriotes, le Parti Rouge*, or *l'Institut Canadien*, became strongly opposed to the political role of the clergy, and produced a powerful movement of anti-clericalism that was defeated in 1870, but which up to that time had made a deep impression on Quebec society:

An intellectual, liberal, and anti-clerical bourgeoisie was in opposition to the whole of the clergy. There is a tendency in French-Canada to ignore the extent to which the Canadian clergy was rudely attacked by the newspapers, pamphlets, and even by the whole of a political party, during nearly half a century. Inspired by the great republican ideas, and the liberal philosophy of England, France, and the United States, our intelligentsia reproached the clergy at the same time with its obscurantism, its authoritarianism,

---

[6] Fernand Dumont, "Quelques Reflexions d'Ensemble" in Dumont, Montmorency, Hamelin (eds.), *Ideologies du Canada Français 1850-1900* (Quebec, 1971), p. 2.

[7] *Ibid.*, p. 6.

its monarchist spirit and its loyalty to England.[8]

The claim has been made by some English and French-Canadian historians that the Québécois preferred the agricultural life because of their Catholic faith, whereas the English, because they were already imbued with the spirit of capitalism implicit in Protestantism, were able to take over the commercial life of Canadian society and to dominate it.

Yet New France, prior to the conquest, was predominantly a commercial colony, under the control and direction of powerful French mercantile monopolies engaged in the relentless pursuit of furs, and tolerating only the minimum amount of agricultural settlement required to maintain the fur trade. It was this commercial class that was dispossessed by the Conquest and returned to France along with the French colonial administrators, leaving behind the *Canadiens*, habitants, seigneurs and clergy. The void at the top of the economic life was quickly filled by British merchants who, having close commercial ties with British banking and wholesale institutions, took control of the fur trade and formed their own monopoly, the North West Company. By 1820 this Company merged with the other British fur trading monopoly, the Hudson's Bay Company, which went on to play a decisive role in the eventual formation of a Canadian capitalist class, on the basis of the initial capital accumulation which the profits from the fur trade had accomplished.

The lack of participation by the *Canadiens* in commercial leadership after the Conquest was not due to philosophical, ideological, or religious characteristics. It was due mainly to the fact that the French commercial élite had left the colony capital poor. The society they left behind had never been given a chance to accumulate some of the profits garnered from the fur trade.

Radicalism in Quebec

French-Canadian society, however, did not stand still after the Conquest. It had to reconstruct its élite, and re-define its ideologies in face of the fact that it was now a colony of a foreign

---

[8] Dumont and Rocher, "An Introduction to a Sociology of French Canada", in Rioux and Martin (eds.), *French-Canadian Society* (Toronto, 1969), p. 190.

power. A new bourgeoisie began to emerge, largely professional and intellectual, but anxious to participate in the economic and commercial life and even, as the economy developed, to control it. They used their control of the elected assembly to push their demands against the Council, Executive, and Governor, who were mostly English. Increasingly, as they defined their outlook, it was liberal, rational, democratic, anti-clerical, and as has been noted above, more and more radical. Their own ideological position was formed in large measure in response to the character of the opposition which combined British power, local anglophone mercantilism, ultramontanist clergy, and the rural French-Canadian landowner, *le Noblesse* or *les Seigneurs*. Thus the enlightened petty bourgeoisie of French Canada had a double struggle to wage, against British Toryism and French-Canadian clerical reaction. Their struggle against British Toryism was for admission to the seats of power, economic as well as political. Their fight with the clergy was for ideological supremacy over the French-Canadian nation.

This latter struggle produced two competing French-Canadian nationalisms: one conservative, the other radical. The defeat of the Rebellions of 1837 and 1838 strengthened conservative nationalism at the expense of the radical ideology. A section of the urban petty bourgeoisie sought to be part of the capitalist development of Canada, broke away from *les Patriotes*, and allied themselves with the conservative clergy.

The clash of the two nationalist ideologies did not abate after the rebellions or even after 1850, although it was becoming apparent that the conservative nationalism was gaining ground. The 1848 Civil War in France gave the radicals a new impetus. They proudly accepted the designation of *le parti Rouge* to declare their ideological affinity with the insurgents of Paris.

Through the *Rouge* members of the Assembly of the Province of Canada, through *l'Institut Canadien* with its dozen or so branches throughout Quebec and its associated libraries (containing many books that were on Papal Index), and through three or four intellectual journals that began to appear regularly, starting in the 1840s, the radicals pressed forward their ideological attack. Their program was an extension of the demands of the *Patriotes* but with some additions, the major one being the repeal of the Act of Union of 1840. Their program was praised by Papineau on his return from exile as being "judicious and truly liberal". It was liberal *and* democratic, calling for universal suffrage, electoral reforms based on population, popular education, local government based on townships rather than parishes, free trade and free navigation, freedom of the press. It included two nationalist declamations: "French-Canadian above everything; encouragement of French-Canadian associations and institutions". Their admiration for United States ideals of democracy, particularly those of Jackson and Jefferson, their frustration over the colonial and undemocratic features of the Canadian political system, their antipathy to English domination, and their impatience over the slow economic progress being made, led many of the radicals to support annexation in the years 1849 – 1851. As for the question of how this fits in with French-Canadian nationalism, the advocates of this option argued that nationality could only gain by the establishment of democracy, that the French Canadians would exist as a nation whether under English or American protection, and anyway, if they were going to be assimilated, they would rather have this happen under the Americans than the English!

It was the *Rouge* members of the Assembly who mounted the main attack on Confederation. They attacked it from several points: the presence in the scheme of significant undemocratic features, its marked centralism and the threat this implied to the French-Canadian nation.

The victory of Confederation seriously weakened the radical elements, but there is no doubt that their criticism did result in some concessions being made in the direction of local government and in the federal, rather than legislative, union that finally emerged.

The defeat of this group was made possible by the triple alliance of the Macdonald Tories, the Cartier *Bleus* and the ultramontanist clergy of the Roman Catholic Church. The Confederation settlement confirmed the original policy of the British authorities at the time of the Quebec Act: to govern Quebec by supporting the established position of the hierarchy in matters of religion, education, and the civil code. This policy had helped defeat the *Patriotes* of 1837, as well as the radical democrats of the 1850s. Among other things, the radicals had waged a long fight against clerical control over education, which they regarded as perpetuating the emphasis on classical training rather than on scientific and technical subjects "to conform to the practice of the century". This position was consistent with the aims of the middle class, which went beyond cultural questions to assert its claim for a more meaningful role in the social and economic life of the Province.

Thus the conservatism which is laid against Quebec as a whole was in fact the product of British colonial policy, and of the Tory elements in Canada who supported clerical reaction against the democratic forces in French-Canadian society. This Tory support was due in large measure to their feeling that what the clergy wanted did not conflict with or in any way challenge the economic domination of the province by the Tory business class, whereas what the Quebec middle class wanted might be a challenge to this domination.

Business and Politics

The Tory business class was motivated by a desire to establish a viable commercial society which it could control. While the French-Canadian intellectuals were debating ideology, the main Anglophone élite in the colony were talking railroads, canals, tariffs, capital, and credit. The business élite was made up of descendants of the merchants who had first arrived in the colony in the wake of the British Army and who had quickly cornered the monopoly of trade. They also included the descendants of the first United Empire Loyalists who came to Canada as emigrés from the American Revolution, many of whom had since become big landowners and businessmen. Together with colonial administrators, army officers, and the Anglican high clergy, they constituted the ruling class:

In a sense, Toryism was the political expression of the province's small upper class, the people who considered themselves the natural leaders of society.[9]

Their policy was to promote economic growth through "mortgaging the public credit" to "supplement and eventually to replace private Capital", particularly in the construction of canals and railroads.[10]

They felt that the government had to play the major role in capital formation, and they saw no obstacles of an ideological

[9] S. F. Wise, "Upper Canada and the Conservative Tradition", Edith Firth, ed., *Profiles of A Province* (Toronto, 1967), p. 24.
[10] *Ibid.*, p. 29-30.

nature to inhibit them in this purpose. *Laissez-faire* had been the slogan of the rising industrial bourgeoisie of England with respect to governments that were hostile to the bourgeoisie and from which they were excluded. But here, in the new society being built in Canada, the bourgeoisie could and would control the government and, therefore, could control and direct the way public funds would be used for economic growth.

The control which they exercised, and fought to retain, was of the most direct nature, with the business elite in most cases indistinguishable from the political elite. One writer describes this relation in the following terms:

Having the power, as the legislative politicians did, to grant to themselves these charters, it was not an astonishing outcome that the promoters should have so often been the politicians themselves. This was particularly so inasmuch as many of the politicians, then so-called, were not politicians in the sense that they exclusively followed politics. Not a few of them were landowners of considerable holdings, and it was not a far step for them to promote railways, the operation of which would increase the value of their timber and their lands. Other members of Parliament were traders, merchants, or shippers, as well as land speculators, and had a personal and immediate interest in bringing about modern methods of transportation. Still other members of Parliament were lawyers, who were either connected with landed or trading families or who were often themselves interested in capitalist undertakings or aspired to become so. [11]

It was this motivation that led to Confederation and nation-building and thereby established the tradition that one recent study called "the primacy of politics over economics", asserting that this represents the "greatest contribution of Canadian Conservatism to Canadian political thought". [12] Frank Underhill, in a much less idolatrous mood, has defined this tradition as "the increasing subservience of the national government to the acquisitive appetites of the big-business-men-on-the-make . . . " [13]

S. F. Wise says that all major political trends in Upper Canada

---

[11] Gustavus Myers, *History of Canadian Wealth* (Chicago, 1914), p. 153.

[12] W. Christian and C. Campbell, *Political Parties and Ideologies In Canada* (Toronto, 1974), p. 110.

[13] F. H. Underhill: "The Conception of A National Interest", *In Search of Canadian Liberalism* (Toronto, 1960), p. 180.

got caught up in this spirit in the 1850s, including the so-called Reform party of Baldwin and Brown:

When in the 1850s, a common political culture emerged in the Canadas, and the major parties, despite their surface antagonisms, came to be in agreement upon the fundamental assumption without which a viable policy could not have existed, the foundations for a Canadian national feeling were laid. In the new synthesis, though both liberal and conservative traditions were considerably modified, it was the values of conservatism that gave coherence to the whole. In this context, it was Macdonald's function to extend the values he had inherited from the Toryism of old Ontario to the rest of the country, in company with these thousands of Upper Canadians who took part in the peopling of the West.[14]

This "common political culture" was, therefore, a modified Tory culture, modified in the sense that it absorbed some of the liberal ideas of the Reformers, but Tory in its rejection of democracy, and its emphasis on rule by elites. As for John A. Macdonald, the real ideological pacemaker of the "Grand Coalition", Bruce W. Hodgins has this to say:

Like all Conservative Fathers, he rejected both the word democracy, and many of those attributes now considered essential for it. He rejected political equality, favoured privilege for the propertied and the well-off, and seemed more concerned about the rights of the minority than providing for majority rule ... To Macdonald democracy was unconservative, illiberal, republican and dangerous; in a phrase it was un-British and hence un-Canadian.[15]

On a world scale, the era from 1859 to 1871 was marked by wars, civil strife and revolutions, resulting in what has been called "the consolidation of large nation-states" (Germany, Italy, Austria-Hungary), the victory of the North in the American Civil War, the end of feudalism in Russia, the opening of Japan to the West, and the creation of the Dominion of Canada "from sea unto sea". All these developments were a response to the rise of the new industrialism with its emphasis on steam, iron, and railroads. Capitalism needed a place to expand and develop, and

---

[14] Wise, p. 32.

[15] Bruce W. Hodgins, "Democracy and the Ontario Fathers of Confederation", *Profiles of A Province*, p. 85.

an extended home market was the indispensable condition for this. It needed political unification, the breaking down of customs barriers and of every other impediment to the political and economic hegemony of the "national" bourgeoisie.

The emergence of the Canadian nation-state at Confederation was relatively peaceful because the violence usually attendant on nation-building had occurred thirty years before. The national unit which came out of the earlier struggle was not large enough to satisfy the ambitions of the bourgeoisie of the Province of Canada, but that conflict did determine that it was this bourgeoisie whose class interest would be ensconced as the "national interest".

The Canadian national state did not come about as a struggle for independence against foreign or colonial rulers. The dominant Canadian bourgeoisie obtained complete jurisdiction over the domestic economy and political life within a colonial relationship that was more formal than real. They ensured that Canadian capitalists would enjoy special and profitable relations with Britain, which, at that time, was the world's leading industrial, mercantile, financial, and military power.

Confederation, therefore, did not come about as a result of a popular movement from below. In fact, to the extent that there was popular agitation it was *against* Confederation, especially in Newfoundland, Prince Edward Island, New Brunswick and Nova Scotia. In the province of Canada, it was deemed unwise to submit the proposal to a vote. Far from being a popular movement, it tended to be a scheme imposed on the provinces which, with the exception of Ontario, appeared reluctant if not actually opposed.[16]

The Canadian nation-state developed after the completion of the commercial and industrial revolutions in Western Europe, where the liberal ideology was already fully formed and dominant. But, while the struggles that marked this development in England had given rise to liberal democracy, no such impulsion was yet present in the Canadian development. In fact, the indigenous forces that might have brought liberal democracy to Canada, the *Patriotes*, the Reformers, and the agrarian radicals, had been defeated. An industrial working class, which in England had been a main contributing factor to liberal democracy, was only in its early formative stages in Canada.

Thus Confederation was brought about at a time when the

---

[16] Peter B. Waite, *The Life and Times of Confederation* (Toronto, 1967), p. 323.

powerful business interests of Montreal and Toronto, who were interchangeably the dominant figures in commerce, banking, transportation, *and* politics, were virtually unopposed. This fusion between government and business from the outset significantly affected the character of the political and ideological superstructure in Canada. The Canadian government at Confederation was completely and openly a businessman's government which could do, and did, what was required to promote the capitalist economy, and which inserted authoritarian provisions in the BNA Act (Senate, Legislative Council in Quebec, power of disallowance, etc.) to safeguard the bourgeois interest.

But it was this group who were the nation-builders, and were thus able for a long time to identify their interests as being, in fact, the national interest. Creighton elevates this to an ideology when he says:

The basic Conservative belief that the nation transcends the group, class, or section lies back of the idea of national union. It is here rather than in any other part of his political thought, that Macdonald approaches British Conservatism most clearly.[17]

The coincidence here between class and nation is regarded by this ideologist as an eternal principle. But the conflicts that followed Confederation soon showed that there were indeed group, class, sectional and even national cleavages, which would challenge the conservative concept of the national interest, and in the process develop or refine ideologies to express these challenges.

The tensions within Canadian society at the time of Confederation were not eliminated, as Creighton seems to suggest, but were only temporarily submerged. In addition, new conflicts arose which could not have existed at that time, except in embryo.

In the first place, the historic split along national lines broke out anew in the struggles with the Métis settlers in Manitoba and the Northwest, culminating in Riel's execution. Despite the shock and anger which this occasioned in Quebec, no attempt was made to conciliate French-Canadian opinion. The colonization of the West immediately after Confederation began as a deliberate policy of encouraging English-Canadians, principally from Ontario, to settle the West and they were offered the best

---

[17] Donald Creighton, *Towards The Discovery of Canada* (Toronto, 1972), p. 217.

lands available. This "assure(d) the triumph of Ontario over Quebec in Manitoba".[18]

The aggravation of this split coincided with the enormous pressure exerted by the British government on its colonies to participate in a number of military adventures overseas, resulting from the new imperialist phase that British capitalism had embarked upon towards the end of the nineteenth century. French-Canadian opposition to this policy was ignored, and by the end of the First World War and the conscription crisis, the English-French rupture had become a permanent feature of Canadian society. The rupture resulted mainly from two characteristics which Canadian Toryism exhibited: a strong and crude Anglo-Saxon chauvinism as an outgrowth of British imperialist ideology, and a disregard of minority rights particularly when the minority in question was constituted along national lines.

It may be true, as Creighton claims, that basic to the conservative ideology is the concept "that the nation transcends the group, class, or section" and that this "lies back of the idea of national union". By failing to recognize that Canada consisted of two nations, not one, this conservative concept, which had supporters in both political parties, led to a massive attempt at imposing by force the Tory idea of national union, with the inevitable result of disruption and disunion. Thus the conservative concept of the national interest, which had triumphed at Confederation, began to come apart shortly afterwards, and insofar as Quebec was concerned became an impossibility after 1917.

Although the split was basically along national lines, it had a religious dimension which often overshadowed or added to the national conflict. The issue of separate schools, for example, was both anti-Catholic and anti-French, and might never have arisen but for the fact that these two elements were intertwined within it. The existence and persistence of the Orange Order must be seen in this context, as has been aptly described by a contemporary historian:

The Orange Order in Ontario provided some of the most vociferous advocates of imperial unity, and it often appeared that to the motto of one race, one flag, one throne, they wanted to add one religion.[19]

---

[18] W. L. Morton, *Manitoba: A History* (Toronto, 1970), p. 233.

[19] Carl Berger, *The Sense of Power* (Toronto, 1971), p. 134.

The attempt to impose an Anglo-Saxon solution to the "French-Canadian problem", was shared by ideologists who are considered to express a liberal rather than conservative political outlook on most other questions. Two of the most prominent, Goldwin Smith, and, much later, John Dafoe, added a "liberal" argument to the Tory critique of Quebec society: that it was inherently undemocratic from a philosophical, religious, and political viewpoint. They both shared in the English chauvinism, but according to them North America, not Britain, was to be "the stronghold of the English-speaking world", and both argued for a continentalist approach. Smith called for outright annexation. He considered that the only way to submerge French Canada was through annexation to the United States.[20] Dafoe, although starting from a critique of Quebec as undemocratic, suggested a solution that was hardly a model of libertarian democracy and free choice:

Make no mistake about it, the English-Canadians will administer Canada and the French-Canadians will be a futile, sullen minority. Do not flatter yourself that the English-Canadians are disturbed by your attitude of injured innocence or your threats of reprisals. You can do precisely as you please; and we shall do whatever may be necessary. When we demonstrate, as we shall, that a solid Quebec is without power, there may be a return to reason along the banks of the St. Lawrence.[21]

The rupture carried with it important ideological connotations in both national communities. In French Canada, it reinforced a besieged fortress mentality. It strengthened the temporal power of the Quebec clergy, which was in the process of creating church-dominated organizations embracing almost every important lay activity of the French-Canadian people. The idea of a separate Laurentian nation was once again heard in the province, now under the persuasive and influential advocacy of Canon Lionel Groulx. To many English Canadians, the rupture was caused by the intransigence of the French Canadians, and among these people the events of the war only strengthened their Anglo-Saxon chauvinism and hostility to the French Cana-

---

[20] Goldwin Smith, *Canada and the Canadian Question* (Toronto, 1971).

[21] John W. Dafoe, in a letter to Thomas Cote, January 1, 1918, quoted in M. S. Donnelly, "The Political Ideas of John W. Dafoe", from J. A. Aitcheson, ed., *The Political Process In Canada* (Toronto, 1963), p. 109.

dians. On the other hand, these events helped bring into play a policy of conciliation towards French Canada, which included the pursuit of Canadian autonomy from Britain, for British policies and the sentimental attachment of English Canada to Britain were held to be at the root of much of the tension in French Canada. This policy of conciliation constituted one of the fundamental tools used to reconstruct the Liberal Party under the leadership of Mackenzie King. But at best it was a blunt tool, for many of the members who returned to the Liberal Party after their brief sojourn as Unionists still retained a basic anti-French outlook, which was to surface from time to time.

This is not to suggest that the policy of seeking autonomy from Britain was merely a device to conciliate the French Canadians. The need to repair the rupture in Canadian society coincided with the desire of a growing section of Canadian capitalists to emphasize strengthened economic ties with the United States at the expense of the old ties across the Atlantic. This was made inevitable for them by the realization that Britain had emerged from the war in a weakened condition and was now a debtor nation, while the United States had become the leading industrial, commercial and financial power in the world. The same circumstances which had made the dependence on Britain once so desirable, now favored a dependence on the United States.

The National Policy had run its course. Innis called this "the end of the period of expansion based on the St. Lawrence and trade with Great Britain".[22] The National Policy had given concrete economic objectives to the essential purpose of Confederation which "was to weld the scattered British possessions in North America into a unity within which Canadian capitalism could expand and consolidate its power, to provide for the capitalist *entrepreneurs* of Montreal and Toronto a half-continent in which they could realize their dreams and ambitions".[23] The ending of this period was signalled by political explosions which showed that, from being an instrument of national unity, the National Policy became clearly and irretrievably a divisive element which shook Canadian society very nearly to its foundations.

The Anglo-French *entente* which, according to Underhill, had been built up by Macdonald and Cartier as the political

---

[22] H. A. Innis, *Essays In Canadian Economic History* (Toronto, 1965), p. 209.

[23] F. H. Underhill, *In Search of Canadian Liberalism*, p. 177.

expression of these earlier objectives, was now to be resurrected by King and Lapointe to express the new orientation of the capitalist *entrepreneurs* of Montreal and Toronto, and to restore the unity which was essential to their rule.

The National Policy did result in an expansion of Canadian manufacturing during the period 1878-1911. This period contained two of the leading decades of Canadian industrial growth, measured in terms of real manufacturing output, between 1870 and 1957. Unlike the industrialization that had taken place prior to this period, which was based on serving the production of staples, the distinguishing feature of the new orientation was the development of a home market economy. This upsurge in industrial activity required the rapid creation of a labor force, which, except for Quebec, where there was a surplus farm population, could not be readily obtained from domestic sources but had to be imported.

The source upon which Canadian industry had come to depend, particularly for skilled craftsmen, was Britain:

In general, English immigrant craftsmen contributed very greatly to make Canada's labour market a modern one, by providing a regular and dependable supply of skilled labour, and by insisting as a counterpart upon a suitable level of wages and conditions.[24]

The Beginnings of Socialist Thought

The British immigrants also brought their ideas and traditions of class consciousness, trade unions, and socialism, which had developed out of a century of working-class struggle in Britain. During that period, the British working class was the first to secure legal recognition of trade unions; it had created a powerful Chartist movement that shook British politics for over a decade; had won male suffrage; had built unions first on craft and then on industrial lines, and at the end of the century was on the threshold of independent labor political action. Such activity created fertile soil for socialist ideas, which, though originating with intellectuals, were linked from the outset with the

---

[24] H. C. Pentland, *Labour and Development of Industrial Capitalism In Canada,* unpublished Ph. D. Thesis, University of Toronto (1960), p. 283.

British labor movement, and became part of its nineteenth-century tradition. Britain was the home of Owenism, much of Marxism, Fabianism, and Christian Socialism. Institutions and organizations reflecting these various socialist trends were integrated in the federated structure of the Labour Party at its foundation in 1900*. It was, therefore, not surprising that the advanced ideas of socialism, including Marxism, came to Canada in the first instance via working-class immigrants from Britain.

But just as the main bourgeois political culture of Canadian society reflects the impact of Britain *and* the United States, so did the development of the Canadian working class and its political outlook. J. A. Hobson, in his travels through Canada in 1905, noted in his book *Canada Today* that "Canada is a generation behind the United States in most lines of industrial development . . . ." This "generation gap" was reflected in the trade-union movement, which in the United States was already quite advanced in comparison to that in Canada. The American Federation of Labor (AFL) at its founding convention in 1886 in Columbus, Ohio, had a membership of 316,469, which practically doubled in the first year. During that same year the older Knights of Labor, which had been in existence for almost twenty years, estimated its membership at between 500,000 and 800,000. This latter body was based on area rather than trade, which meant that production workers as well as artisans could belong, whereas the AFL, by emphasizing craft unions, tended to exclude unskilled workers. In addition to these central labor bodies, there were powerful non-affiliated union organizations like the American Railroad Union, led by Eugene Debs, the Western Federation of Miners headed by William T. Haywood, and the Industrial Workers of the World (IWW) which was jointly founded in 1905 by Debs, Haywood, and Daniel DeLeon, head of the Socialist Labor Party.

These American unions greatly influenced the fledgling Canadian trade-union movement, because they already had a considerable experience in organization, and were radical and militant as a result of two decades of unrelieved and unparalleled violence on the part of U.S. authorities and employers, including armed intervention, murder, imprisonment, and private terror.

The preamble of the AFL constitution dedicated that organi-

---

* The Labour Party name did not come into use until 1906, but 1900 saw the formation of the Labour Representation Committee which six years later adopted the permanent name and party designation.

zation to a "struggle between capital and labor which must grow in intensity from year to year". Its first president, Samuel Gompers, had been a Marxist in London, and is said to have modelled the AFL constitution on that of the British Trade Union Congress. One of its first actions, which won it considerable status on both sides of the border, was to launch in the United States a nationwide strike for the eight-hour day in 1886, which at its height involved 350,000 workers.

The American unions were considered by many Canadian workers to be more militant and aggressive than most of the indigenous ones. An example, by no means untypical, of the way Canadian workers were attracted to the American unions in the early years involved the coal miners of Nova Scotia. Their union, the Provincial Workmen's Association, proved to be conservative and conciliatory to the employers, and consequently failed to win any important gains for the miners or to lead any struggles for such aims. According to one account:

Unhappy with the lack of fighting spirit in what was supposed to be their *union, the miners began to look for an organization which would really be a defender of their interests. To J. B. McLachlan, J. D. McLennan, Dan McDougall and other strongwilled young miners, the answer seemed to be a union like the United Mine Workers of America, the coal miners' union, which was making great gains in the U.S. coalfields.*[25]

Consequently, in 1908, the miners voted by referendum to dissolve the Provincial Workmen's Association and to invite the American miners' union to represent them.

The other American unions mentioned were even more militant than the AFL, and their impact on the Canadian labor movement was also felt, but for a shorter time. The Western Federation of Miners, the American Railroad Union, and the Industrial Workers of the World (IWW) were particularly active in British Columbia, where they combined aggressive unionism with vigorous and widespread socialist propaganda, and undoubtedly were an important factor in the deep-rooted socialist tradition in that province.

The Knights of Labor was particularly successful in Quebec where its loose organizational structure made it possible to unionize the unskilled, low-wage workers in mass production indus-

---

[25] *The Peoples' History of Cape Breton* (Halifax, n.d.), p. 6.

tries that had sprung up in the French-Canadian districts of Montreal, the Eastern Townships and the Lower St. Lawrence: garment, leather, shoe, textile, tobacco, and food processing. In its formative years in the United States, it was greatly influenced by the International Workingmen's Association of Marx, particularly through refugees of the Paris Commune who had emigrated to America and had become active in the leadership of the Knights of Labor in New York. The Knights flourished in Quebec during the last two decades of the nineteenth century, but began to decline under heavy attacks from the Catholic hierarchy in Quebec and the hostility of the AFL, which succeeded in getting the Knights expelled from the Trades and Labour Congress of Canada in 1902.

The growth of trade unionism in Canada, which, notwithstanding what has been said above, was relatively slow*, was accompanied by the first ideological and institutional developments of socialism. This was not a fortuitous coincidence because, as has been noted, many trade-union bodies, including the AFL and Knights of Labor, carried in their program an ideological attack on the capitalist system, and many trade-union organizers, including some of the more prominent leaders like Debs and Haywood, were also proselytizers for the American socialist movement. Marxian ideas began to enter Canada, however, much earlier than that, primarily through British immigrants, and through the work of Marxists who had emigrated to the United States from Germany in the 1850s, including some of Marx's closest colleagues. We know from his book *The Politics of Labor*, published in 1887*, that Phillips Thompson, the Toronto labor journalist, had by then been exposed to at least some of Marx's works. An article in the *Canadian Magazine* of August 1894 entitled "Canadian Democracy and Socialism" testifies to the growing influence in Canada of Marx's ideas:

Karl Marx (1818-1883) is the author of the famous book: "Das Capital"—the Bible of social democrats and a book which has now great influence in the United States and Canada.

There appears to be some dispute as to where and when the

---

* The Trades and Labour Congress of Canada, which was the major trade union center in Canada, had a membership of 13,465 by 1902.

* This book has now been reprinted by the University of Toronto Press (1975).

first socialist group got started in Canada, although there seems to be agreement that groups began to appear in the last two decades of the nineteenth century, and by 1900 there were at least sixty branches throughout the country. Most of them accepted Marx's ideas as they were currently understood, and propagated them; but there were widely differing interpretations, primarily over the kinds of activity which were most likely to lead to socialism in Canada.

The important feature of these early socialist groups was their close links with the developing trade-union movement. Most of the members of socialist organizations were workers, many of them leading trade unionists, and they directed most of their socialist propaganda to the organized labor movement. There was a growing acceptance among them of the importance of labor contesting parliamentary elections at all levels. Many of the socialist leaders became candidates, and some were elected to provincial legislatures and local councils, either as straight socialist or labor representatives.

The early formation of central labor bodies that united trade-union organizations for legislative action reflected an awareness by the unions of the need to combine the political struggle with the purely economic: a realization that the things labor wanted for itself, besides higher wages and better working conditions, went beyond the contestation at a factory level between the employer and his employees. These needs became translated into such political issues as the nine-hour day, trade-union legal rights, compulsory free education, and factory reform legislation. By taking up these and other similar questions and embodying them in the legislative programs of the central labor federations, the trade-union movement in Canada became the first, and remained consistently the major force agitating for a welfare state.

The violent reaction of the Canadian industrialists to the first stirrings of the working class, and the ready support given them against the unions by the state, produced "a record of labour unrest and industrial conflict with illegal and violent overtones, second only to the United States and far greater than that of most west European countries".[26]

According to one historian, the Canadian militia between

---

[26] Stuart Jamieson, *Times of Trouble: Labour Unrest and Industrial Conflict in Canada, 1900-1966* (Ottawa, 1968), p. 7.

1876 and 1914 was used on thirty-three different occasions to intervene in strikes.[27] The Winnipeg General Strike of 1919 was one in a long series of such confrontations, and certainly the most spectacular. The three levels of government involved combined to defeat the strike. The decision to do this was made by the Federal Government, which was the wartime Unionist coalition that united the Conservatives and a majority of the Liberals. The actual instrument to accomplish this defeat was the Committee of 1,000, representing the capitalist class of Manitoba, which was given such close support by the state that the Committee chairman was appointed special Federal Deputy Minister of Justice. On the other side stood the vast majority of workers of Winnipeg, organized and unorganized, demanding what is now considered a basic democratic right: collective bargaining; and exercising the only power they had: withdrawal of their labor.

The prevailing view of the strike by the business élite of Canada was that it was an attack on the very existence of the system, and that any concessions to the strikers would only kindle the fires of revolt all over Canada. This was the view not only of the government, but of every newspaper in the country except two* and of the courts which tried and convicted most of the arrested strike leaders.

This event contained within it all the elements of classical class confrontation and seemed to confirm Marx's description of the state as "the executive committee of the bourgeoisie". This aspect made a deep impact on working-class consciousness, as Kenneth McNaught, the historian, shows:

Out of the strike, the trials, and the jail sentences grew an intensified class feeling, deepened suspicion of the elite-controlled state violence, a fresh drive for independent labour politics and thus a principal tap-root of the CCF—NDP.[28]

The violence directed against labor in these formative years,

---

[27] Desmond Morton, "Aid to the Civil Power: The Canadian Militia In Support of Social Order 1867-1914", *Canadian Historical Review* Vol. 50 (1970), p. 407.

* *The Toronto Star* and the *Ottawa Citizen* disputed the authorized version and held to the belief, now no longer in dispute, that the Winnipeg General Strike was a genuine struggle for trade-union rights.

[28] Kenneth McNaught, "Violence in Canadian History", John S. Moir ed., *Character and Circumstance*.

by an employing class and government which had not yet adjusted its own thinking as to how to cope with the trade-union movement, tended to increase the militancy of the institutions and ideas which expressed the working-class interest.

The separation of a working-class interest, as a distinct ideological element in Canadian political thought, had been gestating at least since the last quarter of the nineteenth century. It was implicit in the very first trade union locals that were established in the first quarter, but the open expression and awareness of a class distinctness does not appear until later. Marx described this process in general terms pertaining to all industrial societies in an article in the *New York Tribune* in 1851:

The working class movement itself never is independent, never is of an exclusively proletarian character until all the different factions of the middle class and particularly its most progressive faction, the large manufacturers, have conquered political power, and remodeled the state according to their wants. It is then that inevitable conflict between employer and employed becomes imminent and cannot be adjourned any longer; that the working class can no longer be put off with delusive hopes and promises never to be realized; that the great problem of the nineteenth century, the abolition of the proletariat is at last brought forward fairly and in its proper light.[29]

Marx was referring here to the German Revolution of 1848 in particular, and to the English and French revolutions as well, in which the middle class fought the aristocracy for political power, and in so doing counted on the proletariat for support. There was, of course, no parallel development in Canada. The bourgeoisie that created Confederation was largely a mercantile and financial elite, which later stimulated and participated in the growth of secondary manufacturing. All sectors of the economy —trade, transportation, manufacturing, primary production, finance—were enhanced by the National Policy, although not uniformly. The National Policy became the motif, the theme song, and the ideology of Canada's ruling circles, and to the extent that it continued to work, or to appear to do so, it was accepted, or at least not challenged, by the population as a whole. The industrial working class, which was largely brought into being by the National Policy, shared in the general euphoria, and felt that

---

[29] Karl Marx, *Revolution and Counter-Revolution* (Chicago, 1907), pp. 22-3.

its own interests were tied to the success of this policy. In this sense, therefore, Marx's observations about the proletariat in Europe applied to Canada.

From the start, both parties wooed the trade-union movement for working-class votes, but Macdonald's appeal appeared more effective. This was initially due to Macdonald's skillful use of a strike at George Brown's *Globe* in 1872 to sponsor an Act giving a qualified legal status to trade unions. But it probably was due even more to the credit that accrued to the party in power as the nation-builders. This situation changed in the 1880s when there took place a substantial defection of labor from the Conservatives either to the Liberals or to a condemnation of both "old parties".[30] This was due to a number of factors: the failure of the Conservatives to sponsor any labor legislation during the entire decade, the "re-imposition" of curbs on trade unions which had antedated the Act of 1872, disenchantment over the failure of the National Policy to prevent a depression, and the "terrible plight of the industrial workers" which was exposed to the public by the report of the Royal Commission on Capital and Labour published in 1889.

Writing about the importance of this report, one author sums up as follows:

The important but implicit conclusion of the Commission's Report was that a rift had come into the open during the past decade between the people and interests masked by the then newly fashionable abstractions Capital and Labour. Though the rift was not described as a Marxist "class struggle" an increasingly self-conscious and aggressive proletariat was seen to have been growing up, fostered, paradoxically, by the National Policy of which one great arm was national unity. Moreover, this group was coming more and more to equate the interest of Capital, its alleged enemy, with the National Policy, and even with the spirit of patriotism.[31]

Thus it appears that one of the first expressions of ideological independence within the labor movement comes with the recognition that the National Policy, far from expressing the working-class interest, assumed that this interest in wages, working condi-

---

[30] Bernard Ostry, "Conservatives, Liberals, and Labour in the 1880's", *Canadian Journal of Economics and Political Science*, Vol. XVII, No. 2 (May 1961), p. 157.

[31] Frank W. Watt, *Radicalism in English-Canadian Literature Since Confederation*, unpublished Ph.D. Thesis, University of Toronto, 1957, p. 94.

tions, and social measures must be subordinated to the more abstract values of a non-class national character. This note of rejection of the National Policy and of its concomitant appeal to patriotism and nationalism is to be found with increasing frequency in the several labor periodicals which began to appear in the late seventies and early eighties. On the basis of this evidence, F. W. Watt comments:

As the first phase of national building continued, the disturbing pressure of contradictory ideals was to come not within the cultivated classes, but from the proletariat.[32]

One of the first Canadian advocates of working-class political independence was Phillips Thompson, Toronto labor journalist. His major theoretical work, *The Politics of Labor*, published in 1887, was addressed to the labor movement of Canada and the United States. His themes were not original: most of them were in fact borrowed from Marx, although he only mentions Marx once. But his book is important as a historical signpost of a new phase in the thinking and direction of part of the labor leadership in Canada. Trade unionism is not enough; the workers must engage in political action on their own behalf, must challenge the capitalist system itself, and, in so doing, give leadership to all other strata which are also exploited by capitalism:

Labor, in working out its own emancipation, will regenerate the world. In solving the labor problem, the other vexed questions which have so long pressed for solution will be settled. All the various forms of social and moral evil which afflict humanity are traceable to caste rule and the spoilation of the laboring class. War, intemperance, prostitution, and crime are due either to greed begotten of Capitalism, the selfishness, arrogance, and luxury of the moneyed and influential class, or the abject necessity, ignorance, and debasement of the disinherited. With social and political equality established, and every man and woman secured in the enjoyment of the full earnings of their labor, the motives which prompt and the conditions which foster these evils would largely cease.[33]

Obviously Thompson's influence, and for that matter the

---

[32] *Ibid.*, p. 18.

[33] Phillips Thompson, *The Politics of Labor* (Toronto, 1975).

trade unions' influence, at this time was not great. But what is important is to see in these movements and in the positing of a socialist alternative, the beginning of what would become a genuine counterculture in Canada, based in the first place on the proletariat. Thompson's book appeared just at a time when socialist groups and independent labor parties were springing up in many urban centers of Canada.

The period between 1896 and 1921 saw the simultaneous and parallel growth of the trade-union movement, various socialist organizations (mainly the Socialist Party of Canada and the Social-Democratic Party), a number of independent labor parties, a plethora of labor periodicals, and some successful electoral contests in which labor increased its representation in parliamentary bodies. There was also an increase in strike struggles, of violence on the picket lines, and of militancy on the part of organized workers. This militancy was particularly conspicuous on a regional basis, occurring most frequently in Nova Scotia and in the West.

A main reason for this appears to be as a response to the endemic regional disparities which were already beginning to show. Industrial entrepreneurs in those regions sought to compete with the advantaged manufacturing establishments in Central Canada by increased exploitation of their workers. Another factor was that primary production in those regions lent itself to industrial unions, such as in mining and lumbering, which everywhere in the industrial nations have been much more militant than the craft unions.

All this was taking place against a background of an unprecedented growth of all sectors of the economy, sustained by great waves of immigrants brought here to meet the need for an expanded labor force, both industrial and agricultural. The working class grew tremendously as a result of this influx of skilled workers from the traditional source, Britain, and unskilled laborers from a new source, Central and Eastern Europe. This in turn strengthened the trade-union movement and its socialist counterpart, not only in numbers but in radicalism. A further impact of this immigration was the number of immigrants, particularly from Britain, who quickly rose to leadership in these bodies on the basis of the political and trade-union experience which they had acquired in their homeland. Their influence was particularly felt in two directions: increased pressure for legislation to protect trade-union rights along lines already achieved in Britain, and for the establishment of a Canadian Labour Party patterned on the British model.

While the Canadian Labour Party was officially launched by the Trades and Labour Congress at its National Convention in 1917, it never succeeded in becoming the third party in Canada, mainly because the British model, based on a working class that was the numerical majority in the population, could not be duplicated in the different Canadian environment.

The rise of the working class, as Phillips Thompson had predicted, had a major impact on Canadian society as a whole. Its most obvious impact was the negative one, a violent Toryist reaction to labor's claims. This was the predominant reaction of the capitalist class and most provincial as well as federal governments until the explosion of 1919. This was aggravated and fed by the Russian Revolution of 1917, which at that time had evoked a warm response from Canadian workers. The experiences of the war led directly and immediately to heightened radicalism among the workers, for whom, here as elsewhere, the impact of the war engendered bitter feelings of cynicism, disgust, and disillusionment with the leaders of society, that bordered on revolt. This in turn influenced two developments that were to have a major political importance thereafter: the movement among Protestant ministers known as the social gospel, and the emergence of liberal reformism as a response in bourgeois circles to the claims of the working class.

The social gospel, according to a recent history,[34] was a movement, primarily in the Protestant church, that sought to relate the principles of Christianity to industrial society by emphasizing the need for social reform and human welfare as valid goals for the Church's concern. It began in the last decade of the nineteenth century and reached its apogee during the war and immediately thereafter. This historical account identifies three wings which crystallized within the Canadian movement: conservative, progressive, and radical.

The radical wing arose within a group of Methodist ministers, primarily in the West, who had connections with the labor and socialist movements, who were greatly influenced by those connections, and who became dominant figures in Canadian radicalism. The most prominent among this group were J. S. Woodsworth, William Irvine, William Ivens, Salem Bland and A. E. Smith. They also had close links with the western farm

---

[34] Richard Allen, *The Social Passion* (Toronto, 1971).

movement, which was already showing signs of revolt, and they "could move back and forth between farm and labour groups with relative ease. . . ."[35]

The turning point for these men was the Winnipeg General Strike. All except Irvine were directly involved in the Strike. Ivens and Woodsworth were arrested and Ivens was convicted and imprisoned for one year. Ivens and Smith were elected to the Manitoba Legislature in the aftermath of the Strike as candidates of the Manitoba Labour Party, and Woodsworth and Irvine were elected to the House of Commons in 1921, where they constituted themselves the "Labour Group". Thus their identification with the labor movement was complete, and their influence in shaping an ideological outlook for labor began to be decisive.

As was to be expected, they brought to Canadian socialism the impress of their religious background and the ideas of the social gospel. By resigning from the church they went beyond this movement because, according to Woodsworth's letter of resignation, "anything like a radical program of social reform became in practice almost impossible" within the church.[36]

Woodsworth was one of the principal advocates of what later became the social-democratic and dominant outlook in Canadian socialism, as distinct from the Marxist revolutionary approach. The actual differentiation, although it may have been implicit in many of the debates within the Canadian socialist movement, started to take shape only after the Russian Revolution. Woodsworth preferred what he called "the British Way", by which he meant the postwar platform of the British Labour Party entitled *Labour and the New Social Order*, which contained a set of far-reaching proposals for the social reconstruction of Britain, to be brought about through Parliament. In an article in the *Winnipeg Strike Bulletin* Woodsworth called this approach revolutionary in its goals but constitutional in its methods. He thought that this approach suited Canadian needs, but he did not rule out the possibility of violence:

Do our Canadian business men suppose that with revolutions going on all over Europe and with the program offered in England as a substitute for sudden and perhaps violent revolution that we in

---

[35] K. McNaught, *A Prophet In Politics* (Toronto, 1963), p. 81.

[36] J. S. Woodsworth, *Following the Gleam* (Ottawa, 1926), p. 15.

Canada are to be permitted to go with undisturbed step along the accustomed ways?

No! We, too, must face the new situation. Whether the radical changes that are inevitable may be brought about peaceably, largely depends on the good sense of the Canadian business men who now largely control both the industry and Government of this Country.

We confess the prospects are not overly bright.[37]

King and Liberal Reformism

But Woodsworth's pessimism was unfounded. Even as he wrote that passage there were signs of an impending shift in top Canadian political circles towards a more conciliatory approach to labor and a readiness to accept some reform measures. These ideas were contained in Mackenzie King's *Industry and Humanity*, published in 1918.[38] King too had read the British Labour Party's platform, and had been impressed with it. He thought that its approach, which called on the government to guarantee a "national minimum standard of life", was practical and just. He had also read the mood of the working class in Canada, and had concluded that an effort had to be made to satisfy some of their claims and to adopt an approach that conciliates rather than confronts. A typical theme in this book is expressed in the following paragraph:

Whilst it is unlikely that Socialism in the form of the omnipotent and ever-present State or Industrial Unionism controlling Industry in conjunction with a democratized State, will ever permanently succeed the present order, it is altogether probable that Collectivist ideals, and in particular what they represent of the community idea and improvement in the status of Labor, will vastly expand their influence in the years to come. This is but continuing a natural evolution which experience has wholly justified. A belief in the

---

[37] *Ibid.*, p. 15.

[38] W. L. Mackenzie King, *Industry and Humanity* (Toronto, 1918).

wisdom and justice of a measure of State interference succeeded the older conception of laissez-faire, which looked to unrestricted competition as the ideal in matters of industrial organization. Regulation, especially as respects a minimum of Social well-being, is more and more the accepted order of today.[39]

King warned that the alternative to such an approach would be strife, disorder, and industrial upheavals. The Winnipeg General Strike seemed to confirm this prognosis, and he felt that this event, coming as it did two months prior to the Liberal leadership convention, would strengthen his credibility as a candidate for that post. In a letter written to his brother in June 1919 King confided that "it is possible that the labour unrest of the West may cause some of the Party to be disposed towards my leadership. . . ."[40]

He was right. His speech at the Convention focused on labor and social reform. This message caught the mood of the Convention, which infused large doses of welfare and labor legislation into the Liberal platform. One observer makes this comment about the Convention:

Indeed, some of the planning for the Convention suggests that it was to be a rally of Canadian progressivism, with the right to send delegates being extended to the Trades and Labour Congress of Canada, the Railway Brotherhoods, the Council of agriculture, and the Great War Veterans Association. Industry and Humanity, it would seem, was neither too radical for these, nor for the new businessmen. As far as the Canadian world of liberal social reform was concerned the book, like the man, was in the right place at the right time.[41]

The significant turn which this Convention represented has been described by Horowitz in the following terms:

King's Industry and Humanity *and the Liberal platform of 1919 mark the transition of English Canadian Liberalism from the old individualism to the new Liberal Reform.*[42]

---

[39] *Ibid.*, (from revised and abridged edition, 1947), p. 179.

[40] Quoted in F. A. McGregor, *The Fall and Rise of Mackenzie King, 1911-1919* (Toronto, 1962), p. 335.

[41] Richard Allen, *The Social Passion*, p. 198.

[42] G. Horowitz, *Canadian Labour In Politics* (Toronto, 1968), p. 30.

Yet it would be less than accurate to see this turn only in terms of the Liberal party seeking political advantages, or Mackenzie King using this type of appeal to further his leadership campaign. It also showed that a substantial section of the Canadian capitalist class recognized and responded to the need for change in view of the shattering effects the Tory ideology had produced. In this regard they were repeating the experience of Western Europe and Britain, where democratic liberalism arose as a bourgeois response to the emergence of the working class and the rise of the socialist idea.

While the Tory government was talking itself and the nation into the spectre of a workers' revolt, what actually took place was a political revolt of the farmers of Ontario and the Prairie provinces. In its wake the revolt destroyed the two-party system federally, produced third-party regimes in Ontario, Alberta, and Manitoba, and established a tradition of agrarian discontent expressed through farmer-dominated provincial regimes.

The distinctive feature of Canadian agriculture, based on the independent petty producer who holds his land as a proprietor but who is dependent on the mercantile, financial, and industrial interests for his survival, has produced agrarian radicalism as a constant theme in Canadian political and ideological development. This radicalism was basic to the ideas of the frontier democracy which led to the rebellions of Upper and Lower Canada. It was an important factor in the reform movements in Ontario after Confederation. George F. G. Stanley asserts that the "*métis* movement of 1884-85, was also an agrarian protest movement".[43] But the creation after Confederation of the West as a colonial hinterland for economic exploitation by Central Canada magnified the inherent conflict by giving it a regional basis. This conjunction of class and regional conflict has been analysed in C. B. Macpherson, *Democracy in Alberta*.[44] It produced a farm movement which, because it was directed at the railroad, banking, and industrial monopolies, touched many demands that the labor and socialist movements were also raising. Yet in spite of this programmatic coincidence, there had been little or no connection between them. What seemed to be a breakthrough in this regard came with the Ontario election of 1919 when 43 United Farmers

---

[43] George F. G. Stanley, "The Western Canadian Mystique", David P. Gagan ed., *Prairie Perspectives* (Toronto, 1970), p. 14.

[44] C. B. Macpherson, *Democracy in Alberta: Social Credit and the Party System* (Toronto, 1962).

of Ontario and 11 Ontario Labour Party elected members joined to form the first farmer-labour government in Canada.

The links were more irregular however in the West. In Alberta, the first electoral success of the United Farmers of Alberta came about in a by-election in April 1921, where a farmers' candidate won the federal seat with the cooperation of organized labor in the city of Medicine Hat. It took some years and much effort, particularly of an ideological nature, to form viable and lasting links between agrarian radicalism and labor-based socialism. This task was accomplished mainly by the ministers or ex-ministers of the social gospel who had a foot in both camps, particularly William Irvine and J. S. Woodsworth. Their moves to solidify such links led them to a realization that what Woodsworth called in 1933 the "Canadian Way", as distinguished from the British way or the American way, was the combination in one political movement of farmers and workers, with an ideological mix to reflect this alliance.

This combination, which had evolved particularly during the twenties, attracted a section of the academic community, notably at McGill and Toronto Universities, and resulted in the first public appearance of Canadian academics in the socialist movement. They made an important contribution to this movement, especially in the thirties. They established the right of intellectuals to involve themselves in radical politics, although it almost cost some of them their jobs.

Summary

The main ideological themes of Canadian society were shaped during two fairly distinct periods: from Conquest to Confederation, and from Confederation to the immediate aftermath of the First World War.

The Toryism which the British authorities implanted after the Conquest merged with the clerical absolutism of the remnants of the ruling élite of New France to establish a structure of government and social institutions even more rigid and authoritarian than had existed before. The conflicts and struggles which ensued challenged that authoritarianism on behalf of the French and English-Canadian petty-bourgeoisie, who drew much of their inspiration from the liberal and democratic ideas of the revolutionary and reform movements of Britain, France, and America.

Confederation climaxed these struggles with the establishment of the modern Canadian state largely reflecting the interests of a business class that was predominantly Tory in outlook, but with that outlook modified somewhat as a result of absorbing some of the ideas of the reformers, while rejecting liberal democracy.

The common political culture which emerged at this time was expressed in programmatic terms by the National Policy, which, so long as it resulted in economic expansion, tended to unify the nation, and to reduce to a minimum the differences between the two major parties. But sectional, group, class, and national differences began to erupt, threatening this unity, and by the end of the First World War fracturing it.

The inability of the Tory idea of national union to accommodate these differences led to several explosive confrontations, with the inevitable result of disruption and division. These divisions were indicators that the National Policy had run its course. A new policy began to emerge, and with it a liberal reform ideology based on conciliation rather than confrontation.

Liberal reformism arose as a response to the emergence of an industrial working class, an organized labor movement; and the development of the socialist idea. The socialist idea became a part of the Canadian ideological spectrum at the same time as liberal reformism was becoming the predominant outlook of Canadian society.

The socialist idea at this point was exclusively working-class and largely Marxian. But as a reaction to the Russian Revolution, and impelled by the impact of the agrarian revolt, there began a shift toward a distinctive Canadian social-democratic expression, more and more in the direction of bridging the labor and farm movements with an ideological mix to make that possible.

CHAPTER THREE

THE SOCIALIST IDEA IN CANADA: ORIGINS AND GENESIS TO 1921

At the outset the socialist idea in Canada comprised a number of trends: Marxism (particularly embodied in the Socialist Labor Party, an American-based organization), various forms of Christian socialism, Henry George-ism, Utopian socialism based on Bellamy's *Looking Backward*, and laborism. All of these were represented in the Canadian Socialist League (CSL), which by 1900 had "seventeen branches in various parts of the Dominion".[1] These ideas were implanted largely through contact with British and American thought, and the influence of immigrants, particularly workers from Britain. But G. Weston Wrigley, one of the leaders of the CSL, identified another source of the socialist idea as an emanation of the rebellions in Upper and Lower Canada:

Many of the descendants of the rebels of 1837 are taking an active part in socialist propaganda in 1901, the grandfather of the writer being one who had the honour of serving three months in jail as a rebel.[2]

---

[1] G. Weston Wrigley, "Socialism in Canada", *International Socialist Review* (Chicago, 1900-1901), Vol. 1, p. 686.

[2] *Ibid.*, p. 685.

Another of these descendants who was said to have had some contact with the socialist movement was Mackenzie King who, according to a member of the socialist movement, attended meetings of the Toronto Socialist group during his undergraduate years at the University of Toronto and "sometimes" took part in its discussions.[3]

With the merging of the Canadian Socialist League and the Socialist Party of British Columbia in 1903 to form the Socialist Party of Canada, Canadian socialism became predominantly Marxist in character and remained so until 1921. At the same time it became overwhelmingly proletarian in its composition, so much so that it was regarded by some as an adjunct to the trade-union movement. Its chief advocates were workers, most of them active in the unions. Socialism attracted very little support from outside the working class. There was a complete absence of any intellectuals in the socialist ranks, even though the two countries which influenced Canadian socialism the most, Britain and the United States, could boast of a host of academics, poets, novelists, playwrights, essayists, who took up the socialist cause and became identified with it.

It is difficult to explain this absence with certainty, yet with the exception of the support of a few ministers of the social gospel this situation persisted until the thirties. J. A. Hobson in his study of *Imperialism* (1902) mentions intimidation at Canadian universities but does not elaborate:

The interference with intellectual liberty is seldom direct, seldom personal, though both in the United States and Canada some instances of the crudest heresy-hunting have occurred.[4]

Hobson goes on to say, however, that "the real danger consists in the appointment rather than in the dismissal of teachers, in the determination of what subjects shall be taught, what relative attention shall be given to each subject, and what text-books and other apparatus of instruction shall be used". Using these criteria, it is instructive to go through the calendars of the University of Toronto's Department of Political Economy for the

---

[3] James McArthur Conners, *The Labor and Socialist Movements In Canada*, unpublished manuscript, undated in "Woodsworth Collection", University of Toronto, p. 2.

[4] J. A. Hobson, *Imperialism: A Study* (London, 1968), p. 219.

years 1894–1917. Not one subject relating to socialism or Marx is listed, nor is there a single volume of reading recommended which deals with this subject.

On the other hand, Canada did have a number of intellectuals who distinguished themselves as vociferous foes of socialism. Goldwin Smith in many of his essays and public lectures warned the working class against "the spectre of Socialism". James Mavor, once prominent in the British socialist movement and a colleague there of Sidney Webb, became a specialist "in the denunciation of socialism, criticism of the trade union movement and academic politics",[5] after taking over the post of Chairman of Political Economy at the University of Toronto in 1894. Professor O. D. Skelton, later to become one of the key civil servants in the Mackenzie King regimes, published in 1911 his massive assault on Marxism which three years earlier had won him an award from an American corporation for the best essay on the subject "The Case Against Socialism".

The Proletarian Character of Canadian Socialism

This circumstance accentuated the proletarian character of the Canadian socialist movement in its early years. Most of the writers and lecturers propagating socialist ideas were workers, with little formal education, self-instructed in Marxism and related topics, working at their jobs full-time and teaching, studying, and organizing in their spare time. Their attraction to Marx's works whetted their appetites for general education and many became very literate in philosophy, anthropology, and history. W. A. Pritchard, a surviving member of this group of worker-intellectuals, describes the educational program that he first encountered when he joined Local 1 of the Socialist Party of Canada in Vancouver in 1911:

The Local possessed a good library with all the socialist classics and a great number of scientific works on various subjects on the tables in the reading room—or area set aside for such—displaying current magazines and journals. In the winter months an economics class was held, Sunday afternoon moderated by George Mor-

---

[5] H. S. Ferns and B. Ostry, *The Age of Mackenzie King* (Toronto, 1976), p. 5.

*gan. Tuesday was local business meeting, Thursday a class on
History by J. D. Harrington, and for a time there was a Friday
night class for those interested in becoming party speakers, conducted by the irrepressible red-headed orator, H. M. Fitzgerald.*[6]

In a series of interviews for the CBC in 1960, Paul Fox asked
a number of veterans of the Canadian socialist movement about
the nature of early socialism here, and invariably they described
this emphasis on socialist education. The names of the leading
propagandists most often mentioned were Harrington, Kingsley,
Pritchard, Morgan, Fitzgerald, O'Brien, Kavanagh, Pettipiece,
Lefeaux. Angus MacInnis, M.P., told Paul Fox these were "probably some of the ablest speakers I have ever heard". Lefeaux,
himself one of the most talented of these pioneer socialists, says
about E. T. Kingsley:

*. . . A real philosopher and scientist. Self-educated I would say. He
was the most widely read man I have ever met on socialism and
general philosophy. He was a Marxist.*

Outside speakers were brought in to address public forums
on socialism. Ramsay Macdonald and Keir Hardie from England, Eugene Debs, Daniel DeLeon, and Professor Scott Near-
ing from the United States, were the most popular. But the main
work of implanting the socialist idea in Canada during this
formative period was done by these self-educated people, all of
them members of the working class.

This had its positive side but also some understandable negative features. It produced a body of men who were looked up to
in the labor movement even beyond those who agreed with their
socialist views. Their emphasis on education made them stand
out among their fellow workers as exceptionally gifted people.
At the same time it gave others a feeling of self-confidence.
After all, if their peers could master philosophy, history, and
economics without formal training, so could they.

On the other hand, their writings and speeches tended to
have an abstract and doctrinaire quality, repeating Marxist postulates over and over again, but giving little attention to the
possible use of Marxism as an analytical tool for the critical
study of Canadian society. Their writings were confined mainly

---

[6] W. A. Pritchard, *Letter to Norman Penner*, August 6, 1974.

to socialist and labor periodicals or small five- and ten-cent pamphlets. With two exceptions no major works were produced by or for the Canadian socialist movement during this period, and the two exceptions are themselves instructive.

The Politics of Labor, a substantial work by Phillips Thompson, a Toronto socialist, appeared in 1887. It was a critique of American capitalism and its political institutions, was published in the United States, and did not contain a single reference to Canada. The other work, *History of Canadian Wealth*, was written by Gustavus Myers, an American writer, and published by Charles H. Kerr in Chicago in 1914. It was an economic history from a Marxist viewpoint of the formation of the Canadian capitalist class. Although it was distributed by the Socialist Party and the Social-Democratic Party of Canada, as were all Kerr publications, no special attention was drawn to it except through routine ads listing books available, nor did it appear to carry any political implications for the work of Canadian socialists. In the 1917 issues of the official socialist party organ, the *Western Clarion*, a series of weekly lessons for readers on the topic "Materialist Conception of History for Beginners" was begun. Not until lesson 19 did the author deal with Canadian history. He acknowledged his debt to Myers and urged his readers to study Myers further.

Perhaps this lack of intellectual support could have been somewhat overcome had the Canadian socialist movement affiliated and taken part in the International Socialist Congress, otherwise known as the Second International, which brought together on a regular basis some of the most imposing intellectual figures of European and American socialism. But the relationship of the Canadians to this body was at best tenuous and vicarious, and for all practical purposes, nonexistent. In 1904 Daniel DeLeon of New York presented credentials to the Amsterdam Congress, claiming to represent the Socialist Labour Party of Australia and of Canada as well as of the United States.

In his report to the Canadian membership after the Congress, DeLeon explains that though the Socialist Labour Party of Canada was accepted as a separate entity on the list of parties present, it was not accorded a proxy vote. DeLeon went on to inform his Canadian members that even their right to be separately represented was challenged by the British Social Democratic Federation which claimed that since Canada was a colony of Britain it really did not have a legal identity of its own; and consequently the Socialist Labour Party of Canada was not entitled to "separate recognition".[7]

But the Socialist Party of Canada (SPC) had already come into existence at this time and before long was the main socialist organization in Canada. In 1909 its Dominion Executive Committee, in response to enquiries from within Party ranks, adopted a resolution against joining the Second International. The main reason given was that "the International Socialist Bureau has seen fit to admit to membership ... certain non-Socialist bodies particularly the British Labour Party, and such parties are not only ignorant of the principles of Socialism, but practice openly the most shameless policy of fusion and compromises with capitalist parties ... ".

This resolution is significant for a number of reasons. It refutes the easy assumption made by some Canadian historians that the working-class immigrants who carried socialist ideas to Canada from Britain brought the idea of the British Labour Party and of its Fabian wing. Most of the British socialists who came to Canada during this period were in fact staunch opponents of laborism and fabianism. This resolution further provides an interesting commentary on how rigid the approach of the SPC was in contrast to the stand of the European socialist parties on the British Labour Party's application to affiliate.

Lenin and Kautsky were quite prominent in that debate, both advocating the acceptance of the Labour Party even though that party did not officially recognize the principles of the class struggle nor call itself socialist, in accordance with the International's rules of admission. Kautsky took the view that while the British Labour Party "does not directly recognize the proletarian class struggle, it nevertheless wages the struggle ... ". Lenin declared that the British Labour Party was "taking the first steps towards socialism and towards the class policy of the proletarian mass organization" and that by accepting the application of the Labour Party, the International would be encouraging that party to take further steps along that path. Lenin in particular attacked H. H. Hyndman of the British Social-Democratic Federation for "acting in a sectarian spirit", by adopting a position which in fact the Socialist Party of Canada copied in its Resolution of 1909.[8]

---

[7] Daniel DeLeon, *Flashlights of the Amsterdam Congress*, New York Labor News (1929), p. 6.

[8] See Lenin's account of this debate in the collection *British Labour and British Imperialism* (London, 1969), pp. 93-8.

The Split in Canadian Socialism

The position taken by the Dominion Executive of the Socialist Party of Canada roused considerable opposition in the party. This became one of the issues in the split in the Socialist Party of Canada and the formation of the Social-Democratic Party of Canada (SDPC) in 1911. At its founding convention the SDPC affiliated to the International. In 1914, by a referendum vote of 933-127, the SDPC decided to send a delegate "for the first time in the history of socialism in Canada" to a Congress of the International to be held that August in Vienna and at which this delegate "would be mixing with the most pronounced socialists in the world".[9] The delegate (first H. Martin, Executive Secretary of the Social-Democratic Party, then replaced by runner-up James Simpson) had to turn back as the war broke out while he was *en route*. Thus the Canadian socialist movement remained separated from the International socialist movement until confronted with the issue once again as a result of the formation of the Communist International in 1919. Its only connection was through the *International Socialist Review*, a monthly periodical published by Charles H. Kerr in Chicago from 1901-1918. This periodical served the leading cadre in the Canadian socialist movement as a source of information about the socialist movement elsewhere. But Canadian contributions to the magazine were minimal: three articles by G. Weston Wrigley, in 1901, 1903 and 1904; an article by Roscoe Fillmore of Nova Scotia in 1915, and an article about Canada by Gustavus Myers in 1913.

Except for a short period when the Socialist Labour Party was the main Marxist group in Canada, the socialist movement here was independent, both main socialist parties being autonomous and unaffiliated national organizations. The platforms of the two socialist parties were similar. Both were based mainly on general statements from the *Communist Manifesto*, with no attempt made to speak in specifically Canadian terms.

The Social-Democratic Party of Canada at its unity convention in Port Arthur, December 30 and 31, 1911, adopted a platform and constitution, the operative statement of which was as follows:

---

[9] *Cotton's Weekly*, June 4, 1914.

The object of the Social-Democratic Party is to educate the workers of Canada to a consciousness of their class position in society, their economic servitude to the owners of capital, and to organize them into a political party to seize the reins of government and transform all capitalist property into the collective property of the working class. This social transformation means the liberation not only of the proletariat but of the whole human race. Only the working class however can bring it about . . .

The "Platform" or "Manifesto" (the two terms are used interchangeably) of the Socialist Party of Canada was finalized in 1910 and contained this version of the Socialist revolution:

The interest of the working class lies in the direction of setting itself free from capitalist exploitation by the abolition of the wage system under which is cloaked the robbery of the working class at the point of production. To accomplish this necessitates the transformation of capitalist property in the means of wealth production into collective or working class property.

The irrepressible conflict of interest between the capitalist and the worker is rapidly culminating in a struggle for possession of the reins of government—the capitalist to hold, the worker to secure it by political action. This is the class struggle.

Therefore, we call upon all workers to organize under the Socialist Party of Canada with the object of conquering the public powers for setting up and enforcing the economic program of the working class . . .

Both programs were vague as to how the transformation was to be brought about. The SDPC used the phrase "seize the reins of government" and the SPC talked about "conquering the public powers . . . " by "political action" of the workers. The Social-Democratic Party did not state that it regarded itself as necessarily the party that would lead this process, whereas the Socialist Party was quite explicit on this question. Both did agree that the path to power included supporting proposals of an immediate reform nature so long as the workers or the objective conditions were not ripe for socialism. But while not opposing activity around immediate questions, both socialist parties relegated this to a subordinate rank. Although they inscribed in their platforms general demands of a democratic and pro-labor nature, they did not formulate a distinctive *party* position on current political questions, but generally left it up to their elected representatives to respond to issues as they arose. They tended to feel that any other attitude might create illusions among the workers and get in the way of "informing the rest of our class that they can expect no redress from the enemy, the capitalist class".[10]

Nevertheless, the work of the elected socialist members was not ignored by their parties. In 1910, for instance, the Socialist Party of Canada issued a pamphlet describing the legislative performance of J. H. Hawthornthwaite, Socialist Party member of the B.C. Legislature since 1901. It was an impressive performance in which the Socialist Party took pride and for which it accepted credit. Yet the relationship of the parties, and of the measures their representatives advocated or supported, to the cause of socialism continued to trouble the socialist movement, in which unease was regularly expressed over "palliatives that do not palliate".

Yet it is clear from documents of the SPC that they viewed all their work as contributing to the education of the workers and did not regard propaganda for socialism in a narrow sense as had been interpreted by some historians. A 1919 editorial in *The Red Flag*, which was for a short period the name of the official organ of the party, explains it in the following terms:

It is frequently asked in a more or less deprecatory spirit: why confine yourself to education? Is there nothing more the Socialist Party can do?

The answer is emphatically no! . . .

It must be understood, however, that education which in the language of the proletariat means class consciousness—and what inevitably follows upon class consciousness, namely class solidarity—can be and is being accomplished in many different ways. The socialist party has its particular methods, namely propaganda meetings and distribution of literature. Labour unions, craft or industrial, revolutionary or otherwise, consciously or unconsciously are all contributing their quota, insofar as they educate the masses to a realization of their position in human society. Strikes, riots, industrial disputes or incipient revolutions contribute nothing to-

---

[10] From a 1914 pamphlet written by T. Pilkington and published by the Socialist Party of Canada.

wards the downfall except in so much as they promote class con-
sciousness and class solidarity . . .

Whether this way of looking at the question was shared by
all the socialist party leadership is doubtful. But what appears
certain is that while not at all opposed to supporting immediate
demands, they did not think that it was the business of the
socialist party to formulate such demands. They felt it necessary
to be uncompromising towards capitalists and capitalism, to condemn in totality the basic features of the system, and thereby to
appear before the workers of Canada as the irreconcilable foe of
capitalism and the only real alternative to capitalist parties and
governments.

This image which the socialists projected was summed up in
1909 in the Alberta Legislature by C. M. O'Brien, a socialist
MLA:

Every member of this Assembly, Liberal, Conservative or Inde-
pendent (I do not know what this independent means; he may be
independent of the Liberals or the Conservatives, or even both, but
he is not independent of the rule of capital). I say every member of
this Assembly, except myself, was elected to defend and uphold the
present social system, to defend its foundation-capital, and there-
fore to justify the capitalist class in their ownership of all the
essential means of wealth and production.

We Socialists have our platform "the transformation of capitalist
property into the collective property of the working class"; So Mr.
Speaker, it is easy to see that the interests represented by the other
members of the Assembly are absolutely opposed to the interests I
represent, and vice-versa. True, we are all interested in having good
weather in sunny Alberta, in being free from pestilence, disease,
and natural calamities, but economically and politically we are
enemies.

It has been argued that the split in 1910 which resulted in
the formation of the Social-Democratic Party of Canada reflected in large measure opposition to the doctrinaire approach
to "immediate demands" taken by the Socialist Party of Canada.
Ostensibly, then, the activity of the new socialist organization as
well as its platform ought to clearly show greater emphasis on
reform measures. This difference is, however, not sharply deline-
ated in the platform of the Social-Democratic Party. It does state

that the Social-Democratic Party of Canada "will support any measure that will tend to better conditions under capitalism, such as: 1) Reduction of hours of labour; 2) The elimination of child labour; 3) Universal adult suffrage without distinction of sex or regard to property qualifications; and 4) The Initiative, Referendum, and Right of Recall".

But this is really no different from the platform of the Socialist Party of Canada. There were, to be sure, differences in emphasis and in practical activity, but these were far from one-sided. In the 1911 Federal Election, the Socialist Party of Canada denounced Reciprocity as "a red herring devised to draw away the awakened proletariat from its pursuit of Capital"; whereas the Social Democrats "favoured it as a step in the direction of free trade". Yet the Socialist Party of Canada nominated eight candidates in that campaign whereas the Ontario Branch of the Social Democrats, the largest section of the Social-Democratic Party in Canada, did not nominate a single candidate. The Socialist Party of Canada tended to ignore municipal elections whereas the Social-Democratic Party began to nominate and elect representatives to civic bodies in Winnipeg and Toronto.

But it was the labor movement that the socialists regarded as their special and most important constituency and in which they exercised an influence far exceeding their strength in the general body politic of the country.

This influence has been attributed to the role of British immigrants who came in to replenish the labor force as the industrialization of Canada got underway, particularly after the inauguration of the National Policy. Certainly the socialists who became prominent in the trade-union movement in the first two decades of this century were mostly Britons, who had brought with them a well-developed socialist and trade-union consciousness, along with their technical skills.

But the process by which socialism and unionism in Canada became intertwined in those years also owed much to the penetration into Canada of the American trade-union movement.

The Knights of Labor and the American Federation of Labor owed their original stimulus in large measure to socialists, including at the start Samuel Gompers. The Preambles and Constitutions of these bodies, with their Marxian flavor and language, reflect this influence. So did the smaller U.S. trade union centers which had some impact in Canada during this period: the Western Federation of Miners, the American Labor Union, and the Industrial Workers of the World. The militancy of the American trade unions stood out in contrast to the conservatism of the Canadian unions, and the early socialists from Britain felt much more comfortable in the American-based unions.

In much of the literature dealing with the so-called International unions in Canada attention is focused on the role of Samuel Gompers after he ceased to be a socialist and became a vigorous exponent of "business unionism", and a foe of socialism. But what is largely ignored in this respect is that the socialist influence *inside* the U.S. labor movement remained strong in spite of Gompers, and in some of the powerful unions was even predominant during this period, making it easier for socialists in these unions in Canada to become and remain leaders in their locals. A recent study of the trade-union movement in the United States identifies five major unions there in which socialism was strong in these years: United Mine Workers (AFL), International Ladies Garment Workers Union (AFL), International Association of Machinists (AFL), United Brewery Workers (AFL), Amalgamated Clothing Workers (Ind) and Western Federation of Miners (Ind).[11] With the exception of the brewery workers, these unions in Canada were also led by socialists. In addition to these unions, Canadian socialists were influential in the International Longshoremen's Association in British Columbia, the International Typographical Union in Toronto, the United Brotherhood of Steamfitters and Plumbers in Montreal, several of the American-based Railroad Brotherhoods, as well as in many of the Trades and Labour Councils and Federations. From 1911 to 1918 both the President and Vice-President of the Trades and Labour Congress (TLC) in Canada were socialists: J. C. Watters and James Simpson, respectively.

The socialist parties directed their main propaganda efforts towards the labor movement. In 1913 they sponsored and succeeded in passing a resolution at the TLC Convention instructing all trade union locals to conduct classes based on Marx's *Value, Price and Profit*. In 1912 they secured, through a referendum of the unions affiliated to the B.C. Federation of Labor, adoption of a resolution endorsing socialism. By then the *B.C. Federationist*, the official organ of the B.C. Federation of Labor, was under the editorial direction of members of the Socialist Party of Canada and its contents, which regularly featured theoretical essays on Marxism, were often indistinguishable from the socialists'

---

[11] William M. Dick, *Labor and Socialism In America* (New York, 1972), pp. 72-5.

own periodicals. In Ontario, *Cotton's Weekly**, which in 1911 had become the organ of the Social-Democratic Party, had reached a circulation of 30,000 by 1913, much of it among trade unionists.

In their propaganda work socialists tended to belittle wage struggles and wage gains as illusory "palliatives". Yet as trade unionists they distinguished themselves in these battles. They advocated independent labor political action, but were unclear and divided as to whether that activity should take place through the socialist parties, or through labor parties on the British model in which the socialists would take part. The advocates of the latter course seemed to have achieved a major breakthrough when in 1917 the annual Convention of the TLC committed it to the building of a Canadian Labor Party. In its report to the 1918 Convention, the Executive Council of the TLC was able to say that this decision

has led to the uniting of Trade Unionists and Socialists for united action and the prospects for a strong and aggressive National Labor Party were never brighter than they are today.

Although the optimism of the Executive Council proved to be unfounded, this statement does constitute an acknowledgement of the effectiveness of the socialist parties up to that date in their relations with the labor movement, and in particular of the pioneering they did in the eventual establishment of a political center outside the two-party system. This was the first explicit declaration by an important body that the existing two-party system did not express the interests of a substantial segment of the Canadian people, and that the opposition to that system was in some way associated with the socialist idea.

Socialists and the Trade Unions

But there were differences and division over what attitude, if any, the socialist trade unionists should have to specifically trade-union questions. Two of the most persistent questions were trade-union autonomy and union structure, both of which be-

---

* In 1914 the paper's name was changed to *The Canadian Forward.*

came especially prominent during the war, reaching a climax in the revolt of the Western trade unions, the emergence of the One Big Union* (OBU) and the Winnipeg General Strike. There was disagreement on these and related matters not only between the socialist parties, but also within their ranks.

There was no doubt that members of the socialist parties were prominent in the Western trade union revolt, the OBU, and the Winnipeg General Strike. Their participation in the latter was decisive through their leadership of the Machinists Union, whose dispute with the metal trades manufacturers was the spark that ignited the Strike. But there is no conclusive evidence to indicate that the launching of the OBU was a policy adopted by the Socialist Party of Canada, and carried out by members acting under its direction. A dispute over an editorial in the Socialist Party of Canada organ throws some light on this question. In the *Western Clarion* for April 1, 1920, an editorial discussing the Winnipeg Strike trials dropped a remark almost casually to the effect that "it is not our function to proclaim the superiority of one form of industrial organization over another, if any exists . . .".

This was a specific reference to the OBU and this remark, particularly the last three words, occasioned a sharp rejoinder in the April 9 issue of *Searchlight*, an OBU paper published in Calgary. This in turn elicited an editorial in the *Western Clarion* discussing this subject and expanding its answer to include a statement or restatement of the policy of the Socialist Party of Canada to the labor movement. The editorial, which appeared May 1, was an important statement of socialist policy towards the trade unions. It said in part:

All that was implied by the complete statement of policy was that the comparative merit of various forms of industrial organizations did not come within the field of the Socialist Party of Canada activity, but that such matters were specific business for the organized labor movement to consider, decide and act upon as effecting its members in their immediate struggle over conditions of work and wages. Such matters are the business of the Socialist Party of Canada only insofar as to take cognizance of for its own general purpose of bringing all social phenomenon within the focus of a revolutionary socialist viewpoint. . . .

---

* Although the OBU was projected at the Western Labour Conference held in Calgary, March 1919, it was not founded until June 11. No one from Winnipeg attended the inaugural convention.

The form of labour organizations structurally adapted to conform to the state of the physical organization of capitalist industry will be of value to its members when bargaining over work and wages with the employers. Its value, however, in a revolutionary sense lies but little in its specific form, but arises from the number of the class conscious workers within its ranks. We assert, that to the Socialist, Non-Socialist, and Anti-Socialist members of the organized labour movement must be left the form of that movement's responses to the immediate conditions in our present industrial and social life.

On the other hand, the business of the Socialist Party is the propagation of Socialism which is ultimately to emancipate the race from such conditions. The Socialist Party of Canada best serves the interest of the working class by concentrating its energies exclusively in that business.

Yet this policy was found to be easier to state in theoretical terms than to apply in practice. Up to a point both the trade-union movement and the socialist movement had a tacit division of labor whereby one carried out the economic battles and the other the political. But this relationship broke down under the impact of the pressures and conditions created by the War. The result was sharp divisions within the TLC with the socialists, especially those from the West, ranged against a significant and ultimately decisive section of the trade-union leadership in the East. The issues which came to a head at the 1918 Convention included conscription, industrial unionism, and trade-union and civil rights which militant trade unionists felt were being eroded by the War Measures Act. The result of that battle was the defeat of the President and Vice-President, both socialists, the alienation of the Western trade unionists, and the election of a TLC leadership more liberal than socialist.

But the socialists, while defeated at the Convention, took the issues to the trade union membership and to the workers at large and engaged in a whole series of movements, political and propagandist as well as economic, which in the subsequent three years helped radicalize the working class. The highlights of these activities included the Western Labour Conference of 1919, the launching of the OBU, the Winnipeg General Strike, the election of a farmer-labor government in Ontario in 1919, the election of eleven Labour Party candidates in the Manitoba Provincial Elections of 1920, the far-reaching impact of the nationwide movement in support of the arrested and imprisoned leaders of the Winnipeg General Strike, and the election of two labor members to the House of Commons in 1921.

A number of historians writing about this period declare that the Socialist Party went on "a syndicalist binge" which ended in disaster, thus demonstrating "the futility of syndicalist tactics". Desmond Morton, one of those making this charge, defines syndicalism as "the doctrine that labour struggle can short-circuit the familiar institutions of parliament and government".[12] Martin Robin claims that syndicalism represented "a long-standing dispute" between "the direct actionists" and "the political actionists".[13]

There are a number of assumptions made in these analyses that cannot be sustained historically. One is that the so-called "political actionists" and "direct actionists" were different people, or that the activities in which one group was involved were different from the activities of the other. There is no doubt that within the socialist movement there had always existed differing perceptions of the relative importance of various forms of working-class activity, but there is no evidence that one group rejected political action or that the other rejected labor struggle. Moreover, the main activities that highlighted the period, the Winnipeg General Strike, the Western Labour Conference, the OBU, and the defence campaign around the Winnipeg trials, brought about a degree of unity between socialists of all persuasions which had not existed heretofore. So did the electoral activity, in which leaders of *all* socialist groups were represented among the candidates which the various labor parties fielded.

The socialists themselves participated in and stimulated a wide variety of actions and they felt that the radicalization that was taking place was the result of the total impact of *all* these forms. This is certainly how W. A. Pritchard explained it in his *Address to the Jury* in 1920. These activities were not separated in fact, nor in the perceptions of the principal actors at that time.[14]

---

[12] Desmond Morton, *NDP: The Dream of Power* (Toronto, 1974), p. 4.

[13] Martin Robin, *Radical Politics and Canadian Labour 1880-1930* (Kingston, 1968), p. 199.

[14] See "Excerpts from W. A. Pritchard's Address To The Jury March 23-24, 1920" in Norman Penner, ed., *Winnipeg 1919, The Strikers' own History of The Winnipeg General Strike* (Toronto, 1975), pp. 243-284.

The Impact of the Bolshevik Revolution

The factor that undoubtedly played the biggest role in galvanizing the disparate elements in the socialist movement, and which accounts in large measure for the increased militancy and radicalism of this period, was the electrifying impact of the Bolshevik revolution in Russia.

Canadian socialists were virtually unanimous in support of the Bolsheviks, particularly in the period when the beleaguered Soviet government was fighting off an interventionist army made up of troops from fourteen nations including Canada. A substantial number of socialists began to look towards the Soviet experiences and the Soviet ideas for possible answers to questions of strategy and tactics which had troubled them for years. The socialist, as well as the trade-union press, began to devote an ever-increasing amount of space to items about the Russian events and particularly, as they became available, to the works of Lenin, who had been unknown to Canadian socialists until the revolution.

Most of the Canadian socialists were quite unprepared for the Bolshevik uprising. At the time of the overthrow of the Czar, seven months before the Bolsheviks took power, an editorial in the *B.C. Federationist* (obviously written by the socialist editor R. Parm Pettipiece) predicted a long period of capitalist development:

A capitalist regime must ensue before the ground can be properly prepared for the working class revolution. Out of the present and rapidly growing confusion, a capitalist constitutional state will probably come in time. That there will be setbacks in periods of reactionary ascendancy is almost certain, but that the general trend will always be onward and upward is also sure. Either that or all theories regarding the growth and development of human society go for naught.

On the other hand a leading member of the Ukrainian Branch of the Social-Democratic Party in Winnipeg was more sanguine, probably because he was better acquainted with the actual situation in the Russian socialist movement.

I am confident that the workers and peasants, our class brothers,

*will not stop. Now that the tsarist autocracy is cracked and Nicho-
las has abdicated, the people will go from the provisional government forward to government by the working people and thus forward to Socialism.*

In the year following the Bolshevik revolution, the *Western
Clarion* carried news and articles from and about the Soviet
regime in every issue. Although banned by Order-in-Council,
November 13, 1918, it reappeared on December 28, 1918, under
the name *The Red Flag*, continued this heavy emphasis on popularizing the Bolshevik progress, and became the first publication
through which Lenin's works were introduced to the Canadian
public. Among these were: *Chief Tasks of Our Day* (December
28, 1918); *The International Revolution* (January 11, 1919); *State
and Revolution* (serialized, commencing March 22, 1919). *The
Western Clarion* (reappearing under its own name since 1920
when the ban was lifted) began on March 1, 1921, to publish
Left-Wing Communism, An Infantile Disorder. Also carried in the
columns of the Socialist Party organ were reports and verbatim
accounts of the speeches and activities of European socialist
figures who were regarded as holding views similar to those of
Lenin: Karl Liebknecht, Rosa Luxemburg, Clara Zetkin, Franz
Mehring. As well, they published the words of leading figures of
the Russian Revolution: Trotsky, Kamenev, Chitcherin, Kollon-
tay, Litvinov.

The other socialist journal of the time, *The Canadian For-
ward*, organ of the Social-Democratic Party of Canada, pub-
lished in Toronto, likewise gave considerable prominence to the
Russian Revolution and was no less jubilant about the success of
Lenin and his followers. Some issues featured editorials greeting
this victory: "Radicals Rule Russia" (December 24, 1917); "The
Bolsheviki and World Peace" by Leon Trotsky (February 10,
1918); "The Bolsheviki—What Is It?" (March 24, 1918); "Red
Russia" by John Reed (May 24, 1918); "The Main Problem of
Our Day" by N. Lenin (September 10, 1918).

Not to be outdone in enthusiasm, trade-union journals also
devoted considerable space to the events in Russia. In its first
issue after the Bolshevik victory, the *B.C. Federationist* proclaimed in a front-page editorial the "Vitality of the Great Russian Revolution", and thereafter carried regular items of news
and comments on the progress of the Soviet regime. The *Western
Labour News* which in 1918 became the official organ of the

Winnipeg Trades and Labour Council, and the *Industrial Banner* of Toronto, did the same.*

The Manitoba Social-Democratic Party held a provincial convention on March 3, 1918, and endorsed a resolution which expressed "its willingness to unite with the Socialist Party of Canada on the basis of the Bolsheviki program."

This despite the fact that there was as yet very little information about the program of the Bolsheviks in Russia, nor any discussion as to what parts, if any, of that program, could be applied to Canada. The convention also instructed the Dominion Executive to "take the necessary steps to affiliate this party with the Zimmerwald Conference" as "the nucleus of the Third International".*

At the same time another event occurred abroad which was to have an important impact on the Canadian socialist movement: the drafting in March 1918, and the adoption in June of that year, of the British Labour Party's manifesto called *Labour and the New Social Order*. This followed a conference held in December 1917 at which for the time the British Labour Party explicitly adopted socialism as its aim. A front-page article in *The Canadian Forward* by John Alexander, on January 10, 1918, explained the significance of that for Canadian socialists:

The movement in Britain, it seems to me, is the one next to our own, that is of most account to us, as its success would undoubtedly react most favourably on the movement in Canada. Its progress now takes on an added interest since the adoption in the new Constitution of the British Labour Party of a definite socialist objective.

James Simpson attended this December Conference and carried the message back to Canada with characteristic enthusiasm. The Social Democratic Party organ serialized the entire Labour Party manifesto. The manifesto contained a sweeping program for restructuring society, calling for "socialization of Industry", nationalization of land, railways, mines, electric power, and the

---

* The *Western Labour News* was then edited by Rev. William Ivens, and the *Industrial Banner* by James Simpson.

* The Zimmerwald Conference was the name given to three meetings of left-wing socialists held between 1915 and 1917, which denounced the Second International for not opposing the War. Lenin played a prominent part in Zimmerwald although he did not regard it as "the nucleus of the Third International".

adoption and enforcement of a national minimum standard of health, education, leisure and subsistence for every citizen. It seemed to offer another polar attraction to Canadian socialists who had hitherto been critical of the British Labour Party, or who were seeking a model of socialism different from the Russian one.

In February 1918, shortly after his return from Britain, James Simpson gave a speech to over 3,000 people in Montreal in which he directly linked the Bolshevik program with that of the British Labour Party:

There are not many differences between the Bolsheviks and the British workers. The press has tried to belittle the Bolshevik Government, but it is well to recognize that the sentiment of the Russian people is at bottom that of the British workingmen.

They were wearied of Czarism in Russia. They had enough of capitalism. The workers have torn power from the capitalists which the latter have tried to seize at the revolution. They have dethroned the bourgeoisie for fear of a second French Revolution. What the British workers want is just what the Bolsheviki have attained—the nationalization of all great public institutions—such as railways and banks.

These two events, the Bolshevik Revolution and the British Labour Party Conference, occurring at the same time, gave a considerable boost to the propaganda efforts of the Canadian socialists. In fact, they transformed these propaganda efforts from small circles of sympathizers to audiences of thousands who came out regularly to hear about the spirit of socialism that was "sweeping the whole earth".

From March 1918 on in Vancouver, separate forums of the Federated Labor Party and the Socialist Party of Canada were held on Sunday evenings. They attracted such crowds that at one point they were running four and five meetings simultaneously. Speakers included J. S. Woodsworth, E. T. Kingsley, and Doctor W. J. Curry for the Federated Labor Party, and W. W. Lefeaux, W. A. Pritchard, J. Kavanagh for the Socialist Party. Similar meetings were held in Victoria and Nanaimo, although not on such a scale.

The following report appeared on the front page of the *B.C. Federationist* for January 17, 1919:

WOODSWORTH TALKS TO A CAPACITY HOUSE
Speaker at Rex Theatre Explains the Question. What do we Want? Complete Overthrow of the Present System of Production is Advocated.

Last Sunday evening was no exception to the state of affairs which had prevailed for weeks past at the Rex Theatre, as hundreds were unable to gain admittance.

Mr. Woodsworth, in opening, stated that he had been at the Broadway Theatre continuously for the last seven Sundays. He referred to the significance of the fact that it was possible to carry on four large meetings in Vancouver theatres at the same time on Sunday evenings in the working class interest. These were more than propaganda meetings, they were centres of expression. The press controlled and the pulpits catered largely to one class in society. It was encouraging therefore, that so many were found to be actually clamouring to give expression to the sentiments and desires of the great masses of people.

Similar meetings were being held across the country, of which the famous Walker Theatre meeting of December 1918 in Winnipeg was a highlight. It featured speakers from the Socialist Party of Canada, the Social-Democratic Party of Canada, the Independent Labor Party (ILP), and the TLC. Its message was socialism, support to the Bolsheviks, and militant demands for the restoration of civil and trade-union rights. There were similar meetings in Montreal, Toronto, Kitchener, London, and Glace Bay, all expressing the same interest and showing the same enthusiasm.

The events which inspired these meetings were felt not only in the increased scale of propaganda activity but also in stimulating the search for new paths of socialist political activity. On the one hand, the Bolshevik revolution and especially the increasing availability of the writings of Lenin now suggested new approaches to the role, character, and tasks of a Marxist party. On the other hand, the British Labour Party's adoption of socialism in its postwar program increased the attractiveness of founding a Canadian labor party on the British model. By September 1918, provincial labor parties had been established in Ontario, Quebec, British Columbia, Alberta, Manitoba, and Nova Scotia, and the outgoing TLC executives proposed calling "a convention to organize a National Canadian Labor Party ... at as early a date as practical". The Ontario section, which had been formed on

March 29, 1918, went beyond the confines of labor and socialist groups to include the United Farmers of Ontario. The B.C. Federation of Labor reported that its political arm, the Federated Labor Party, formed in January 1918 "has advanced by leaps and bounds and is now established in all parts of the province ... and at the next provincial elections there will be candidates under the auspices of the party in most of the constituencies".

These were indeed heady times for the socialist movement and their mounting optimism was expressed in the words of Dr. W. J. Curry, a Vancouver dentist who was one of the popular speakers on the propaganda circuit. In an address given at one of the Federated Labor Party forums entitled "Social Revolution" he concluded a Marxist analysis of the capitalist society with these words:

The empire of capitalism is about to perish, just as other empires have perished in the past. Capitalism has been weighed in the balance and has been found wanting. The capitalist class will be deprived of its power and the kingdom given to the working class. (Much applause).

This feeling of optimism was enhanced by the Winnipeg General Strike and its aftermath. While the strike itself had been defeated and some of the main leaders arrested, the general feeling in the Winnipeg General Strike Committee as expressed in its post-strike statement was that the strike had been a political and moral victory:

Labor was not prepared for the long, bitter struggle which was forced upon her by the bosses six weeks ago, but in spite of her unpreparedness, labor made a magnificent fight. Now get ready for the next fight.

... The Government should learn from the Strike that the soul of the people is rising; that the people will no longer be satisfied with lip service. Labor and returned men have stood shoulder to shoulder because both are suffering injustice ...

... the time is now ripe to curb exploiters and ensure workers better wages and conditions of life. The great producing class will take the ballot in hand and clean up the law-making factories. People are going to have more say in the Government and the sooner the Government learns this, the better it will be for all concerned.

This message was carried across the country at huge and enthusiastic gatherings addressed by some of the leaders of the Strike. The *Toronto Star* of July 15, 1919, carried a report of a public meeting in Queen's Park attended by 5,000 people and addressed by Alderman John Queen and Alderman A. A. Heaps, arrested strike leaders: "It is doubtful whether the staid Queen's Park has ever been the scene of such an enthusiastic meeting."

In Glace Bay, Nova Scotia, the Mayor declared a Civic Holiday known as Winnipeg Strike Day to coincide with a visit there of Alderman Heaps. According to the *Lethbridge Herald* of July 12, 1919, J. S. Woodsworth declared at a special meeting of the Lethbridge Trades and Labour Council that "the only way labour can get what it wants is to some way get control of the military and courts of Canada". In November 1919, William Ivens gave a report of his six weeks "triumphal tour" through Eastern Canada at a meeting in Winnipeg before "an audience of about 5,000 . . . ". The repercussions of the Winnipeg General Strike continued to agitate the labor and socialist movement for almost two years. The trials, which took place between December 1919 and April 1920, were front-page news in the Canadian press during this period, as well as the subject of constant editorial comment, which according to the *New York Post* of January 15, 1920, reflected "the intense interest not only in Winnipeg but throughout Canada".

On his release from prison in 1921, after completing his sentence, W. A. Pritchard was greeted by a crowd between seven and twelve thousand at the railway station in Vancouver, and welcomed at a whole series of festive celebrations lasting for a week.

But differences began to develop within and between the socialist parties about the future of the socialist movement in Canada, and in particular over whether they should affiliate to the projected Canadian Labour Party. A new socialist party, formed in Toronto in 1915 and called the Socialist Party of North America (SPNA)*, was quite unequivocal in its attitude. Its 1918 *Declaration of Principles* contained the following passage:

---

* It consisted of the SPC branches in Toronto, Guelph, Kitchener, and Hamilton which broke away from the parent body in January 1915. Mainly composed of trade unionists, it was, in spite of its name, an independent organization, functioning only in these centers.

The Socialist Party of North America, therefore enters the field of political action determined to wage war against all other political parties, whether alleged labor or avowedly capitalist, and calls upon the members of the working class of this country to muster its banner to the end that a speedy termination may be brought to the system which deprives them of the fruits of their labor, and that poverty may give place to comfort, privilege to equality, and slavery to freedom.

The Canadian Forward of February 24, 1918, published on its front page an article by James Simpson entitled "The Future of the Social Democratic Party of Canada". Stating that the SDP now faced "a new political situation in Canada" with the possibility of "one strong working class party embracing trade unionists, socialists, cooperators, Fabians, farmers", Simpson urged his fellow socialists to grasp the opportunity which now existed and give all possible support to the formation of the new party. According to Simpson there were three alternatives to choose from: the complete merging of the SDP into the new party thus "losing its identity entirely"; the SDP retaining its identity as a vehicle for "carrying on distinctive socialist propaganda activity"; or the SDP affiliating to the new party, accepting its decisions as to candidates, while at the same time retaining the right "to carry on its educational work as locals of the SDP". Simpson argued for the third alternative:

The experience of the British Labour Party proves that the intimate association of the Trade Unionists and Socialists in one political organization is mutually advantageous. Trade unionists get a clearer vision of their duty to those of their own class and socialists become more sympathetic with the psychology of the working class movement, thus compelling them to adopt methods of education through their propaganda that are sanely adopted to the real conditions that have to be faced.

But it became clear that the party was sharply divided on this question. A letter from Jacob Penner of Winnipeg in March 1918 put this position forward:

The locals* in Manitoba will hold a Provincial Convention on the

---

* Locals of the Social-Democratic Party of Manitoba.

3rd of March. The most important question that this convention will deal with is "what attitude should the SDP assume in regard to the newly-formed Labor Party?" The opinion most prevalent here on the question is that the Party should not affiliate with the Labor Party. Personally, I think that the composition of the Labor Party here in Winnipeg and its rather conservative tendencies, leave no other path given to us but to reject the invitation to affiliate.

The Manitoba Convention upheld Penner's views, leaving the question of affiliation "in abeyance . . . until such time when the latter [Labor Party] will have adopted a platform and constitution". Yet at the same time it endorsed the Bolshevik program without having much information about it, and voted to affiliate to the Third International which was not even formed yet!

A similar view was held by the Socialist Party of North America which at the Convention launching the Ontario Labour Party on March 29, 1918, moved the following amendment:

Only a political party of the working class based upon a recognition of the class struggle with its immediate aims the abolition of the capitalist system and the establishment of the Cooperative Commonwealth, can permanently benefit the condition of the working class.

Although there were only three delegates directly representing the SPNA, its amendment received thirty-five votes but was defeated by a majority of over one hundred.

The debate over the nature of working-class political action foreshadowed the eventual split in the Canadian socialist movement. Those who were enthusiastic about the new turn in the British Labour Party favoured a Canadian party along similar lines. Those who were attracted to the Bolshevik regime and Lenin were hesitant, sceptical or opposed to the Canadian Labour Party.

At the outset the debate was mainly around questions of efficacy rather than philosophy. All sides supported the Bolshevik regime but divided on the question of which model would be more effective in the Canadian setting. But gradually, as information about the Soviet party and particularly the writings of Lenin became available, fundamental theoretical questions were injected into the discussion.

The concept of "the dictatorship of the proletariat" seems to have been the first new theoretical postulate coming out of the Russian Revolution to attract the attention of Canadian socialists. The publication in English of Marx's "Critique of the Gotha Programme" in *The Canadian Forward*, June 26 and July 10, 1917, in which Marx specifically used that term, did not arouse any comment at the time in the socialist press. That phrase appears to have been ignored until after Lenin's rise to power. *The Red Flag* on March 1, 1919, carried a front-page article entitled "Through Dictatorship to Democracy" by Clara Zetkin. In the next issue there appeared a front-page article by Trotsky called "The Principles of Democracy and Proletarian Dictatorship". Two weeks later, on March 22, 1919, *The Red Flag* began serialization of Lenin's "State and Revolution" which was his key work on the subject of the proletarian dictatorship. At the Western Labour Conference, which began on March 13, 1919, the following resolution was put and unanimously adopted:

. . . this Convention declares its full acceptance of the principle of "Proletarian Dictatorship" as being absolute and efficient for the transformation of capitalistic private property to communal wealth, and that fraternal greetings be sent to the Russian Soviet Government, the Spartacus in Germany, and all definite working class movements in the world recognizing they have won first place in the history of the class struggle.[15]

There appeared to be fairly general support for that idea in the Socialist Party of Canada, the Socialist Party of North America, and among a large minority of the Social-Democratic Party.

This included the idea put forward by Lenin that "A Marxist is one who *extends* the acceptance of the class struggle to the acceptance of the dictatorship of the proletariat."

However, not all of those who agreed with the concept of proletarian dictatorship were prepared to accept the conditions laid down by the Communist International at its Second Congress in Moscow, July 19 to August 7, 1920, and first published in Canada in the *Western Clarion*, January 1, 1921. There was no Canadian present at that Congress, nor at the founding Congress held a year earlier. But W. W. Lefeaux, a leading member of the Socialist Party of Canada, was in Moscow just after the Congress and had extensive contact with two leading American delegates to that Congress, John Reed and his wife Louise

---

[15] See N. Penner, ed., *Winnipeg, 1919*, p. 29.

Bryant. Lefeaux also met Bela Kun, the leading Hungarian Communist, and met and talked with Lev Kamenev, a member of the Political Bureau of the Russian Communist Party. He returned favorably impressed with the Soviet regime, and wrote the first account of the new Russian regime by a Canadian visitor. In it he recognized its difficulties and believed that its "theory and philosophy are those of Marxian socialism" although "all Marxian socialists do not agree as to the methods of putting the doctrine into practice".[16]

He brought with him a copy of the Conditions of Affiliation which he submitted to the Socialist Party of Canada and which he opposed in the subsequent debate and referendum in the Party. In later years he summed up his principal objections as follows:

Several of the Conditions of Affiliation most of us strongly objected to. One was that the party should be known as the Communist Party of Canada. Another was that we should be absolutely controlled by the Executive of the International which was at that time in Moscow.... [17]

This latter claim became the main argument advanced in the Socialist Party of Canada debate by those opposed to affiliation. In an article in the *Western Clarion*, February 1, 1921, J. Harrington, the editor, elaborated on this objection:

... acceptance of the 18 theses ... could involve accentuating factional disputes in the socialist movement between right, left, and centre, which divisions do not exist in the socialist movement in Canada. This, therefore, would be an artificial division based on external considerations having little or nothing to do with the situation in Canada.

He objected to the second condition, which called for the systematic removal of all "reformist" elements from responsible positions in the trade unions, party press, and parliamentary factions and their replacement by Communists. This, he said, "would involve us in a series of bitter struggles that would hamper and in the end nullify our educational work", work

---

[16] W. W. Lefeaux, *Winnipeg-London-Moscow: A Study of Bolshevism* (Winnipeg, 1921).

[17] Minutes of a meeting called by the B.C. Provincial Executive, CCF, October 15, 1943. Angus MacInnis Collection: Box 31, Folio 4.

which Harrington believed was of the utmost importance.

He objected to the condition which required members of the Communist International to support the colonial liberation movements which, according to Harrington, "are of no importance ... to the main struggle of the working class which is against the Capitalist class".* Harrington closed with the following disclaimer: "I do not consider rejection of these terms implies any disagreement with the methods and purposes of the Bolsheviks."

Yet even though all members who participated in the debate remained supporters of the Bolsheviks, the debate, as it progressed, became increasingly acrimonious and, in the end, completely disrupted the party. That this was not entirely fortuitous but an aim sought by the supporters of the Communist International is suggested by a bitter attack on the Socialist Party in the first issue of a new publication called *The Communist*, which appeared May 1, 1921. Published "by authority of the Third Communist International in Canada" but containing no other identification, *The Communist* accused the Socialist Party of Canada of being interested only in propaganda and never in economics or the day-to-day struggles of the working people. The *Western Clarion* declared that this "was a lie and should be scotched immediately" (June 1, 1921).

W. A. Pritchard replied to *The Communist* in a vitriolic and sarcastic letter in the *Western Clarion*, July 16, 1921, which among other things expressed a western Canadian hostility to socialists in Toronto:

Yet, for all that, there can be discerned more revolutionary knowledge and instinct out in the West, than can be found in the East, despite the latter's preponderance of population, which brings me to remark somewhat upon the grotesque attitude adopted by our unknown and apparently hitherto unheard-of critics, the "sewer-pipe" revolutionist of The Communist *published as far as can be ascertained in Toronto ...*

Our friends of the "rat-hole" persuasion with a heap of choice cult phrases ... have discovered that some years of painful prodding in the realm of propaganda is of no avail, that the Socialist Party of Canada is reformistic, that Harrington, whose record is ... as clean as any in the movement, East or West, is a Kautsky.

---

* No one else appeared to have raised this as an objection.

And this committee of the Third International of Canada, who are they? We know not . . . I protest against the insipid yet insidious attacks of noisy unknowns, against those who are known to the authorities as outspoken protagonists of the class struggle . . .

But many of the key people in the SPC opted for affiliation. Among them were J. Kavanagh, H. Bartholomew, W. Bennett, J. Knight and Roscoe Fillmore. R. B. Russell of Winnipeg was still in jail during most of the debate and did not make his mind up until later, when he refused to accept the demand of the Third International that he work for the dissolution of the OBU in favor of a return to the ranks of the AFL. While the opponents of affiliation carried the referendum by a small margin, a large section of the party did secede and formed the Communist Party. The Socialist Party of North America, which included people like Tim Buck, Tom Bell, Jack MacDonald, in its entirety joined the Communist Party. The Social-Democratic Party of Canada, by then the biggest section of the socialist movement, split, with the majority joining the Canadian Labour Party or its provincial counterparts, and the remainder, including all the language branches, joining the Communist Party.

By the end of 1921, the Canadian socialist movement had been decisively transformed. The Social-Democratic Party and the Socialist Party of North America had ceased to exist. The Socialist Party of Canada was reduced in numbers and in influence. The Communist Party had emerged with a new brand of Marxism based on the Russian experience and the teachings of Lenin. The Ontario section of the Canadian Labour Party, the Independent Labor Party in Manitoba, Saskatchewan and Alberta and the Federated Labor Party of B.C. became the repositories of the British labour-socialist idea, but were not ready for some time to coalesce into a nationwide political entity.

Thus a period which began on a crest of militancy and radicalization in the labor movement, unprecedented to that date, ended in a splintering of Canadian socialism. Only the Communists seemed to know where they were going, but their enthusiasm and optimism, still riding on the high hopes of the Russian Revolution, were to prove illusory.

Yet in spite of divisions and setbacks, Canadian socialism had by then made an impact on Canadian political thought and had established itself as a definite part of the Canadian ideological spectrum.

This can be partially seen by the reaction of the orthodox or established political cultures to socialism. The spirit of authoritarian Toryism, out of fear and contempt, adopted the approach of intellectual suppression, and later, as the socialist idea became stronger, state repression. Reference has already been made to the treatment of Marxist ideas at the academic level. This was seen to be mainly one of refusal to accept Marxism as a subject worthy of inclusion in the university calendars, to kill it by silence. Ferns and Ostry in their biography of Mackenzie King describe a student strike that was precipitated at the University of Toronto in 1895 over the refusal of Professor James Mavor, then Chairman of the Department of Political Economy, to allow a socialist speaker to address a meeting of the Political Science Club on the campus.[18]

In Quebec, socialism was proscribed by the Church at an early stage, as was "neutral" or international unionism which was seen to be synonymous with socialism. In a paper presented to the Royal Society of Canada in 1894, Joseph Royal maintained that the danger of socialism comes from the importance and character of labor unions which

... have crossed the border to be implanted amongst us. These appear to be irreproachable in themselves, but their origin is foreign and that is the most serious objection. They are American in character and spirit.

The tendency to regard socialism and unionism as synonymous was held by many in government, as well as in the press and at universities. Much of the violence directed at unions in this period stemmed from a fear that every strike was in fact a miniature socialist revolution or an anarchist plot. If, as M. Royal claimed, the American unions brought socialist ideas into Canada, it was equally true that some of the attitudes of American employers and governments in fighting unions were also imported.

But it was not until late in the war years that the machinery of government was used more and more against the socialist movement. This was a response to the role which socialists were playing in the growing unrest and turmoil among workers over wartime conditions of conscription and inflation. Commenting on the appeal of the Social-Democratic Party of Manitoba that

---

[18] Henry Ferns and Bernard Ostry, *The Age of Mackenzie King* (Toronto, 1976), p. 23.

workers should refuse to register, the *Toronto Telegram* had this to say:

Socialism in Winnipeg has disgraced organized labor as socialism everywhere disgraces organized labor.

The National Government of Canada has the power to teach the Winnipeg socialists a lesson that should also have been taught to Quebec anti-recruiters and every other class of shirker who refuses to even supply the information demanded by his endangered country.

The Canadian Government should fill the jails so full of these people that their feet would stick out of the windows.[19]

The demand for repressive action increased after the Bolshevik revolution and the enthusiasm which that event generated in socialist and labor circles. In September and October 1918, Orders-in-Council were passed which banned all socialist publications and many of the socialist organizations in Canada.* Amendments to the Immigration Act and to the Criminal Code passed in June 1919 and directed at the Winnipeg General Strike were so worded that they could be used, and in fact for many years were used, against the propagation of socialist ideas.

An irrational anti-socialist hysteria seemed to have gripped the Federal Cabinet when in April 1919 it despatched an urgent telegram to Borden in Versailles, asking him to get the British to station a cruiser off Vancouver as "a steadying influence" against "socialism" and "Bolshevism" which were "rampant in Vancouver, Calgary and Winnipeg". This feeling was reflected in the government speeches made during the House of Commons debate on the Winnipeg General Strike, June 2, 1919. Meighen contended that his actions in Winnipeg were designed to save the country from "Bolshevism" which among other things he defined in the following terms:

If you are going to have a combination of all organizations of labour in the Dominion taking part in and determining the event of every dispute as to labourers' conditions and wages here, there, at

---

[19] Quoted in *The Canadian Forward*, January 13, 1917.

* Although its paper was banned, the Socialist Party of Canada was not itself banned. The Social-Democratic Party was banned, but this was later lifted except for language branches of the SDP which remained under the order. The SPNA was banned and remained so for the duration of the War Measures Act.

*any other point, why then you have the perfection of Bolshevism. It
could be nothing less.*

A member of the government benches (whose speech in that
debate was praised by Meighen) declared:

*Sedition must be stamped out. It is all very well to talk of free
speech, but to talk of Bolshevism and riots and overthrowing the
Government is a different thing, and I think the Sedition Act
might well have been amended four years ago instead of now; but
better later than never. Radical socialist leaders must be interned
or deported.*

This spirit found further expression in a curious publication
issued in August 1920 by the Department of Labour and widely
distributed. Entitled *Information Respecting the Russian Soviet
System and Its Propaganda in North America*, it painted a hor-
rendous picture of a wide Bolshevist propaganda network, operating all over Canada and receiving funds through the Russian
Trade Mission in New York. Among those cited in the documents as being wittingly or unwittingly disseminators of Russian
propaganda were the One Big Union and the Labour Church, R.
B. Russell, J. S. Woodsworth and Rev. William Ivens.

Another quite different approach to the growth of socialism
and the labor movement in Western countries has been the
advocacy of liberal reformism which in British political theory is
associated primarily with the teachings of John Stuart Mill. One
of the early expositions of this approach in Canada was an interesting essay entitled "Canadian Democracy and Socialism," published in the *Canadian Magazine* in 1894. Written by John A.
Cooper, a lawyer and frequent contributor to this publication, it
describes the growth of socialism in Canada, and, acknowledging
the "great influence" which Karl Marx was already exerting here,
concludes with this statement:

*No radical changes are immediately needed, but many measures
which will tend to elevate the masses, press for immediate consider-
ation. The growth of great and soulless corporations must be prevented; the massing of much wealth in the possession of single
families must be avoided; disputes between capital and labor must
be settled by arbitration, so that the harmony between capital and
labor will be preserved; the education of the masses must be
pressed with renewed vigor, so that anarchism cannot be begotten*

amidst ignorance and superstition; the crowding of the poor into unhealthy portions of great cities must be avoided, because a pure mind exists only in a pure body. These are a few of the socialistic schemes which can be undertaken to discount the troubles of the future. With these undertaken and successfully carried out, extreme socialism would cease to be a menace and anarchism cease to be a nightmare.

A powerful exponent of this thesis appeared later in the person of Professor O. D. Skelton, who wrote an article for the Canadian business journal, *Monetary Times*, January 1913, entitled "Are We Drifting Into Socialism?" Just two years after the publication of his book *Socialism: A Critical Analysis*, in which he dismissed socialism in Canada as of little importance and without prospects "for further expansion", he now saw socialism as a force to be reckoned with. To meet its challenge he outlined a series of reform measures that needed to be undertaken by the various governments in Canada: limited degree of state ownership; more government regulation of industry, old age pensions, free education, free parks, higher taxes on the rich. He then argued:

Not only are these policies not necessarily socialistic; they are the best bulwarks against socialism. They are homeopathic cures, vaccinations against its growth. For private property today is on the defensive. It has no heaven-born sanction. It will endure only so long as it proves socially beneficial. The hour of social as well as political democracy has come. The ideal which will prevail, the ideal shared by socialists and individualist reformers alike, is the organization of industry in the interest of the masses of the people. Our existing order will endure if it can be made and can be shown to be true, that private property is a better means of attaining this end than collectivist property. It must be shown that within the existing framework of society we can combine private initiative and private energy with social control and social justice. Every tax-dodging millionaire, every city slum, every instance of shady high finance, or of overworked and underpaid employees, is a potent argument for socialism. Remove the grievances, and they are many, even though exaggerated by the socialist out of all perspective—and the socialist has lost his best ammunition.

This idea was further developed in a series of lectures given to the Royal Canadian Institute in 1918 by Professor R. M.

MacIver, newly-appointed Chairman of Political Economy at the University of Toronto, and later expanded into a book by him, published April 1919, called *Labour in the Changing World.* A summary of his lectures appeared in the University of Toronto Monthly under the title "Capital and Labour—the New Situation". His opening paragraph states the theme for his work:

The new situation of labour, its new power and its new challenge, form a subject which all who speak or think of "reconstruction" should seek to understand. A century ago labour was fighting, fighting blindly and chaotically, for the mere right to organize, fighting almost as an outlaw in society, the Government openly on the opposing side. Today labour feels a consciousness of power due to many causes, not least to the great war itself, and its challenge is more confident. Its horizon is no longer limited to the living wage. It has widened its claim. It demands a share in prosperity and a voice in the control of industry. The attitude of labour has changed, and since labour is the challenging party we cannot understand the issue between capital and labour without a knowledge of this change. It is mere foolishness to talk, as some still talk, of the essential unity of interest of capital and labour, and to preach mutual goodwill as if that alone would see us through. For labour is beginning to attack the bases of the present system, and to demand a new foundation on which common interest can be built.

In his book he advocates the adoption in Canada of the British Labour Party manifesto *Labour and the New Social Order.* Locke's "frankly materialistic individualism of a bygone age ... is at war with the ideal of labour ... for it places property above persons and it venerates the competitive principle", and therefore must be discarded. Labor's goal of industrial democracy will end a situation in which "the children of labour are deprived by economic necessity of the opportunity to develop, for their own and the common good, their natural powers". He calls frankly for a change in the system, but not through revolutionary means:

Thus roughly stated, the ideal doubtless suggests revolution. But revolution as a result and not as a means, revolution as the significance of a new order duly established by intelligent process, not the blind catastrophe of despair.[20]

---

[20] R. M. MacIver, *Labour in the Changing World* (Toronto, 1919), p. ix.

The Canadian Forward, organ of the Social-Democratic Party of Canada, commented favorably on MacIver's ideas, which were presented in a series of articles in the *Toronto Daily Star*. In its issue of July 1918, the *Marxian Socialist* of the SPNA attacked them, stating that they had "a two-fold purpose, to confuse the workers and make them think our masters are willing and anxious to bring about a state of affairs in industry, which will be of real benefit to the working class, and at the same time warn some sections of the capitalist class that they will have to concede to a great many changes if they want to enjoy the profit system still longer."

But the most important advocate of liberal reformism as the answer to socialism and radical laborism was Mackenzie King, whose career had been mainly in labor matters. As a result he had acquired expertise in the technical aspect of labor-capital relations, but more importantly he had developed a shrewd awareness of the political importance of the working class. His book *Industry and Humanity*, published in 1918, and his success at the Liberal leadership convention in August 1919, assured the adoption of reformism as the credo of the Liberal Party. It was the result of the impact that the labor and socialist movements were making on Canadian society. Liberalism in its new reformist garb provided the alternative to authoritarian Toryism, which it replaced as the main ideology of Canadian capitalism. But it also provided an attractive alternative to socialism for some sections of labor and for a large section of the Canadian electorate. Inside the TLC it helped in the rise of Liberals to the dominant executive posts over Socialists, a situation which endured for the ensuing thirty years.

Summary

Socialism came to Canada as a world idea, described by O. D. Skelton in the first decade of this century as "the most remarkable international political movement in history, commanding the adherence of eight million voters, representing every civilized country under the sun".[21] Marxism was the dominant characteristic of that movement in Canada as well as in

---

[21] Skelton, *op. cit.*, p. 15.

most countries until after the Russian Revolution.

However, within the general theoretical propositions of Marx and Engels there were differences and variations between countries, and within them as well. Canadian socialism was doctrinaire and sectarian as compared to the socialist parties in most other countries. It was also more proletarian than the movements in most other countries. One of its major shortcomings was its inability to use Marxism as an analytical tool to better understand the specificities of the political, social, and economic environment of Canada.

The early socialist movement in Canada was made up largely of British working-class immigrants, although second and third generation Canadians were also present, some of them descendants of the rebels of 1837.

From the outset there was a close liaison between the Canadian socialist and labor movements and this connection was helped by the presence of American-based trade unions, many of which had socialists as leaders.

Gad Horowitz in his essay *Conservatism, Liberalism and Socialism in Canada: An Interpretation*, puts forward this explanation of why socialism was more successful in Canada than in the United States:

In Canada, socialism is British, non-Marxist and worldly; in the United States it is German, Marxist, and other worldly.

He goes on to personalize the differences in these terms:

The socialism of the United States, the socialism of DeLeon, Berger, Hillquit and Debs, is predominantly Marxist, and doctrinaire because it is European. The socialism of English Canada, the socialism of Simpson, Woodsworth, and Coldwell, is predominantly Protestant, Labourist, and Fabian, because it is British.[22]

The American socialists named by Horowitz dominated the socialist movement there until the end of the First World War, whereas the Canadian figures he lists came to dominate Canadian socialism after, and in the case of Coldwell quite a bit after, the war. To make a historical comparison one must list the dominant Canadian socialist figures of the same period as DeLeon and Debs: Hawthornthwaite, Kingsley, O'Brien, Pritchard,

---

[22] G. Horowitz, *Canadian Labour in Politics* (Toronto, 1968), p. 24.

Russell, Queen, Lefeaux, Simpson, all of whom considered themselves Marxists. Those that came from Britain were mainly from the Independent Labor Party, not the Fabians, and that party according to its chairman, Keir Hardie, considered itself Marxist.

The socialist movement during this period registered two main achievements: implanting and popularizing Marxist ideas, and building the trade-union movement. It regarded itself as the repository of a counterculture: a whole system of ideas and activities directed against the prevailing philosophy of the capitalist society. In line with this, it developed various forms of independent labor political action, which had moderate successes, and in the course of this activity pioneered the idea of a third political party based on the socialist idea.

The rise of Canadian socialism had an impact beyond the direct success it had in the labor movement. It influenced the social gospel movement which was taking shape during the war. It also helped crystallize the reform-minded elements within the conventional party system and in this way contributed to the defeat of Toryism and its replacement by liberal democracy as the predominant ideology in Canadian society.

The split in the Canadian socialist movement that later became permanent started with two events which at their inception caused enthusiasm and jubilation in all socialist ranks: the Bolshevik Revolution of 1917 and the adoption of the British Labour Party manifesto, *Labour and the New Social Order*. It soon became clear that these two events represented two distinct paths to socialism, one based on the dictatorship of the proletariat, and the other on a constitutional transformation of one system into the other. But even those who favored the dictatorship of the proletariat as the road to socialism were not all prepared to accept completely the strategies and tactics which Lenin laid down and which were embodied in the Statutes of Affiliation to the Communist International. The socialist movement thus splintered, with the pro-Soviet group, for the time being, the most certain of its path.

The other elements, while definite about their rejection of the Soviet path, were not so sure about the alternative. The British path had been regarded as the model by most of them, but with the emergence of a strong farmers' party in 1919-1921, some doubts were raised, and when a viable social democratic party on a national scale finally emerged in 1932-1933, it was not based on the British model but on what its President described as the "Canadian Way".

CHAPTER FOUR

THE COMMUNIST PARTY OF CANADA, 1921-57: THE NATIONAL QUESTION

Origins

The Communist Party of Canada was made up at the outset of former members of the three socialist parties in existence at the time of the Russian Revolution: the Socialist Party of Canada, the Social-Democratic Party of Canada and the Socialist Party of North America—a majority of the first, a minority of the second, and almost the entire membership of the third. This was reflected in the first nine-member Political Bureau of the Party which was the effective and operative leadership, resident in Toronto, and made up entirely of full-time "functionaries", to use the Party's term. Two had been members of the Social-Democratic Party, three were from the Socialist Party of Canada and four from the Socialist Party of North America. Out of the nine, eight were British-born, seven of them workers who had been active in the Canadian trade-union movement as well as in socialist circles prior to taking over full-time posts for the Communist Party. One, Maurice Spector, born in Russia of Jewish parents, a student at the University of Toronto at the time of the formation of the Communist Party, quickly became, in the words of *The Communist International* magazine of October 7, 1929,

77

"the theoretical leader of the Canadian party".

The Communist Party of Canada emerged out of the Canadian socialist movement on the basis of a conviction that the problems which had bedevilled the movement from its inception could be solved by the teachings of Lenin and by affiliation to the Communist International, whose main attraction was that it would be dominated by leading members of Lenin's own party. The conviction that Lenin's principles and methods (which had worked in Russia) could work in Canada began to grow among Canadian socialists almost from the first news of the Bolshevik uprising and the rise to fame of Lenin, who had hitherto been unknown to Canadian Marxists. As described in the previous chapter, the Manitoba section of the Social-Democratic Party had voted in March 1918 in favor of affiliation to the Communist International a year before the International was formed, and two years before the Conditions of Affiliation had been drawn up. Whatever the relationship between the Communist International and the Communist Party of Canada became after affiliation, the desire to associate the socialist movement in Canada with the successful Russian Revolution came from within Canada, as a response to the difficulties, doubts and disagreements which had plagued Canadian socialists up to that time. There was intense interest within the socialist movement in all the writings and speeches of Lenin, which were reprinted in Canadian labor and socialist journals as fast as they became available. Many of the socialists accepted Lenin's statement in *"Left-Wing" Communism, an Infantile Disorder*: " . . . at the present historical moment the situation is precisely that the Russian model reveals to ALL countries something that is very essential in their near and inevitable future." In accepting this model, without too much information, they fitted the description that Lenin makes in the very next sentence: "The advanced workers in every land have long understood this; most often they did not so much understand it as grasp it, sense it, by their revolutionary class instinct."

The first big "discovery" they made was the emphasis that Lenin put on the concept of dictatorship of the proletariat.

In an article referred to in the previous chapter, the Winnipeg Local of the Socialist Party of Canada, in January 1919, called the dictatorship of the proletariat "a new phrase which has come into common use," but declared that the concept which the phrase expresses was already contained in *The Communist Manifesto* of 1848.

However, in *The State and Revolution*, which was serialized in the Canadian socialist press later in 1919, Lenin for the first time called this the touchstone of Marxism. In fact, it was the touchstone of the new Marxism which was emerging out of his writings and the experiences of the Russian Bolsheviks and which would eventually be associated with his name. Its newness as far as Canadian socialists were concerned was indicated by the way they highlighted it in their press, speeches, and resolutions.

But an even bigger impact was made by the publication in 1921 in both the *Western Clarion* and the *B.C. Federationist* of *"Left-Wing" Communism, an Infantile Disorder*, subtitled "A Popular Essay in Marxist Strategy and Tactics". It seemed to be directed at many of the problems which Canadian socialists had experienced. It was an attack on what Lenin called "left doctrinairism", on the substitution of revolutionary rhetoric for "the utmost flexibility in tactics". It ridiculed the prevalent practice of repeating well-known Marxist postulates, instead of concretely "taking account of *all* the forces, groups, parties, classes, and masses operating in the given country". It called for participation in parliamentary activity instead of "hurling abuse at parliamentary opportunism". It called on Communists to repudiate the tactic of creating "new artificial forms of labor organizations" and instead urged them to participate in reactionary-led trade unions because "it is imperatively necessary *to work wherever* the masses are to be found". Lenin rejected the notion that Communists never compromise, calling this "childishness which is difficult even to take seriously.... One must be able to analyse the situation and concrete conditions of each compromise, or of each form of compromise". He projected in a way new to Canadian socialists the idea of a "vanguard party" disciplined and centralized, exercising "political leadership" over all the activities of its members.

While these new postulates were acceptable to many in the socialist movement, the Conditions of Affiliation to the Communist International published in the *Western Clarion* on January 1, 1921, were hotly debated, and some of the key figures rejected them, mainly on the grounds that the authority which the International would have over all decisions of member parties would constitute intolerable and potentially harmful interference by an outside body.

Those who formed the Communist Party as the Canadian branch of the Communist International did so not only because they did not object to this intervention but also precisely because they welcomed it, hoping that in this way they would be given the answers to their problems. This attachment to the Communist International was, in fact, an attachment to the Soviet Union as the model, and this relationship continued up to the present even though the Communist International was formally disbanded in May 1943.

After Lenin's death in 1924, this new Marxism became known as Leninism and Marxism-Leninism, both phrases originating with Stalin. This new concept of Marxism, however, consisted more of Stalin's views of Lenin, than of Lenin's additions to Marx. As Stalin's power and prestige grew in the Soviet Party through successive purges, it was Stalin's theoretical leadership that imprinted itself on the world Communist movement, Canada included.

Stalin's theoretical impact on Canadian Communism was expressed in the first place through his leadership of the Communist International. This leadership became absolute by the Sixth Congress of the Communist International in 1928 which confirmed Stalin's defeat of Trotsky and Zinoviev. With the expulsion of Maurice Spector, long recognized as its theoretical leader, in 1928 and of Jack MacDonald, its General Secretary, in 1929, the Canadian Communist Party swung behind the Stalin leadership and henceforth never wavered from that position.

Stalin's particular theoretical contributions were expressed mainly through a number of small pamphlets all of which, with one exception, were written after Lenin's death, and through his reports to the Congresses of the Communist Party of the Soviet Union (CPSU) especially the Sixteenth in 1930, the Seventeenth in 1934, and the Eighteenth in 1939. The pamphlets were *Marxism and the National Question* (1913); *The Foundations of Leninism* (1924); *The Problems of Leninism* (1926); *Economic Problems of Socialism in the USSR* (1952). In addition, Stalin supervised the writing of the *History of the Communist Party of the Soviet Union (Bolsheviks)* (1938) and personally wrote the section entitled "Dialectical and Historical Materialism".

Probably the most important of these writings from the standpoint of impact on world communism was the *Foundations of Leninism*. Here, in a series of lectures given in April and May of 1924, Stalin codified in catechismal fashion what he considered to be Lenin's thought. Whereas Lenin in *"Left-Wing" Communism* claimed international validity for only "some of the fundamental features" of the Russian experiences, Stalin in the *Foun-*

dations claimed that all of these features are valid in *all* countries, and that this is what constituted the term "Leninism".

This all-inclusive definition of Leninism by Stalin was immediately challenged by a number of critics in the Russian Party including Zinoviev who stated that "Leninism is Marxism of the era of imperialist wars and of the world revolution *which began directly in a country where the peasantry predominates.*"[1]

Stalin's argument against Zinoviev is quite interesting not so much because of its substance, but mainly because of what it reveals about Stalin's methodology:

What can be the meaning of the words underlined by Zinoviev? What does introducing the backwardness of Russia, its peasant character, into the definition of Leninism mean?

It means transforming Leninism from an international proletarian doctrine into a product of specifically Russian conditions.

It means playing into the hands of Bauer and Kautsky, who deny that Leninism is suitable for other countries, for countries in which capitalism is more developed.

. . . How can the nationally restricted definition of Leninism be reconciled with internationalism?[2]

Stalin's method of arguing, as shown here, starts by defining the purpose of the argument and then rejects all considerations that do not serve this purpose. He summed up this point by positing the choices that faced the disputants:

EITHER the peasant question is the main thing in Leninism, and in that case Leninism is not suitable, not obligatory, for capitalistically developed countries, for those which are not peasant countries.

OR the main thing in Leninism is the dictatorship of the proletariat, and in that case Leninism is the international doctrine of the proletarian of all lands, suitable and obligatory for all countries without exception, including the capitalistically developed countries.

Here one must choose.[3]

---

[1] J. Stalin, "*Works*" (Moscow, 1954), Vol. 8, p. 14.

[2] *Ibid.*, p. 15.

[3] *Ibid.*, p. 18.

This subordination of theory to tactics is basic to Stalin's methodology and greatly influenced the Communist Party of Canada in its theoretical work.

At the outset of the *Foundations*, Stalin stated that the problem with defining Leninism was

. . . to expound the distinctive and new in the works of Lenin that Lenin contributed to the general treasury of Marxism and that is naturally connected with his name.

His one-line definition of Leninism using this criterion then became:

Leninism is Marxism of the era of imperialism and the proletarian revolution. To be more exact, Leninism is the theory and tactics of the proletarian revolution in general, the theory and tactics of the dictatorship of the proletariat in particular.

Lenin's major work on this question was *The State and Revolution*, written and published on the eve of the October uprising. But in 1938, Stalin, in his Report to the Eighteenth Congress of the CPSU (B), dismissed this book in the following terms:

Lenin wrote his famous book, The State and Revolution, *in August 1917, that is, a few months before the October Revolution and the establishment of the Soviet State. Lenin considered it the main task of this book to defend Marx's and Engel's doctrine of the state from distortions and vulgarizations of the opportunists. Lenin was preparing to write a second volume of* The State and Revolution, *in which he intended to sum up the principal lessons of the Russian Revolution of 1905 and 1917. There can be no doubt that Lenin intended in the second volume of his book to elaborate and develop the theory of the state on the basis of the experience gained during the existence of Soviet power in our country. Death, however, prevented him from carrying this book into execution. But what Lenin did not manage to do should be done by his disciples.*

After stating in 1924 that Lenin's main original contribution to Marxism was his elaboration of "the theory and tactics of the dictatorship of the proletariat," Stalin, fourteen years later, asserts that Lenin did not really add anything to this theory and did not have time to sum up or interpret the experiences of the Russian Revolution on this question. What he is really saying is that Leninism is the experience of the Russian Revolution as seen by Lenin's "disciples", mainly himself. In his argumentation leading up to this remarkable passage, Stalin declared that what is new in the Russian experience with the dictatorship of the proletariat is that it was applied "to the partial and specific case of the victory of Socialism in one country..." which neither Marx, Engels nor Lenin lived to experience.

The Communist Party in Canada worked, studied, and did its theoretical work, especially after 1928, in the Stalin frame of reference, which means Stalin's definition and conception of Leninism, and particularly Stalin's "practical" approach to the "theory and tactics" of the proletarian dictatorship.

Moreover, the Communist Party of Canada, to the extent that it did try to assimilate at least the outlines of Marxist philosophy, did so under the tutelage of Stalin. Stalin's main work in this field was his twenty-five page essay entitled "Dialectical and Historical Materialism", which was inserted as part of Chapter 4 of the *History of the Communist Party of the Soviet Union*, published in 1938. This was a highly mechanical, simplistic, and didactic reduction of what Marxism was supposed to mean philosophically. As a matter of fact, this essay was an elaboration and restatement of Stalin's first attempt at theoretical writing, an essay entitled "Anarchism or Socialism?" which appeared in 1906. As a first work this was a creditable effort at presenting the main features of the Marxist method for propaganda purposes. But when republished in almost its original form, but presented as the "latest" work of the leader of world communism in 1938, and vigorously promoted as a theoretical masterpiece equal to the Marxist classics it claimed to explain, it was a crude and heavy-handed effort. It purported to give the reader in twenty-five pages an instant view of highly complex philosophical and scientific concepts, all of which were marshalled in such a way as to prove that Communism was as inevitable a qualitative leap as was the transformation of boiling water into steam. Yet this essay became a major source of study in the Canadian Communist movement and virtually replaced all other Marxist works on philosophy.

Probably of greater consequence to the Communist Party of

Canada was Stalin's presentation of Lenin's conception of the Party. Here, in place of Lenin's emphasis in *"Left-Wing" Communism* on flexibility in tactics and structure, Stalin's definition is of a rigid, military-like apparatus controlling all the activities of its members, subordinating them to the higher committees (which he called the general staff), and making no allowance for adaptability to different countries with varying traditions and cultures. Stalin's work on the party which appeared in *The Foundations of Leninism* was undoubtedly influenced by the conception, still held then by the Communists, that this period was one of impending revolutions, wars, and civil wars. But Stalin's definition was never modified or altered in any way, even after the revolutionary upsurge had waned.

Stalin's prestige in the Canadian Communist movement was enormous. He was looked upon as the fountain of all wisdom, and his leadership was never questioned in the slightest. This must be kept in mind in any appraisal of the Communist Party of Canada which grew up and developed in the era not of Lenin but of Stalin. What was eventually called Marxism-Leninism was in fact Stalin's Leninism, the claims of which to world leadership he first staked out in *The Foundations of Leninism*.

The Communist Party of Canada was markedly different from the socialist parties which preceded it and out of which it sprang. The first distinguishing feature was its international connections, which were not those of fraternal liaison between equal parties, but were those of subordination willingly entered into by the Canadians, and equally willingly sustained by them throughout the Party's history. The Party was regarded by its members as a national section of a world party which was to be monolithic, disciplined, and guided by the authority of the leading world committee.

The second feature, which was a derivative of the first, was in the structure of the Party and its perception of its role. It was to be a highly-disciplined and tightly-structured organization, with its leading committees and officers wielding immense power within the Party. Every activity in which members were engaged, such as trade unions, parliaments, mass organizations, was to be guided by the Party through its committees and leaders. The Party regarded itself as the vanguard, leading all the political struggles of the working class and its allies within the overall framework of the struggle for the socialist transformation of Canada. Unlike their predecessors who were unclear and dubious about the interaction between nonrevolutionary struggles and the revolution, the Communists felt that Lenin's prescription for the Party gave them the answers to these vexing questions. At any rate, the solutions worked out by the Central Committee and "Politburo" under the guidance of the Communist International would be obligatory on all members of the Party in whatever field they were engaged. Interminable debate would be ended; members would cease acting on their own. To the Communists, the revolution was if not an immediate possibility yet the main task of the contemporary historical epoch, thereby conferring upon them great responsibilities as the revolutionary party.

A third feature of the Communist Party of Canada was its attempts to apply its general theoretical framework to the Canadian society in which it lived and worked. While accepting this general framework as being primary, the Party also accepted Lenin's admonition to try to concretize the general strategy and tactics of the proletarian revolution to national circumstances. This effort was launched from the beginning and party journals and resolutions increasingly dealt with specifically Canadian issues in Marxist terms. The main theoretical problems which engaged the Party's attention were the status of Canada (colony or self-governing nation), French-Canada, the trade-union question, federal-provincial relations and the agrarian question. These theoretical issues were the backdrops for vitally important tactical questions: united front, relations with Social-Democrats, the relation of reformism to revolution, and the Party's attitude to parliamentary and electoral activities. Although these might appear to be two separate categories, theoretical and practical, in the Communist perception they were an integral whole, so much so that it was often difficult to assess whether theory preceded tactics or vice versa.

It is interesting to note that the Party and its international advisors did not consider it necessary to do an in-depth study of the Canadian political economy at the outset, although they never ceased to point out how Lenin at a very early stage in his political life considered it essential to write "on the basis of precise data" the *Development of Capitalism in Russia* (1905). In fact, the Canadian Party never did undertake such a study, although in most of its important works, policy statements, and convention resolutions it did present a critique of current material on the state of the economy and class relations. That it did not have such an overall study, however, proved to be a major handicap.

The Status of Canada, Independence, and the National Question

In the March 1925 issue of the *Workers Monthly* and the March 21, 1925, issue of *The Worker*, Tim Buck, then trade union secretary of the Communist Party of Canada, published an article entitled "Canada and the British Empire". It sought to come to terms with the question of the status of Canada. This article began a discussion on a theme which was to surface as an important and sometimes dominant one for Canadian Communists throughout their subsequent history.

His main thesis was that Canada was "still a colony, still part of the Empire upon which the sun never sets". He supported this assertion with these arguments:

The political status of the Dominion of Canada and the internal and external powers of its governments are defined and limited by the British North America Act, enacted by the British Government in 1867. No amendments of any importance has (sic) ever been made to it, and because of the legislative and technical impediments—the fact that Canada has no machinery for registering opinions on the matter, and has no recourse beyond appeals to the British Government, which hitherto have proved useless—none are likely. With the slightest modifications effected by "precedents and interpretations" of which much is made of by Canadian "statesmen", the British North America Act pins the Dominion of Canada, firmly down to the position of a British Colony.

There is not a line or a letter in the act that authorizes the Dominion Government to negotiate a treaty with the foreign power. The Federal Government cannot legislate in connection with internal affairs except within the limits set by the Act, it cannot amend the constitution of the Senate, "Canadian edition of the House of Lords", and may not change the constitution of any Province or take action which would effect (sic) the Office of Lieutenant-Governor, who is the "impersonation of the King in each Province".

On top of that, the Dominion Government has no jurisdiction over Canadian citizens outside Canada. When Britain is at war, Canada is at war also, and Canadian ports must always be open to British ships-of-war.

Politically therefore, Canada is still a colony, still a part of the Em-

pire upon which the sun never sets.

Buck then pointed to the rising economic power and influence of the United States, which, he argued, had replaced Britain as the leading foreign investor in Canada. Moreover, while "British capital invested is in governmental and municipal securities, the greater part of the American investments are in industry", with over "800 branch factories operated by U.S. concerns in Canada".

At first glance one would assume that it matters very little to the revolutionary movements, whether England or the United States rules Canada, openly or in veiled form. Capitalism is capitalism and so far as the average worker is concerned this struggle for political control has little more than a sentimental appeal.

In a very real sense, however, the winning of complete independence from British political control means a great deal to the revolutionary movement of Canada and to the labor movement as a whole. In substance, it means the repeal of the British North America Act. It will strip the capitalist government of their everlasting excuse of powerlessness, and bring the workers of the country face to face with realities.

He therefore suggested that the Communists should support that section of the bourgeoisie which is striving for independence from Britain, even though this group, headed by Mackenzie King, "is serving American interests well today".

In their fight for complete independence from Downing Street, the Communists of Canada will help them with all their might. Having won independence, however, when they attempt to turn over Canada, lock, stock, and barrel, to Wall Street, they will find in us their bitterest opponents. Independence is only a step for each of us. For the dominant economic interests it is a step toward Americanization. To us the Communists, it is a step towards a Workers' and Farmers' Republic.

Buck referred to the movement toward independence as being "just now so much to the front". The movement that Buck was talking about centered around Mackenzie King who, during his four years in office up to that time, had asserted Canadian sovereignty over matters of foreign policy on several notable issues, and was obviously going to do the same on every appropriate occasion. The most vociferous intellectual exponents of this movement in English Canada were John W. Dafoe, editor of the *Winnipeg Free Press*, who is considered to be "the father of Canadian nationalism", his publisher Sir Clifford Sifton, and J. S. Ewart, an Ottawa lawyer whose *The Kingdom Papers* and current speeches contained the most clear-cut expositions of Canadian autonomy. Even Arthur Meighen, leader of the Conservative Party, had just stated what was for his party a startlingly new doctrine that, if Britain went to war, Canadians would be consulted by a referendum as to whether Canada was at war also. And of course French-Canadian opinion led by Henri Bourassa was more strongly than ever in favor of Canadian autonomy as a result of the traumatic experience of the conscription struggle of 1917. At the same time as Tim Buck's article appeared, a similar expression of opinion by J. S. Woodsworth, M.P., was published in *The Canadian Forum*: "We have not outgrown either our colonial status nor the colonial psychology."

In his unpublished draft of the article quoted above, Buck commented on the wide appeal which the movement for autonomy had in parliament, embracing "public men of all parties right through from the laborites to the conservatives". But "outside of J. S. Ewart, the Canadian authority on international law, the Communists are the only ones to openly advocate complete independence".

This article was written outside the usual Communist frame of reference. It did not refer to anything that Marx or Lenin said on the national question. It did not contain a worked out analysis of class relations in Canada. It did not define colonialism in Communist terms even though Lenin had defined it in his speeches to the Communist International. Its definition of colonialism was that of J. S. Ewart, for Buck's description of Canadian "colonial" status follows to the letter Ewart's argumentation in *The Kingdom Papers*. Buck attempts to give it a working-class orientation by referring to the jurisdictional disputes between federal and provincial governments over matters of concern to the workers: labor laws, unemployment relief, and the eighthour day. A repeal of the BNA Act would put an end to the political football that is made of these issues, he asserts. But the bulk of his argument is in support of constitutional procedures of some importance to the bourgeoisie, but of little immediate concern to the working class. Years later Buck did admit that "our demand for Canadian independence was for bourgeois independence—freedom from British rule".[4]

But it did have a curious application at that time to the Party's approach to the trade-union movement, the work in this field being directed by Tim Buck himself. In his pamphlet *Steps to Power* published that same year (1925), he outlined the Communist tactics and policies in the trade-union movement. While advocating complete independence for Canada in the article we have been quoting, Buck limits himself in the pamphlet on trade-union tactics to advocating "autonomy" for Canadian branches of U. S. unions and he cautions the workers that "autonomy for Canadian trade unionism does not mean narrow nationalism ... ". Undoubtedly the main reason for this tactic was Lenin's admonition to Communists to stay in the established trade unions, even the most reactionary ones. But it also seems to be related to the "two-step" tactic, which Buck had outlined in his earlier article, for achieving Canadian independence. The main immediate target for independence, he argued, is Britain, and Communists must be prepared to have as allies even those whose interests are tied to the United States. Only at a later stage, when Canada had won independence from Britain, would the main struggle shift against the United States.

Two other members of the Political Bureau joined Buck in stressing this line. They were Maurice Spector, Chairman of the Party and editor of the Party's weekly organ *The Worker*, and Stewart Smith, Secretary of the Young Communist League, who was elected in 1924 to the Party's top political committee at the age of 16 and remained on that body until 1956, when he resigned from the Communist movement. In August 1926, Smith circulated a document entitled *History and Present Economic Background of the Struggle for Canada* in which he attempted a Marxist analysis of the history of Canada to buttress the argument for the slogan of Canadian independence. But in it he began to shift his ground somewhat by providing statistics showing the rising impact of U. S. investments in Canada which have reached a point where

... not only has American capital as such more strength in Canada, but American capital is for the most part in control of the so-called Canadian capital. . . . In direct opposition to this, stand the interest of British capitalism and British Capital.

---

[4] Tim Buck, *Lenin and Canada* (Toronto, 1970), p. 71-2.

He was suggesting here, in very tentative terms, that there was a growing clash in Canada between American and British capital and vicariously between sections of the Canadian bourgeoisie which are tied to either great financial power.

But in an article published a month later (September 1926), Maurice Spector reaffirmed the earlier position:

Despite all statements to the contrary, Canada is still a colony of Great Britain, a part of the British Empire. . . .

That is why the Labour Party* takes a position in favour of complete self-determination of Canada, and why the left wing of the Labor Party, headed by the Communists, takes a more specific position for the annullment of the British North American Act, the separation of Canada from the Empire, and Canadian independence.

However, within a year Spector, Buck, and Smith had completed the shift which Smith had foreshadowed in his article quoted above. Spector, now the editor of the new theoretical organ of the Party, *The Canadian Labor Monthly*, used its first issues, January and February 1928, to develop a new thesis in an article entitled "Canada, The Empire and the War Danger". He described the Anglo-American rivalry as "one of the basic imperialist antagonisms of today", which was being fought throughout the world and which had found a particularly important battleground in Canada and in the other British dominions: "The dominions are no longer dependent chiefly on British capital for development. The United States is nowadays the great provider of capital." This rivalry had enabled an indigenous bourgeoisie to develop, particularly in manufacturing, which was now pressing its claims for "national autonomy" and an end to "colonialism in their political relations with the 'Mother Country' ".

This striving, according to Spector, explained the moves that King had made to assert Canadian autonomy first in international and then in internal affairs, as witness the "Byng versus King" issue:

But for an independent tariff policy, a free hand in the exploitation of the workers at home, commercial treaty-making power, diplo-

---

* The Canadian Labour Party to which the Communist Party was affiliated at this time.

matic representation and a seat in the League of Nations, the Dominion bourgeoisie do not need secession.

According to Spector the main section of the Canadian bourgeoisie was now as independent as it wanted or needed to be vis-à-vis Britain. Therefore a new formulation of party policy was needed and it was defined in these terms:

The fight of the workers and farmers of Canada against the imperialist war danger must, therefore be aimed against the Canadian bourgeoisie as joint partners of British Imperialism. But there is another imperialism that is penetrating Canada, seeking to strengthen its financial and diplomatic bonds, and that is American imperialism with its "fine record" in Latin America. The workers and farmers of this country must oppose American imperialism no less than British.

Spector closed his article by asserting that a rereading of Lenin's *Imperialism* had shown the Canadian Communists that in the period of imperialist capitalism there are "transitional forms of state dependence. And the division into two principal groups of countries—possessors of colonies and colonized areas—is not sufficient to characterize the period. It is necessary to take into account the various kinds of dependence of countries which are politically independent in form but are surrounded in reality with a fine network of financial and diplomatic bonds". This quotation from Lenin had convinced Spector that Canada was one of those transitional forms of dependency and that "real independence" would be won only by overthrowing "the capitalist government of this country" and establishing "a workers and farmers republic".

This position was confirmed later that year at the Sixth Congress of the Communist International in Moscow. In its resolution on the colonial question, September 1928, the Communist International said this:

It is necessary to distinguish between those colonies which have served the capitalist countries as colonizing regions for their surplus population, and which in this way have become extensions of the capitalist system (Australia, Canada, etc.) and those which are exploited by the imperialists primarily as markets for their commodities, as sources of raw materials, and as spheres for capital investment.

Colonies of the first type became Dominions, that is members of
the given imperialist system with equal or nearly equal rights.[5]

On the basis of this resolution, the Executive Committee of
the Communist International (ECCI) in April 1929 addressed a
"closed letter" to the Canadian Party on the eve of its Sixth
Convention. It was a long letter, covering all phases of the
Party's work. In its section on the status of Canada, it asserted in
part:

On the basis of Canada's development into a definite capitalist
country the Party must put emphasis on the Canadian bourgeoisie
as the main enemy of the Canadian proletariat. The ties between
Canada and the British Empire are not ties of compulsion but of
mutual interests in exploitation . . . the Canadian proletariat there-
fore cannot attribute to the Canadian bourgeoisie the role of an
anti-imperialist class fighting for national freedom and a bour-
geois-democratic republic. The Canadian bourgeoisie is the chief
and most active agent of the imperialists in their attacks upon the
Canadian working class. The Canadian bourgeoisie takes advan-
tage of the conflict between British and American Imperialism for
influence in Canada and the weakening of the strength of the
British Empire to assert an ever growing measure of administrative
independence . . . In these circumstances the slogan of "Canadian
Independence under a workers and farmers government" . . . can
only confuse . . . and lead the working masses to believe that they
are oppressed more by the British Imperialists than by the Cana-
dian bourgeoisie.

This statement was followed by two articles written by John
Porter* which appeared in the *Communist International* magazine June 30, 1929, and October 3, 1929. Both articles were
heavily statistical and represent an advance in the kind of analysis on Canada that had been done by Communists up to that
point.

The first article talks about "the existence of a growing Canadian bourgeoisie" that utilizes "the Anglo-American rivalry in
Canada" for its own benefit. This bourgeoisie is not only in

---

[5] Jane Degras, ed., *The Communist International Documents*, Vol. II, p. 534.

* John Porter is a pseudonym that some sources say represents the collective name of
John Weir, Leslie Morris, and Sam Carr, young Canadians studying at the Lenin
School in Moscow, and subsequently used by the Communist International to refute
the Buck-Smith-Spector line.

control of the Canadian economy but is increasingly investing capital abroad, particularly in Latin America.

Porter denounces "a conception ... held in many circles of the Comintern that Canada is virtually a colony of the United States".

The truth of the matter is that Canada, since its bourgeois revolution of 1837, has ceased to be a colony, has developed since that time in the sphere of complete capitalist relations ... Canada is developing its own imperialist interests (and) is seeking a place on the world market....

The increase of American capital and influence in Canada combined with the decline of the British Empire and of British capital investments in Canada, and the industrialization of Canada, has caused a change in the policies of the Canadian bourgeoisie as evidenced by the role of the King Government:

Representing the most powerful Canadian interests, it seeks to utilize the Anglo-American conflict for the benefit of the Canadian bourgeoisie as a whole; in this sense it is playing a flagrantly opportunist role and one that will lead to disaster. Necessary to both British and American imperialism, it plays the game of granting concessions and at the same time resisting both groups, the while seeking to build a powerful national economy and to assume a somewhat independent imperialist attitude in the struggle for markets for Canadian manufactured and agricultural products.

This new situation called for a change in party policy. It must struggle "against both American and British imperialism, and against being dragged by the Canadian bourgeoisie into either one of the two imperialist camps". At the same time, the Party must avoid raising the slogan of "Canadian Independence" so as "not to repeat the past error of placing the Party in the camp of any bourgeois opposition movement".

The second article was a sharp attack on the Canadian Party for its previous policies and for not having fully corrected these past errors.*

---

* These errors are blamed entirely on Maurice Spector who had been expelled from the Party in November 1928 as "a renegade Trotskyist". Porter quotes Spector's article of September 1926 but ignores Buck's essay of March 1925. However, it is quite clear from the inner party debate that the Communist International considered Buck and Smith equally with Spector as culprits in initiating and promoting this policy.

For years the Party ascribed to the Canadian ruling class, a revolutionary role, and remained silent upon the question of the proletarian revolution! The basis of this theory was the conception of Canada as a colony.

At the same time, Porter accused the Canadian party leadership of retaining vestiges of the old position by emphasizing the Anglo-American conflict and ignoring the independence role of the Canadian bourgeoisie. He calls on the Party to abandon all references to the confusing concept of "Canadian Independence" and concentrate its attention on the direct confrontation between workers and bourgeoisie.

This correction was adopted by the Sixth Convention of the Communist Party of Canada in June 1929. But at a plenary session of the Central Committee of the Party in January 1930, Tim Buck, now the leader of the Party, made a spirited defence of his position prior to that Convention, and attacked some of the statements made by Porter and the Lenin school students. Buck said that his own position was to draw attention to the "peculiarities of Canada" which were "different from the perspectives and tasks of such parties as the Communist Party of Great Britain and the United States". In Porter's position, Buck asserted, "there is the danger of completely ignoring the significance of the Anglo-American conflict to Canada, and the revolutionary perspective that an Anglo-American war raises before the Canadian Party". He criticized the statement for ignoring the fact that "the Canadian bourgeoisie are free from British domination because of the growing strength and influence of the United States. . . . " He asserted that Porter's postulation that "Canada has become transformed from a raw material hinterland to an exporter of manufactured goods" was false and he cited statistics to disprove that assertion. He also rejected Porter's argument "that native capital has freed itself from the domination of foreign finance capital".

Comparison, therefore, of the total national wealth with the total of foreign capital invested in Canada does not prove the superiority of native capital, but on the contrary shows that the $5,750,000,000 of foreign investments are a decisive factor in the productive industries. . . .

Further analysis shows that British and United States capital each tends to go in the direction of the interests of their respective imperialist development. Thus for example, the railways were built

*and the wheat producing country developed under the hegemony of
British finance capital which is still strongly entrenched on the railways. American capital, on the other hand, seeks control of important basic industries, such as newsprint paper production, nickel,
copper, electrical industry, etc. And furthermore, the most important
industries still tend to pass into United States control when their
development reaches a certain point . . .*

He pointed out that U.S. branch plants in Canada had a
tendency to set up Canadian boards to disguise American control, "but control is absolutely in the hands of the parent companies in each case, and the major portion of shares not held by
the parent companies, is held by American investors". He then
cited as an example of American influence in Canada the visit of
J. P. Morgan* to Ottawa in 1919, which motivated the Dominion
Government in Ottawa "to adopt drastic and ruthless measures"
to crush the Winnipeg General Strike.

It is evident, said Buck, that Canadian industry is still dominated by the imperialist finance capital of Britain and the United
States, while there is going on at the same time a fairly rapid
development of native capital, particularly in manufacturing.
"Today Canada is ruled by the Canadian bourgeoisie" but this
bourgeoisie is divided between those sections which are linked
with American capital and those with British. "Canada cannot
be characterized as a colony. On the other hand, it is incorrect at
the present time to categorically designate Canada as an imperialist country. . . . " Furthermore, though the Canadian bourgeoisie rules this country there are still vestiges of colonialism in the
retention of the British North America Act "which cannot be
amended or modified by the Canadian Parliament". Buck closed
his statement by reiterating his view of the peculiarities of the
Canadian situation while formally accepting the line of the Communist International that Canada is a fully independent capitalist state.

Buck came under heavy attack after that speech. He was
accused of resisting the criticism of the Comintern, particularly
by Leslie Morris and Sam Carr, who had just returned from two
years at the Lenin School in Moscow, and who together with
John Weir had authored an attack on the Canadian Party's
position. At the end of the discussion, Buck retreated completely

---

* Prominent U.S. banker and industrialist.

from his position, admitted to having collaborated with Smith and by inference with Spector on this "erroneous" thesis, and pledged to go to the membership and lead an ideological campaign of explaining the correct, that is, the Comintern, analysis of the status of Canada. But Buck in his retraction did not deal with the substance of the argument which he had advanced in his opening remarks. Smith was not present at this Plenum, having stayed in Moscow, and Buck had to deny in his closing remarks the rumor that Smith was being held in Moscow "against his will", to undergo a period of re-education. But in a recent interview, Smith claims that while he likewise retracted under heavy Comintern pressure, he still believed his position to be correct, and asserted that he was in fact vindicated in 1955 when the new party program embodied the position "that I had fully developed in 1929".[6]

This controversy was still haunting the Communist Party a year later when the Party's Political Bureau issued a "draft statement" which is published in *The Worker*, January 3, 1931.

In this situation, it is of vital importance that every party member understand the significance of the correction of the false conception previously held by the Political Bureau of the Party, concerning the path of the proletarian revolution in Canada.

This position which was maintained by our Political Bureau for a period of several months even after the Comintern had denounced it as incorrect, was a modification of the original theory that Canada was a colony, and that the path of our struggle lies thru a struggle for "Canadian Independence".

The Canadian bourgeoisie is an imperialist bourgeoisie. And Canada (their country) is an imperialist country. The Canadian bourgeoisie are imperialists, because of their economic, financial, and therefore political interests arising out of the highly concentrated character of Canadian industry with its high degree of technical development and its important role in the export of capital . . . All the characteristics of imperialism defined by Lenin with the sole exception of the possession of Colonies, are present in the Canadian economy . . .

In view of the importance that this question had in party

---

[6] Stewart Smith: Taped interview with S. R. Penner, 1972, and deposited in I. M. Abella, ed., *Oral History of Canadian Radicalism*, at York University.

history, especially with its revival in the post-World War II period, it is interesting to see Tim Buck's perception of this debate in later years. In 1970, he published a work in connection with the centenary celebration of Lenin's birth, entitled *Lenin and Canada*. In it, Buck says that the demand for Canadian independence was "our demand" and that it "was acclaimed by many people, particularly among middle class radicals."[7] A review of the party's official organ *The Worker* from March 1925 to January 1928 shows that far from influencing the middle-class radicals on this question, the Communist Party was in fact influenced by the bourgeois spokesmen such as Henri Bourassa, J. S. Ewart, J. W. Dafoe, Clifford Sifton, and Mackenzie King; and among the middle-class radicals it was influenced by J. S. Woodsworth whose weekly column on the House of Commons was carried regularly by *The Worker*. The content of its position was not qualitatively different from the position taken by these spokesmen except perhaps in the demand for the abolition of the post of Governor-General following the Byng episode, or in the call for the abolition of the Senate, although that demand had been in the legislative program of the Trades and Labour Congress from its inception. Buck was much closer to the truth when, in an earlier book *Thirty Years* (1952), he characterized the party's error in these words:

The effect of this false theory [Canadian Independence] was to make the Communist Party an ideological ally of bourgeois nationalism which developments had already made reactionary.

Buck is right, however, in stating that the issue of Canada's relations with Britain and the United States was then very much to the fore in Canadian political and intellectual circles, and the Party was reacting to this. The agitation around this question reached a boiling point with the refusal of Governor-General Byng to grant Mackenzie King a dissolution, which set into motion the dramatic events that led to the famous "Byng versus King" election of 1926. The party's leadership was caught up in this turmoil and its excitement was reflected in the headlines of *The Worker* of July 19, 1926, which declared:

CANADA UNDER THE BYNG DICTATORSHIP
Is Dominion Second Egypt or Shall the BNA Act be Scrapped?

---

[7] Tim Buck, *Lenin and Canada* (Toronto, 1970), p. 72.

The Party was able to discern, at least in outline, that the issue had come to the fore under the pressure of growing American investment in Canada. Buck in particular saw this, even though he was unable to convince his colleagues in Canada and in the Communist International of its importance, nor was he able to overcome his own fascination for the formalities of Canadian independence as they were expressed in the British connection. But some non-Marxist spokesmen on the left were already convinced by this time that the real threat to Canadian independence was embodied in the growing American presence. An editorial in the February 1926 issue of the *Canadian Forum* gave this warning:

Accurate figures are nowhere obtainable, but there is no doubt that a large proportion of Canadian industry is owned or controlled by American capital and estimates have been made placing this percentage as high as forty or fifty per cent of the total. . . . If this flow of capital from the United States to Canada continues at the same rate for another ten years, practically all our manufacturing plants and the greater part of our mineral and timber limits will be owned or controlled by American capital. Under such a regime the successful Canadian will aspire to the position of branch manager of an American Corporation, while the less ambitious will become day-workers in a plant controlled by absentee owners. This picture may seem overdrawn and fantastic, but such an end is well on its way to consummation, and once American capital assumes a dominant position in our industrial life it is idle to imagine that we can retain complete control over our political destiny.

The question of Canada's status seemed to have been settled at last in the ranks of the Communist Party by the definitive statement of the Central Committee meeting of February 1931. That cleared the way for what was projected as "the major task confronting the Party". This was defined as "the concentration of all its forces for a counter-offensive" against "the attempts of the Canadian bourgeoisie to further reduce the living standards of the workers". At least the question did not surface in any major way during the thirties. A faint echo of it appeared in the *Manifesto of the Seventh Convention of the Communist Party of Canada*, July 23 – 28, 1934. Written by Stewart Smith, who was acting party leader in the absence of the imprisoned Tim Buck, it accused British imperialism of bringing the world "to the brink of a new world slaughter" and asserted that "the Canadian

HX 102.B8   Lenin + Canada .   .

HX 106. P45 The Canadian Left

HX 104.5 W45   The Strangest Dream

ST.LAWRE
UNIVERS
Canton, New York 13

INTERNATIONAL EDUCATI

All recognized St. Lawrence University Programs Ab
comprehensive fees they would pay on campus. How
spending money (in all cases) are additional costs. S
continue to receive it and may often increase their lo
order to help with the cost of airfare for students on
an **International Education Scholarship Fund**. On
students may apply for the scholarship funds. Finan
selection. The amount of this fund is limited and, in
round trip airfare for the program.

This application must be submitted to the Center for
**February 28 *for Year or Fall Semester Programs* o
Programs.** Students must have a current financial a
to qualify for this scholarship.

APPLICAT

I hereby apply to the International Education Scho

ruling class and its Bennett Government" was supporting the "war preparations of Britain" and for this purpose was conducting "a campaign of patriotism and imperialist propaganda" and spending millions "to re-equip the military forces and militarize the youth". But within a year, as a result of the major shift in tactics proclaimed by the Seventh Congress of the Communist International held in Moscow August 1935, the Party adopted a moderate and conciliatory position with respect to Britain, the British Empire and even with respect to pan-American continentalism. In his major speech to the Eighth Convention, October 8, 1937, Buck said:

The most effective role that Canada can play in the British Commonwealth of Nations is the role of a true democracy. The representatives of Canada must express the will of the Canadian people in the Councils of the Commonwealth instead of being, as they are now, instruments of British imperial policy in Canada.

Canada should play her rightful part as an American country and join hands with other peace-loving nations of the Western hemisphere in making America a force for peace.

The manner in which Canada can best be an influence for peace in the British Empire is by loyally and honourably fulfilling all her obligations as a member of the League of Nations...

There was some bewilderment in party ranks over the extent of the shift that was being made in party policy, but there was fairly general agreement that everything, even Marxist concepts, should be subordinated to the world-wide struggle against German, Japanese, and Italian fascism. Another echo of the previous position, however, surfaced during the period from September 1939 to June 1941 when Canadian communists were opposed to the war.

The party's position as outlined in the *Federal Election Manifesto* of February 1940 condemned British imperialism as being equally responsible with German imperialism for the war, and accused the Canadian Government and ruling class of "being dependent on the hegemony of British Imperialism in Europe" and seeking "the rich profits from war involving British Imperialism". While it is true that this statement did not repeat the conception of Canada as a colony of Britain, it did reflect the continued belief among some members of the party leadership in Canada's dependence on or junior partnership with British imperialism*.

It was not until 1947 that the Communist Party (then called the Labor-Progressive Party), began once again to concern itself with the threat to Canadian independence emanating from U.S. imperialism. The slogan of "Canadian Independence" that was rejected in 1929 reappeared in Buck's address to the National Committee of the Labor-Progressive Party in January 1948, which was published as a pamphlet entitled *Keep Canada Independent*. This became, in fact, the all-pervasive theme of the Party's work from that time on.

The point of departure for this address was a series of measures introduced in 1947 by Mackenzie King's new Finance Minister, Douglas Abbott, ostensibly designed to meet a critical and growing deficit in the U.S. – Canada balance of trade. Its immediate effect was to reduce imports of manufactured goods and fresh fruits from the United States to conserve American dollars, and to increase exports of Canadian goods needed by the United States – mainly raw materials and resource products. In Buck's words it was a plan

to hinge Canada's economy increasingly upon the production of raw materials and specialities, such as newsprint, for United States industry. It is a plan to reduce the weight of finished goods industries in our national economy, even worse. It is a plan to wipe out Canadian sovereignty by giving the United States government a direct voice in deciding the direction and level of Canada's economic development...

... The Abbott plan definitely subordinates both the immediate welfare and the national interests of Canadian people to the imperialistic aims and policies of United States finance-capital.

The Abbott plan, according to Buck, was not some minor government legislation to meet urgent and short-term needs, but a long-term strategy which would change the direction of the Canadian economy:

What has taken place is the breakdown of the mechanism of

---

* In January 1943, the Central Committee of the Communist Party of Canada, which was still illegal, held a closed meeting in Toronto and condemned Stewart Smith for having written this Manifesto without prior agreement of other colleagues, many of whom had already disappeared in expectation of the ban on the Party, which came on June 6, 1940.

capitalist world trade and finance. That mechanism has been a key factor in Canada's economic dealings with the rest of the capitalist world ever since Sir John A. MacDonald introduced his "National Policy" almost eighty years ago. Its breakdown, for Canadians, brings an end to an economic era . . .

Towards the end of his address, Buck outlined what he called a "new national policy" which was designed to develop "broad popular unity". These proposals were of a reformist or social-democratic character, emphasizing increased trade and expansion of Canadian manufacturing. The most radical of these proposals was the demand for nationalization of the banking and credit system, power transmission systems, and the basic steel industry.

Indeed, there was not a hint of either revolutionary analysis or revolutionary action. He did not treat the penetration of U.S. finance capital into the Canadian economy as a historical process, the result of inexorable Marxian laws of capitalist development; rather he considered it completely in relation to circumstances of the post-World War II era. It was presented as a policy of the Canadian Government which could be changed and rectified by another policy. The analysis was geared to the moderate proposals at the end of his discourse. A deeper and more Marxist study appeared later in 1948, with the publication of Tim Buck's most substantial written work: *Canada: The Communist Viewpoint*. It was a compendium of many things: history, political economy, Marxist-Leninist theory, long-term strategy, short-term tactics. In his foreword, Stanley Ryerson described the book as follows:

This book is a landmark in the history of the labor movement of this country, as the first comprehensive study in the light of Marxist-Leninism, of the development and present crisis of Canadian monopoly capitalism. It provides a penetrating insight into the fundamentals of Canada's evolution . . .

Much of the evolution described is taken from standard works in the field, and Buck appears to have leaned rather heavily on O. D. Skelton's *General Economic History 1867-1912*. Buck elaborates his earlier analysis of the Abbott plan, and presents a convincing and prophetic estimate of the short-term effects of the policies of integration on the Canadian economy. In this sense it was a forerunner to such later works on this subject as Irving Brecher and S. S. Reisman, *Canada – United States Economic Relations (1957)* and Walter Gordon, *A Choice for Canada (1966)*. He elaborated his proposals for a new national policy and suggested that "the alternative" to economic dependence on the United States could be achieved "in large part by calculated development of productive capacity now lacking in Canada" through "fostering industries by governmental action". He suggested that at one time the interests of the Canadian capitalists coincided with the national interest but now,

The correspondence which did at one time exist between the aim of Canada's industrialists and the national interest has disappeared. It disappeared with the transformation of Canadian economy from competitive capitalist enterprise to monopoly-capitalism and the assumption of control by the "geniuses of financial manipulation" largely as a result of the influence of foreign capital in its origin. Canadian finance-capital developed as a junior partner of, first, British finance-capital, and now of Wall Street. The aims of its directors have always been, not in development as a nation, but the sale of Canada and her natural resources to the highest bidder – on the terms most profitable to themselves.

The picture which Buck portrays is one in which the Canadian manufacturers developed the country, albeit in their own interests, and in so doing created the nation. Even at the later stage, when individual manufacturers merged with banks to form finance-capitalist monopolies, they continued their drive for Canadian autonomy.

With the rise of finance-capitalist monopolies in Canada and the resulting changes in the structure of our national economy, the dominant interests in the country pressed increasingly for assertion of Canadian sovereignty. One by one, the colonial limitations that were still imposed on Canada after Confederation were eliminated.

At what point and for what reason did the Canadian bourgeoisie change their direction and adopt "the un-Canadian aims of the finance-capital oligarchy which now dominates the economy and the politics of our country"? It was, says Buck, primarily due to the conditions produced by the Second World War, out of which U.S. imperialism emerged as the only imperialist power able and ready to conquer the world markets.

Thus, the Canadian bourgeoisie, fully independent economically and politically, are by deliberate policy selling out to U.S.

capital and thus undermining our national independence. They will be satisfied to occupy the role of junior partners not just in the struggle for world markets but in the economic development of Canada itself. They will make government policy support their aims through both the Liberal and Conservative Parties which they control.

Buck presents a closely argued case to suggest that while Marxists believe in the inexorable operation of economic laws, history shows that "the operation and effects of the economic laws can be influenced by national economic policies".

He cites evidence to show how successive Canadian governments by the judicious use of policy were able to direct Canadian development along certain definite lines. He therefore suggests changing the present direction by the election of a "Dominion Government which will introduce national policies based firmly upon the aims of increasing our economic independence". The measures which such a government would introduce would be designed to increase the Gross National Product by the 50 per cent expansion of manufacturing to be "ensured" by government intervention, trade with all countries, especially the socialist ones, and a vast program of welfare state legislation. There is not any obstacle that Buck envisages to the attainment of such aims. They can be accomplished within the existing framework of society. The most basic change required would be a new constitution which would bring about a "geographically sectional but financially and administratively centralized, modern industrial state". However, the attainment of these "important reforms" is viewed by the Communists, says Buck, as only an intermediate stage on the way to a socialist revolution.

In the ensuing years, the Communists became more and more convinced that the fight for national independence from U.S. domination was the key, opening the path through intermediary stages to a socialist transformation of Canada. A whole series of party programs showing how this would be accomplished were drafted and redrafted between 1952 and 1971: *Canadian Independence and Peoples Democracy* (draft adopted February 1952); *Canadian Independence and A Peoples Parliament* (re-draft adopted March 1954); *The Road to Socialism in Canada* (draft adopted January 1958); *The Road to Socialism in Canada* (redraft adopted October 1959, with amendments made in 1962); *The Road to Socialism in Canada* (draft adopted April 1971); *The Road to Socialism* in Canada (redraft adopted November 1971).

These programs show that since 1948, when the Party revived its interest in the independence issue, it had become much more absorbed in it, and drew ever more sweeping conclusions from successive analyses of this subject.

In a foreword to the 1952 draft Tim Buck likened the Canadian situation to that faced by colonial and semicolonial countries:

These great new issues affect the Canadians of all classes—equally as national subservience before foreign exploitation affects patriots of all classes in colonial and semi-colonial countries.

The program opens on a declamatory note:

From the time of the settlement of Canada four hundred years ago, our people have fought for national independence from France and Britain. Have our people struggled through these centuries only to be swallowed now by the United States of America?

With one voice every patriotic Canadian will answer: NO. To make sure that this will not happen Canadians will wage the greatest struggle of our history as a people. We Canadians are called upon now to win our national independence from U.S. domination, to establish the supremacy of Parliament and to regain sovereign Canadian control over our resources, industries, armed forces and foreign and domestic policies.

To achieve these high patriotic aims Canadians must unite to defeat the numerically small but powerful clique of speculators and monopolists and their political representation who are perpetrating a national betrayal—to hurl us into a third world war for the U.S. trusts.

This was the keynote of the whole program. Every issue and every party task was now to be either subordinated to this issue or judged in relation to it. Canadian trade union independence was raised for the first time in party history to a demand on its own:

"The winning by the Canadian workers of the national independence of their trade unions is part of the struggle for the independence of Canada."

The Party notes with alarm the increasing ' "U.S. penetration into the fields of culture and arts", and calls for "the fullest promotion of Canada's own material forms of literature and art which express the democratic traditions of our people".

The French-Canadian people must be convinced that they "cannot win full national freedom until the domination of U.S. imperialism over Quebec as well as the rest of Canada is broken".

A Peoples' coalition is projected which will not "be dominated by any one party" to bring about new national policies. Its program will be as proposed by Buck in 1948 but with the addition of a Canadian flag, withdrawal from NATO, and restoration of "Canadian armed forces to Canadian Command".

But "the struggle against U.S. domination is at the same time a struggle against the internal enemy, the anti-democratic Canadian monopoly capitalists, the source of reactionary internal and external policy". For that reason, the conflict must advance at a certain stage beyond the winning of national independence to a fight for Socialism. At that point the Communists must and will take over the leadership of the movement.

The program adopted in 1954 was similar to the 1952 draft, although the slogan "Put Canada First" appeared for the first time. It left out any references that would lead one to conclude that, in the Party's estimate, the Canadian situation was similar to that of a colony or semi-colony. It strengthened the section on trade union independence, although, as in the first draft, its use of both "independence" and "autonomy" to represent the Party's trade union aims seems confusing since they are quite different concepts.

The Party was by now firmly committed to the concept of Canadian independence from U.S. domination. This became the all-pervasive theme of every aspect of Party interest. Its press and periodicals were full of the new line. Articles began to appear reworking the interpretation of Canadian history to bring to the fore all the anti-American aspects of Canada's past, and much of this had a curiously non-class character. Though many party members felt uneasy about the slogan "Put Canada First", recalling the reactionary character of the old movement which went by that name, the party spokesmen heavily emphasized this theme.

Much of this was a continuation, in a different context, of a renewed Communist interest in Canadian tradition which began in the aftermath of the Seventh Congress of the Communist International in 1935. At that Congress Georgi Dimitroff, General Secretary of the Communist International, attacked "the national nihilism" of most Communist Parties:

Communists who suppose that all this has nothing to do with the cause of the working class, who do nothing to enlighten the masses on the past of their own people, in a historically correct fashion, in a genuinely Marxist, a Leninist-Marxist, a Lenin-Stalin spirit, who do nothing to link up their present struggle with its revolutionary traditions and past—*voluntarily relinquish to fascist falseness all that is valuable in the historical past of the nation, that the fascists may bamboozle the masses.*

No, Comrades, we are concerned with every important question, not only of the present and the future, but also of the past of our own people . . .

We Communists are the irreconcilable opponents on principle, *of bourgeois nationalism of every variety. But* we are not supporters of national nihilism *and should never act as such.*

This admonition of Dimitroff had been accepted immediately by the Canadian Communists, and in his report to the Canadian Party in November 1935, Stewart Smith expressed it in these words:

It is the Communist movement in Canada today that is carrying forward all the best traditions of the Canadian and British, the French-Canadian, and the foreign-born people of Canada. Our press and agitation has correctly commenced to show the masses that we are the bearers under the modern conditions of the revolutionary tradition of 1837. We carry forward the traditions of the fight for democratic liberties in Canada and Great Britain under the present-day conditions.

The Canadian Communists under this new approach did some prodigious work in new interpretations of Mackenzie, Papineau, and Riel, whom they identified as revolutionary heroes of the Canadian past. By naming the Canadian Battalion that went to fight for the Spanish Republican Government in 1936, the "Mackenzie-Papineau Battalion," they drew public attention to this revolutionary tradition. Now in the postwar period new "heroes" were added to those already mentioned. Brock, Simcoe, and Macdonald were honored for their opposition to U.S. designs on Canada. In 1954, Stewart Smith led a delegation of the Toronto Executive of the Party to place a wreath at Macdonald's monument in Queen's Park. This move, however, met with considerable resistance from party members who found it rather difficult to honor Macdonald after having for many years honored the rebel whom Macdonald had sent to the gallows!

Canadian Communists in the main, however, went along with the Party's new program. They saw it as a necessary continuum in the Party's efforts to interpret Canadian reality in Marxist terms. They also saw it as a means of winning more acceptance for Communism on the basis of merging it with exuberant Canadianism.

The projection of the new stage in the U.S.–Canada relations which Buck began to develop in 1948 proved to be prophetic—Buck's analysis had shown that it was possible to adopt a whole range of immediate solutions to the current problems, brought about by U.S. domination, entirely within the framework of existing capitalist society. A new nationalist sentiment and movement did begin to develop in English Canada among a section of Canadian capitalists who saw their commercial interests jeopardized by U.S. investment in Canada, and among intellectuals who had little or no socialist, let alone communist, involvement. The milieu which was least concerned about the issue was the labor movement, most of whose members worked in U.S. branch plants and belonged to U.S.-based unions.

The criticism that the Communist International had levelled at Buck's earlier nationalism could be seen as being applicable to this latest and most pervasive nationalism. By making its main slogan "Canadian Independence", was not the Party detracting from the revolutionary aims of a truly Marxist movement whose main goal must be Socialism? Moreover, by projecting once again the two-step concept of the struggle for Socialism, was not the Party guilty of suggesting that Canadian society had to achieve a bourgeois-democratic revolution before it could advance further?

There was, however, a basic difference between the Communist view of the earlier period and the current one, and all the Party material made that abundantly clear. This was the period of the cold war in which U.S.–Soviet confrontation was seen as the main contradiction on a world scale, and that conflict pervaded all other issues. Moreover, U.S. imperialism was conducting a many-faceted drive throughout the world to take over the crumbling empires of the old imperialist powers, and was attacking revolutionary and democratic movements everywhere. Therefore, the main task of every Communist party was to organize opposition on its own territory, on the broadest basis possible, against U.S. imperialism and its allies.

That this was, in fact, the basic strategy of the world Communist movement was publicly underscored by Stalin himself. In a brief intervention at the close of the Nineteenth Congress of the CPSU in October 1952, six months before his death, Stalin exhorted the Communist parties in capitalist countries to take up the "banner of national independence".

The bourgeoisie used to be regarded as the head of the nation: it championed the rights and independence of the nation, placing them "above all". Now not a trace remains of the "national principle". Now the bourgeoisie sells the Nation's rights and independence for dollars. The banner of national independence and national sovereignty has been thrown overboard. There is no doubt that it is up to you, the representatives of the Communist and Democratic parties, to lift the banner and carry it forward it you wish to be patriots of your country, if you wish to become the leading force of the nation. There is nobody else to lift it.

It is obvious that all these circumstances should lighten the work of the Communist and Democratic parties which have not yet come to power.

So there is every reason to count on successes and triumph of fraternal parties in the countries where capital holds sway.

Yet the Canadian Communists' position had anticipated Stalin's, and they found evident satisfaction in his confirmation of a theme they had developed since 1948; in fact, one that they had pioneered in the late twenties. Undoubtedly the close and special relationship between Canadian and American capitalism helped them in coming to that conclusion. But their early perception of this relationship arose out of Buck's insistence on studying what he called "the Canadian peculiarities", in spite of admonitions from the Comintern which had ignored these features.

French Canada

The evolution of the Communist Party's policies on French Canada was always intertwined with other related questions, the most conspicuous being the status of Canada, federal-provincial relations, constitutional amendment and repeal. But basically its interpretation of French Canada was conditioned by its long-term strategic aims and its perception of the character, structure, and role of a Leninist party.

As a socialist party, it felt that the measures required for the socialist transformation of Canadian society could be accomplished only through a strong central government having all the powers of economic and social control. But even short of a socialist transformation, the Communist Party had always supported and advocated the grant of stronger powers to the federal authority, as indispensable to the carrying out of its program of immediate demands. In that sense it had positions very similar to those of the CCF.

Its perception of the class struggle in Canada was that the confrontation of the working class and the capitalist class was being fought out on a national scale, and that the regional, national, or other differences were secondary. For this reason, a Leninist-type party with a strongly centralized leadership, and a monolithic structure, was required. There could be no room in such a structure or concept for autonomous or semi-autonomous sections, and all attempts made by French-Canadian party members for such concessions were repulsed.

The theoretical background for the Party's study of the "national question" was provided by the many writings of Lenin and Stalin which stressed the right of "oppressed nations" to "self-determination" as a democratic demand which must be supported by every genuine proletarian party. But the national question to them was *always* subordinate to the class struggle, and thus was regarded as a tactical rather than strategic demand. The Canadian Party was constantly torn between recognizing and supporting the right of French Canada as a nation to "self-determination", and its fear of "bourgeois nationalism", within as well as outside party ranks. Thus the Party's position on French Canada appeared dichotomous and equivocal.

Until 1960 both revolutionary socialism and social democracy were extremely weak in the French-Canadian community in Quebec. This was due to a whole number of complex factors, not the least of which were the power and influence of the clergy, the strength of clerically-oriented nationalism, the outright persecution of communists by the provincial authorities, and the suppression of socialist and liberal thought in the French-Canadian academic institutions.

There were no French Canadians at the Party's founding convention, but, according to Tim Buck, a French section was established in the first year following the foundation.[8] It was headed by Albert St. Martin who had founded "L'Université Ouvrière". According to Buck he had to be expelled from the Party for "extreme petty-bourgeois nationalism", which included favoring the Catholic syndicates over the international unions. Although the Party was able to recruit other French Canadians into the leadership of the Quebec section, that leadership in Buck's words was "guided by Fred Rose" who presumably represented the main body of the Canadian Party.[9]

Buck acknowledged in retrospect a theoretical weakness in the Party when, in discussing the first period of the Party's existence, he says:

While grasping the significance of Lenin's emphasis upon the role of the working class in the struggle to protect the real interests of the nation, the party did not then grasp the full historical significance of the national status of the people of French Canada and therefore failed to put forward the necessary demand for the right of the people of French Canada to national self-determination up to the right of secession.[10]

Indeed until 1929 very little was said or written about French Canada at all. In the two articles published by Buck in March 1925, under the title "Canada and the British Empire", he never once mentioned the status of French Canada, or even listed French-Canadian spokesmen among those who had taken a stand against British domination of Canada. The reason for this may be indicated in a series of notes he wrote in 1926 entitled *Independence*. Discussing various elements of the Canadian population that could be counted on as allies in the fight for Canadian independence, Buck had listed as "d" the following:

French Canadians: Not to be exaggerated. Anti-British tendencies, also chauvinistic tendencies. Against fighting British wars, against France's war also. See in BNA protection their peculiar interests (languages, religion, schools). Must be shown that Independent Canada would give same liberties and guarantees.

---

[8] Tim Buck, *Thirty Years 1922-1952*, p. 29.

[9] *Ibid.*, p. 30.

[10] *Ibid.*, p. 29.

But in the Party's excitement over the "Byng versus King" issue, *The Worker* prominently displayed and praised Bourassa's demand for Canadian autonomy and his denunciation of the Governor-General. Yet a month later in the document which Stewart Smith wrote for the Political Bureau of the Party entitled *History and Present Economic Background of the Struggle for Canada*, the special part which French Canada played in the "struggle for Canada" was completely ignored. In a discussion article in *The Worker* of March 9, 1929, F. Rosenberg of Montreal (later known as Fred Rose) sharply criticized the Political Bureau for issuing a draft resolution for the Party's forthcoming Convention that made "no mention of the French-Canadian question".

In letters addressed to the Party, prior to this Convention, the organizational department and the political secretariat of the Executive Committee of the Communist International (ECCI) advised very strongly that the Party should pay more attention to French Canada. In the organizational department's letter, point 7 of its list of tasks and priorities for the Canadian Party stated as follows:

The Party must immediately set to work amongst the French Canadian masses of Quebec. An organizer should be immediately placed in Quebec province for this purpose; the discontinued French paper should be renewed; special forms of approaching the French Canadian masses must be found in view of religious prejudice, language, etc. Upon no account must the French Canadian units be regarded as "language units" in the "immigrant" sense because Canada is a bi-lingual country and the French Canadians are native masses.

The letter of the Political Secretariat of the ECCI goes further in discussing some of the theoretical questions involved. It drew the Party's attention to "the strong anti-British sentiment among the French Canadians which played a very important role in the last war". It called on the Party to take up the fight for "complete self-determination" for French Canada. It pointed out that "the French Canadian workers in the Quebec Province ... form the most exploited section of the Canadian working class". It called on the Quebec section of the Party to "work within the Catholic unions" although it did not suggest how this would be done in view of another observation in the letter to the effect that the Party in Quebec has "practically no connections with the French Canadian workers".*

Yet, in spite of this admonition from the Communist International, the Convention continued to ignore the French-Canadian question except for a few references to the need to recruit French-Canadian workers. No other reference appeared in the Convention records on the subject of self-determination for Quebec, or indicating any party awareness of the special character of the French-Canadian "nation".

The only decision on French Canada that was carried out after the convention was the resumption of a party organ in the French language, *L'Ouvrier Canadien* (changed to *La Vie Ouvrière* in 1935). Its contents, however, were merely a duplication of the general agitation and propaganda carried in the English and foreign language party press. Nothing special was said about Quebec at the two party conventions held in the thirties: the seventh in 1934 and the eighth in 1937. This reflected the prevailing party attitude which looked upon the differences between French and English Canada as negligible. This was expressed by Fred Rose, then Quebec party organizer, in an article in *The Worker*, January 19, 1935.

In 1867 Great Britain granted executive power to the Canadian bourgeoisie. The English Canadian section being most powerful, grabbed a bigger share in the exploitation of the country's natural resources. This does not place the French Canadians in the category of an oppressed minority. Such was the development of capitalism in all countries. Some sections of the bourgeoisie were in a position to grab and steal more of the people's resources than others. The French Canadian bourgeoisie got its share, either separately or jointly with the English Canadians. As for the "rights" that the masses can enjoy under capitalism the French Canadians have lingual and other so-called "democratic" rights to the same extent as the English Canadians. The Canadian working class can use both the French and English language in the fight against the bourgeoisie.

Rose then attacked L. Taschereau, the Quebec Premier, for calling French Canada a nation. This is "a lie", Rose asserted, because French Canada does not possess all the attributes of a

---

* This was particularly ironic since Albert St. Martin, who had connections with French-Canadian workers, had been expelled for, among other things, advocating work in the Catholic Unions.

nation which Stalin said were necessary to fulfill that definition: language, territory, common economic life, psychological make-up, community of culture. One of these characteristics is missing —namely, a common economic life—and therefore French Canada fails to qualify.

There being no French Canada economy but rather the Canadian economy, it is obvious that there is no such thing as a French Canadian nation apart from Canada as a nation of which the French Canadians (they are the biggest single racial group in Canada) are the basic group . . .

By no means must there be an underestimation of the nationalist sentiments that are deep-rooted amongst the French Canadian workers . . . Revolutionary internationalism is rapidly replacing reactionary nationalism . . . Nationalist separation can bring the French toilers only one thing—increased misery.

This article illustrated the problems that Canadian communists experienced in assessing the French-Canadian question. They were first of all appalled by the reactionary character of Quebec nationalism, dominated as it was by clerical corporatism. Secondly, they could not define the French Canadians as anything more than a "racial group". Thirdly, by judging the class struggle as a unitary struggle, they felt that any concessions to French-Canadian uniqueness would divide and weaken the working class. Though they changed many times since then, they never completely came to terms with these constraints.

Stanley Ryerson began in 1937 a series of works on French Canada that were aimed at overcoming them, yet he, too, was unable to surmount the problem without serious reservations. With the publication of his *1837, The Birth of Canadian Democracy*, which was described by the Party as "the first serious attempt to evaluate an important period in Canadian history in the light of Marxism", Ryerson emphasized the democratic traditions in French-Canadian nationalism.

The 1837 rebellions in both Upper and Lower Canada are considered by Ryerson to be bourgeois-democratic revolutions, part of a world movement which "opened the path to the development of capitalism" and "which brought into being modern democracy." In addition, the rebellion in Lower Canada is part of "the national problem of French Canada" which "dates, of course, from the Conquest. The British policy was from the first based on the assumption that the French nationality, language and religious beliefs would rapidly disappear, and be replaced by those of the conquerors". This assumption had to be discarded in face of the American Revolution, but another attempt to anglicize French Quebec was made and failed after the Durham Report. The English "landlords-merchants" became the "ruling class" of Lower Canada, and found it "necessary to cement an alliance with the pro-feudal Catholic hierarchy and French land-owners, in order to defeat the democratic forces of the French middle class and peasantry".

Yet outside of a few scattered references to "the national problem", "nationality" and "the question of nationhood" (the latter reference applying equally to Upper and Lower Canada) Ryerson does not yet explicitly define Quebec as the French-Canadian nation, fighting for self-determination.

The Communist Party was not ready to go that far, as was evident in its brief to the Royal Commission on Dominion-Provincial Relations (Rowell-Sirois) in 1938. This document, entitled *Toward Democratic Unity For Canada*, was widely praised in sections of the daily press when first presented. It is probably the most detailed study of Canada and of constitutional issues ever done by the Communist Party. It was obviously well researched and documented. Yet for all that, it has an ephemeral character, for many of the proposals and much of the interpretation were to be quickly discarded in favor of new ones. The *Introduction* anticipates this, for it states:

Under one set of circumstances, centralized national government may serve the interests of the democratic masses in their struggle for economic improvement and democratic rights; under another set of circumstances, centralized national government, dominated by reactionary vested interests, may stand as a barrier to democratic progress.

The entire brief argued that the circumstances then obtaining in the country required centralized national government. Its interpretation of Confederation which provided the historical background for this argument, can be summarized in the following extracts:

In its actual form, Confederation represented a compromise of the rising industrial capitalist class, desiring internal free trade and central jurisdiction over external trade, with pre-capitalist and semi-feudal influences, seeking to preserve the powers of landlord-

ism and feudalism in the provinces . . . The semi-feudal system of Quebec was incorporated into Confederation practically unchanged, because the rising industrial capitalist class saw advantages for itself in the maintenance of the degraded position of the French Canadian people. While internal free trade and central control of external trade were essentially attained, the economic disunity of the new nation remained.

National unification was incomplete . . . Quebec has been maintained as an "economic zone" of especially low living standards, deprived of the social and cultural attainments of the rest of the people of Canada.

The brief then goes on to argue that the "French Canadian people have never enjoyed genuine minority rights" which are defined as economic, social, political as well as cultural amenities.

Genuine minority rights involve the granting to the minority by the central government of equal political rights; but the French Canadian people have systematically been deprived of equal democratic rights by restriction of the franchise and oppressive electoral laws. Genuine minority rights require that the central government ensures to the people of the minority the same social services as are enjoyed by the other citizens of the state; the French Canadian people have been denied this . . . The objective of the rising industrial interests and the semi-feudal influences of Quebec in arriving at the basis of Confederation in so far as Quebec was concerned was to prevent the French Canadian people from enjoying equal social, economic, and cultural rights . . . Complete national unification is required to establish the minority rights of the French Canadian people for the first time by guaranteeing to the people of Quebec equal social, economic, and cultural rights and placing upon the central government the obligation to ensure the fulfillment of these rights.

The Communist Party here uses the term "minority" to describe the French-Canadian "people". It has borrowed a term which is common enough in sociological parlance, but strange to Marxism-Leninism, at least in the sense that it is used here. There is no definition in the Party's statement of a minority nor is there a description of the features by which it is distinguished. The concept is all the more startling when the suggestion is made that the Central Government should enforce the rights of the minority by invading provincial jurisdictions in the area where the "minority" is, in fact, the "majority". Part of the reason for this approach is given in a later section of the brief which discussed the growth of political reaction in Quebec:

Thus, Quebec reaction which sets itself against Canadian national unification and loudly proclaims "provincial rights" is invading the national sphere to wrench from Canadian citizens their democratic rights.

At the same time, fascism is encouraged and fostered centering in the Province of Quebec and seeking to spread out across the Dominion.

... Just as in other countries where fascism has come to power, the governmental structure of Quebec is honeycombed with avowed opponents of democracy ... The policy of the government party in the "Padlock Law" and in labor unions is directly approved by the fascists ...

At the conclusion of the brief, the Party repeats what it believes to be

The only sound, principled approach to this problem. The minority rights of French Canadian people are not identified with Quebec provincial rights; but on the contrary, the amendment of the British North America Act to permit the completion of national unification opens the way for the establishment of equality of the rights of the French Canadian people, without which there can be no economic progress and social security for the Canadian people as a whole.

What is involved here is a confusion between theory and tactics. From the tactical viewpoint, a good case could be made, as it was, for the Party's proposals to fight for national programs of economic and social welfare, and to strongly oppose Duplessis's brand of nationalism by which he was attempting to obstruct such legislation. But beyond that, it seems questionable for the Party to devise its basic interpretation of Canadian history and society with a view to bolstering what is at best a question of immediate tactics. This practice was even more conspicuous when Stanley Ryerson published in 1943 his study *French Can-*

ada, which established for the first time the Party's definitive view that the Quebec question was basically a "national question". Sam Carr, national organizer of the Labor Progressive Party*, greeted this book in the *Canadian Tribune*, October 16, 1943, in exuberant language:

The fact that Ryerson's book provides the first thorough-going analysis, economic and political—to the national question of Canada, both provides a striking demonstration of the serious contribution that Canadian Marxists are making to political thought in our country, and a practical measure of assistance to the growing maturity of Canadian labor.

The book was an extension of the study which Ryerson began in 1937 of the French-Canadian democratic tradition. This time, it is seen through five main architects of that tradition: Papineau, Lafontaine, Dorion, Riel, Laurier. Ryerson characterized the essence of this tradition as follows:

It is important to understand the fact that the democratic struggle of the French Canadian people during the whole of the preceding period had been a struggle for the right of national self-determination for their right as a nation to choose their own form of state.

Confederation, he said, bears the imprint of this struggle as it contained many concessions made to French-Canadian opinion led by A. A. Dorion:

The French Canadian popular demand for an autonomous state was conceded by the British North American Act, insofar as a federal system was established instead of a legislative union; and in the granting of powers to the provincial governments in the spheres of direct taxation, administration of public lands, local public works, education, municipal institutions, marriage, hospitals, ad-

---

* The Communist Party of Canada was declared illegal under Section 39 of the Defence of Canada Regulations, June 6, 1940. When the political conditions were favourable to a reappearance of the Communist Party, it was decided to call the party by a different name, mainly to save the Liberal Government the embarrassment of having to rescind the order of June 6, 1940. The Labor Progressive Party was founded June 1943.

*ministration of justice, and "property and civil rights".**

The importance of the concessions to Quebeckers is emphasized by Ryerson:

... the question of French Canadian autonomy, of "Quebec provincial rights", must be recognized by English-speaking Canada for what it is: the expressions of the democratic right of the French Canadians to the choice of their own state.

But the heart of the book is that, for the first time, it invoked Stalin's definition of a nation to apply to Quebec:

*A nation is an historically evolved, stable community of language, territory, economic life, and psychological make-up manifested in a community of culture.**

And yet, having invoked Stalin's definition and declaring that Quebec possessed all these characteristics, Ryerson drew back from the implications of this definition, and produced a startling (for Marxists) conclusion:

The position of the French Canadians is that of a nation which has won the essentials of political equality within the Canadian federal State, but which, heavily handicapped by vestiges of the feudal past, suffers from serious elements of inequality in a whole number of spheres of life.

Between its submission to the Rowell-Sirois Commission in 1938 and the appearance of this book, the Communist Party had undergone a marked change in its policies on French Canada, and particularly in its historical interpretation of French-Cana-

---

* In 1963, Ryerson, while still a member of the Communist Party, admitted that this and similar statements in the book were "overstatements" and a "shade exaggerated". (*Marxist Quarterly*, August 1963, p. 13n). But they shaped Party policy at the time, just as Ryerson's correction of 1963 reflected new policy needs in the midst of the "Quiet Revolution".

* Stalin's definition was not original even when first enunciated in 1913. Goldwin Smith in his book *Canada and the Canadian Question*, written in 1890, declared French Canada a nation because "where one community differs from another in race, language, religion, character, spirit, social structure, aspirations, occupying also a territory apart, it is a separate nation, and is morally certain to pursue a different course, let it designate itself as it can" (p. 168, University of Toronto edition, 1970).

dian society. From a minority seeking "minority rights" French Canada had become a nation which had *always* fought for "national rights". From a minority which had been cheated at Confederation out of its "equal political rights", it now appeared that French Canada had really won "the essentials of political equality" at that time, and now needed only economic equality. Whereas in the Party's brief, economic equality could come only by scrapping "provincial rights" which were regarded as a deception, in Ryerson's book, the question of provincial rights was "recognized for what it is: the expression of the democratic right of the French Canadians to the choice of their own state".

These changes in interpretation were embodied in the program adopted by the Labor Progressive Party at its founding convention that same year (1943):

The Confederation established in 1867, embodied the principle of responsible government won in 1848; it expressed the growing maturity of the industrial capitalist class, the winning of commercial autonomy, the establishment of the statehood of the Canadian Dominion from "Sea to Sea". But in its federal form, the new state acceded to the demand of the French Canadians for their own autonomous state . . .

Other sections of this program threw additional light on the motivation for these changes. The Party had thrown its full weight behind the war effort of the King Government and firmly opposed the nationalist groups in Quebec, especially the Bloc Populaire, which were resisting the war and strongly agitating against conscription (which the party supported). To raise or support the slogan of self-determination under those conditions would only strengthen the nationalists of Quebec and detract from the main task which the Party projected:

National disunity and distrust impede the total mobilization of our country for victory and the enactment of nationwide measures for social security. They endanger both the war effort and our prospects of democratic advance in the post-war world.

This did not mean that the Party was giving up its demands for satisfaction of Quebec needs. It was putting them in a different context. That this was what the Party had in mind in Ryerson's book was clearly stated in Sam Carr's review in the *Canadian Tribune* of October 16, 1943:

Today the grave danger is that unless immediate action is taken, the French Canadian national sentiment may be turned into the path of rabid bigoted nationalism—the incubators of racism and fascism.... A careful reading ... of the work provides us with a proper understanding of French Canadian traditions as they really are. Ryerson's book should also be required reading for those who are under the baneful influence of the corporatists and Bloc Populaire gangs who claim to be carriers of the French Canadian tradition ... the author of French Canada *points to the rise of new forces to give a worthy answer to reaction.... If the Bloc Populaire with its fascist, corporatist program is to be defeated, the trade unions, the CCF, and the Labor Progressive Party must unite ... with pro-war and anti-Bloc sections of the Liberals in Quebec ... This new addition to our arsenal of weapons for democracy should be read by the widest circle of Canadians.*

Thus we have once again the subordination of theory to tactics. The book is seen as "a weapon" for the immediate circumstances, and consequently its basic interpretation is devised to bolster the current tactical needs.

There was no fundamental change in the Communist position on French Canada in the following period, although there were some important differences in emphasis and terminology. In the Party's new program of February 1952, where the focus was on the fight for Canadian independence from U.S. domination, the emphasis was on utilizing the nationalist traditions of French Canada in the service of this new stage:

The French Canadian people cannot win full national freedom until the domination of U.S. imperialism over Quebec, as well as the rest of Canada, is broken. The struggle for Canadian independence is French Canada's path of advance towards the achievement of full national self-determination ... In this common struggle with all other Canadians, the French Canadian workers must not succumb to bourgeois nationalism, but at all times fight for unity with the English speaking workers.

In the 1954 program this point is even stronger:

The defeat of the greatest threat they have ever faced—domination by the United States—must be undertaken by the French Canadian people if they are to preserve their nation and win national equality.

*The betrayal of French Canada to the U.S. has been jointly engi-
neered by the Canadian monopoly capitalists and reactionary circles in French Canada. This combination, which demagogically
exploits the national aspirations of the French Canadian people
has placed in jeopardy the future of the French Canadian nation
by handing over Quebec to the grasping U.S. trusts.*

The succeeding passages on French Canada elaborate on the
anti-U.S. imperialist theme. All problems of French Canada are
now shown to be the result of U.S. control of Quebec and the
rest of the country. Quebeckers are called to struggle against the
United States in order "to save the French Canadian nation".

*In this struggle the long-standing demand of the French Canadian
people for full national equality, unresolved by Confederation, will
be satisfied in the only democratic way—the guarantee of the right
of French Canada to national self-determination up to and including secession. Victory for this democratic principle will open the
way for the free and voluntary association of French Canada with
English speaking Canada in a federal state based upon the complete national equality of both peoples.*

The term "national equality" as used in previous party statements, beginning in 1938, was meant to cover the measures
required to give French Canadians economic and social equality,
in addition to the political equality which they were supposed to
have attained at Confederation. The above passage seems to be
ambiguous on this score. The suggestion that full national equality was not given at Confederation but would be given by a
genuine federal state implies that the national equality referred
to here is primarily a political concept. This interpretation of the
Party's position seems to be strengthened by a passage in its
submission in January 1956 to the Royal Commission on Canada's Economic Prospects:

a) Federal Responsibility for Advancing Canada As A Democratic Two-Nation State

*The urgent need for many nationally financed and administered ser-
vices should not be allowed to lead to any encroachment on the
rights and authority of provincial governments to manage the business of their respective provinces. There should be unequivocal recognition of the full nationhood of the French Canadian people.*

This is an unusual concession by the Party to provincial rights. It also seems to suggest some kind of special status for Quebec, beyond that of the other provinces, although that is not spelled out in explicit terms.

The Party was to change its program on Quebec several times as the movements of popular nationalism and separatism emerged and grew in the sixties and seventies. It should not be understood, however, that the working out of interpretations on French Canada consumed the entire attention of the Party's Quebec section. The membership in Quebec, both English- and French-speaking, were engaged in general party tasks such as trade-union work, electoral activities, peace campaigns, circulating the party press, and raising money to sustain the organization. It must be remembered, as well, that during most of those years the Party in Quebec was under the heaviest attacks of any party section in the country: Duplessis's infamous "Padlock Law", the brutal activities of the Quebec Provincial Police against Communist meetings and demonstrations, and the constant ideological assaults carried on by the clergy.

At the same time, a note must be added about the constant tension which existed between the French- and English-speaking members of the Quebec section. A former leading Quebec Communist, Pierre Gélinas, has written a novel depicting that tension: *Les Vivants, Les Morts, et les Autres* (Ottawa, 1959). The conflict basically revolved around the feeling among the Francophones that they were a permanent minority in the Party, and consequently they demanded some autonomy over policies and activities in the French community. However, the Party would never grant even the smallest concession to this demand, which it labelled as "bourgeois nationalism". In 1947, this demand exploded at a Party Convention with the resultant expulsion of a large number of French-Canadian activists, some of whom had been in the Party since Albert St. Martin had been expelled for similar deviations. One account of the battle asserts that over 300 French-Canadian members quit the Party as a result of these expulsions.[11]

The oscillations in party policy on French Canada reflect, among other things, an endemic fear of overstepping the border line between acceptable nationalism and "bourgeois national-

---

[11] Marcel Fournier, *Histoire et Ideologie du Groupe Canadien Français du Parti Communiste*, 1925-45, in "Socialisme Québécois 69", No. 16, p. 70.

ism", or chauvinism. Yet this fear was much more evident in the way the Party dealt with French-Canadian than with English-Canadian nationalism, which the Party embraced frequently, and with enthusiasm. This was also reflected in the relations between French- and English-speaking members, and the fact that the Party has never (and this has continued to the present day) entrusted the leadership of the Quebec section to French Canadians. At times, French Canadians were promoted to leading positions in the Quebec section, even once to the rank of provincial leader, but on all such occasions the real power was still held by English-speaking representatives of the Party's national leadership, which in all cases was responsible for working out the main lines of the Party's position in French Canada.

CHAPTER FIVE

THE COMMUNIST PARTY, THE TRADE UNIONS, AND CCF

Canadian Communists and the Trade-Union Movement

Canadian Communists have had their greatest success in the trade-union movement. They have paid more attention to that field than to any other. They built and led unions, occupied high offices in the trade-union central federations, did Trojan work in organizing the unorganized, and according to a recent study,[1] played a decisive role in the wave of industrial unionism which swept Canada in the late thirties and forties, and helped bring the CIO into Canada.

From the outset the party's leadership and its membership were largely proletarian. The majority of the first political bureau was made up of active trade unionists who brought with them the tradition of trade-union involvement which had been such a prominent feature of early Canadian socialism. But it was Lenin's prescription on trade-union tactics contained in *"Left-Wing" Communism, an Infantile Disorder* that changed their

---

[1] I. M. Abella, *Nationalism, Communism, and Canadian Labour* (Toronto, 1972).

124

approach to trade union work, and that they attempted to put into practice immediately.

In this work, Lenin conducted a sharp polemic against "left-sectarianism" especially seen in withdrawal from "the reactionary trade unions" and the creation by Communists of new forms of labor organizations under their leadership.

To refuse to work in the reactionary trade unions means leaving the insufficiently developed or backward masses of the workers under the influence of the reactionary leaders, the agents of the bourgeoisie, the labor activists, or the "completely bourgeois workers"... In order to be able to help "the masses", it is necessary to brave all difficulties and to be unafraid of the pin-pricks, obstacles, insults and persecution of the leaders... and it is imperatively necessary to work wherever the masses are to be found.

Lenin makes the point several times that the trade unions are and must remain "the most easily accessible form of organization". They are the most rudimentary class organization and to try and invent "a brand new, clean little 'workers' union', guiltless of bourgeois-democratic prejudices, innocent of craft or narrow craft-union sins" is "foolish". Even under the most severe attacks by the reactionary trade-union officials, or by the governmental authorities, Communists must be prepared to go to great lengths to remain in these trade unions:

It is necessary to be able to withstand all this, to agree to any and every sacrifice and even—if need be—to resort to all sorts of stratagems, maneuvers, in order to penetrate the trade unions, to remain in them, and to carry on Communist work in them at all costs.

Thus Lenin's main message to the newly organized Communist parties of the advanced capitalist countries was to stay in the established trade unions at all costs. But outside of that, Lenin was not too specific as to what he meant by the phrase "Communist work" in the trade unions. Did it mean carrying Communist propaganda to the non-Communist membership of the unions? Yet, if this invited proscription and persecution, did Lenin mean that Communists should drop this activity and even their identity as Communists in order to stay in "at all costs"? If they did not carry on Communist propaganda, would their activity in the trade unions merely be that of militant fighters for higher wages and other reformist demands? These and other vexing questions were to surface many times in the course of the Party's subsequent involvement in the Canadian trade-union movement. But at the outset, the Communist leadership was confident that Lenin's advice was all-inclusive. Jack MacDonald stated in his keynote address to the founding convention of the Workers' Party,* in February 1922, as reported in *The Worker*, March 15, 1922:

What must the militants of the Left-Wing of labor do to win support and leadership? In general they must take the advice of the Grand Old Man of the Revolution, Lenin . . . from . . . what he wrote in his Left-Wing Communism.

But in the immediate aftermath of the founding of the Communist Party, more specific answers to some of these problems were given by the Communist International (CI) and the Red International of Labor Unions (RILU). The latter body was established by the CI in 1921 on the basis of a set of theses adopted by the Third Comintern Congress, and their general direction was embodied in the *Resolution On Policy On The Labor Union* adopted at the founding convention of the Workers' Party, 1922:

. . . the membership of the Workers' Party will work in co-operation with all militant elements in the Unions for the formation and development of a Left-Wing therein.

In all localities and industries where the old trade unions are definitely the predominant bodies, the Workers' Party will oppose all dual unions or secessionist efforts. In localities or industries where the independent unions have achieved some measure of constructive organization and where the old trade unions are weak, the membership of the Workers' Party will work within their respective organizations for the purpose of bringing about united action in all struggles while seeking at the same time to bring about their unification with the general labor union movement.

---

* The Communist Party was founded in 1921 as a secret organization and the Workers' Party was formed in 1922 as the open legal expression of Canadian Communism. This dichotomous situation was ended in 1924, when the Workers' Party changed its name to the Communist Party, and the secret apparatus was eliminated.

... the membership of the Workers' Party will assist in the consolidation of the labor unions on militant lines, by permeating these organizations with a revolutionary spirit, exposing the reactionary and treacherous policies of the labor union bureaucracy, stimulating the sense of aggressive rank and file control, and resisting to the utmost, the expulsion of militants and the splitting up of the union in general.

This resolution was hotly debated because it was primarily directed at the One Big Union, many of whose leaders were present at the convention. Russell, the chief officer of the OBU, opposed the resolution while many of his erstwhile colleagues endorsed it. To them, in the light of Lenin's book and the Trade Union Theses of the Comintern, the OBU was a "dual, secessionist union", and should be led back into the AFL ranks. Maurice Spector called the OBU "the last dying kick of the syndicalists in Canada", while Jack MacDonald said "it may be hard to go back to the AF of L, but the workers are there, and we have got to be manly enough to do it for the consolidation of the industrial power of the workers". Russell, in defending the OBU and his own position, stated that the resolution of the Workers' Party made an important error in failing to recognize "that the sectional needs of the workers differed". He also felt that the AFL was getting steadily weaker and even "dying". In a printed reply to the Workers' Party, the OBU later made the further point that even if they wanted to, the officers of the OBU could not dissolve the organization or lead it back to the AFL: "Unlike the Workers' Party and the reactionary unions, it is not ruled from the top and its policy cannot be directed by one or two super men."

The OBU continued to exist, though in a weakened state, until it merged with the Canadian Labour Congress in 1957. It remained mainly a Winnipeg union which organized the street railwaymen, the service trades, the bakery workers, and a steel mill in Selkirk. After the 1922 Convention, it carried on a continued and bitter polemic with the Communists. But most of its former leaders remained in the Workers' Party and were prominent in carrying through the policies outlined in the trade-union resolution adopted at its 1922 Convention.

This resolution served public notice on the AFL leaders that the Workers' Party was going to work within the AFL to challenge the policies of the "reformist" and "reactionary" bureaucracy, and that the Party would devise its own policies for the trade unions and seek to win support for these policies. On the advice of Earl Browder of the U. S. Communist Party, who was representing the Communist International and the Red International of Labor Unions, the Convention decided to launch a "minority movement" within the AFL unions, which would consist of "cells" or "fractions" operating inside the local unions and central federations. The implementation of this decision led to the creation of the Trade Union Educational League (TUEL) headed by Tim Buck. Through the League Buck would be directing all the cells and fractions of the "minority movement" across Canada. Its implementation had another impact, not intended, but one which could constantly recur in the Party—the confusion between party work and union work. Already in April 1924, the Party's Secretary noted in his *Report* to the Party this tendency which had been drawn to his attention by the Communist International.

It is clear that the work in the trade unions under the auspices of the TUEL, has created the impression, among certain sections that a left-wing block is all that is necessary. And that such a block, with its slogan of amalgamation and a Canadian Labor Party eliminates the necessity for a political party . . . While admitting that valuable work had been done in the trade unions, this work appeared as the independent movement of a left-wing rather than the particular work of the party.

Yet that confusion was inherent in the party's position and this was illustrated in *Steps to Power*, written by Tim Buck and published in 1925 by the Trade Union Educational League. In it an integrated program for the Canadian trade-union movement was spelled out: industrial unionism, Canadian trade-union autonomy, organization of the unorganized, independent labor political action, nationalization of industry with workers' control. These have remained, albeit in changing forms, the main trade-union objectives which the Communists have pursued.

In the form in which they are presented here by Buck, there is nothing to differentiate between the Communist Party and the trade-union movement, nor is there any attempt, as some critics have suggested, to hide the aims, the methods, or the motives of the Party in pursuing these goals. They are intended to be the means by which the Communist Party would win acceptance by the workers of Canada as the vanguard of the class, and as the political "general staff" of the revolution. Buck's book expressed vividly the difference between the attitude of the old socialist movement which did not adopt a party policy on detailed trade-union questions, and the Communist concept which felt that the Party had not only the right but the responsibility to intervene in all trade-union affairs.

Buck calls for a new approach to the winning of industrial unionism. In the past, he says, "owing to the mistaken tactics of radicals and progressives" industrial unionism has been taken to mean secession, but this is not the correct road. Industrial union-ism will come about as a gradual process within the existing shops where craft unions are now operating and craft unions should be encouraged to "amalgamate".

Demonstrate to the average unionist that the natural development of labor organizations is through craft organizations to federation to amalgamation; show him further that consolidation through merging various crafts is the only certain preventative of secession movements, and he becomes immediately a booster for amalgamation.

From that point, the winning of industrial unionism is relatively simple:

One of the first tasks of the militants in the labor movement, therefore, is to crystallize the existing sentiments for solidarity, organize the amalgamationists and their sympathizers, and by co-ordinated effort with the amalgamationists of the other crafts of the same industry, marshall their votes, smash down the barriers between the various executives, elect an executive representative of all crafts, and the battle for industrial unionism is practically won.

Autonomy will take longer to achieve because of the resist-ance of the international officers of the AFL, and because pro-gressives should avoid, as far as possible, "break-aways" as the method of attaining autonomy:

Canadian autonomy does not mean the secession of Canadian locals from the "Internationals", neither does it mean weakening International bonds in any way . . .

. . . There is some danger, in fact, of the developing sentiment leading to secession movements, the only effect of which would be

*to destroy the influence of the radicals within the unions con-
cerned, thereby playing into the hands of the reactionary official-
dom.*

Yet there was no principle involved in Buck's warnings, for
he said he could countenance "the development of non-interna-
tional organizations under certain circumstances and conditions".
But in general he cautioned against it, and advised the radicals
to view the process of gaining autonomy as a long-term struggle,
and urged them to avoid "narrow nationalism".

Autonomy, he goes on to assert, is needed in "the field of
political activity" because some international unions "prohibit
their locals from affiliating with the Canadian Labour Party"
which is supposed to be the instrument for independent political
action of the trade-union movement.

Yet while the Canadian Labour Party (CLP) had been set up
by the Trades and Labour Congress in 1917 and then revived in
1921, the Communists felt that the CLP had to be primarily their
organization:

*But while the federated form of organization gives the CLP, the
mass, its energy and driving power came from the individual membership of political parties affiliated to it, in which are organized
the active politically conscious members of the working class. Of
these parties, the more important and unquestionably the most
influential is the Communist Party of Canada; and while it is
unlikely that the CLP, will become a Communist Party, the logic
of events must inevitably urge it ever closer to the Communist
position. It can in that way avoid the period of illusions and that of
clarification which inevitably follows and march steadily forward,
the revolutionary political wing of Labor's army.*

But all this demands a strategy on the part of the radicals
and Buck was very explicit on this question:

*Few radicals realize the value, in a struggle such as this, of official
positions in local bodies; and yet local officers have, if organized,
tremendous power, and the education and training gained by holding such positions, makes local secretaryships, presidencies, vice-
presidencies, etc., points of strategic importance, possession of
which might easily make the difference between victory and defeat.*

To agitate and propagate for progressive action without taking

every possible care to ensure success would be folly . . . If the mili-
tants in every local of a town or city got together on a common
basis, organized their propaganda so as to create the necessary
sentiment for united action, and draw their locals together there is
no doubt whatever but the rank and file movement locally would be
irresistible. Collect these local groups of militants throughout each
industry, and there is a power and force that could carry all
opposition before it. Add to this the capture of local offices, na-
tional drives on definite propositions, organization of left-wing con-
ferences and left-wing delegates at conventions, and the labor
unions of North America, under the leadership of the militant
section of the rank and file, would march on through nationaliza-
tion of industry to workers' control, through autonomy to the
struggle for power, and through that struggle to a Workers' Repub-
lic.

This approach was generally followed throughout the succeeding years by the Communist Party. The results looked for by
Buck in this book, however, were not forthcoming because the
problem of winning the Canadian workers to socialism was an
ideological rather than an organizational one. But in the course
of trying to follow this path, the Communists did win important
positions in the trade-union movement, became recognized as
capable and militant trade unionists, and above all, with some
exceptions, they managed to stay in "at all costs", most of the
time.

Within a year of the publication of *Steps to Power*, the
Communists began to set up industrial unions under their leadership. The Mine Workers' Union of Canada in Nova Scotia
under the leadership of J. B. McLachlan and the Lumber Workers Industrial Union in Northern Ontario were established in
1926. They joined with the Canadian Brotherhood of Railway
Employees (CBRE), the OBU, the Canadian Pacific Express Employees, the Electrical Communication workers, and the Canadian Federation of Labor in November, 1926 to launch the All-
Canadian Congress of Labour (ACCL) representing 40,000 affiliated members (the Trades and Labour Congress represented
130,000 at that time). In explaining their action, the Communists
had this to say in *The Worker*, December 4, 1926:

The crystallization of this movement of the independents was inevi-
table. The Trades and Labour Congress has ostrich-like obstinately
refused to undertake a move to unite the independents under its

own wing. It has placed jurisdictional loyalties far above the ne-cessity of bringing about co-ordination for action. Year by year the Congress has been getting more and more conservative, more and more out of touch with the growing need of the workers of the Dominion for greater autonomy. It has been, as a result, unable to stem the growth of secessionism. The Trades Congress has insisted on remaining nothing more than a legislative "mouthpiece". Per-haps what constant verbal criticism of the policies of the Congress has been unable to achieve alone, the organization of this bloc of independent Canadian unions will be more successful. Perhaps the Congress will at last realize the need of both national unity and national autonomy.

By the end of 1928, however, the Communist Party was showing signs of disenchantment with the new Canadian trade union center. Reporting on the second annual convention of the ACCL, *The Worker* accused the leadership of bidding "for class collaboration", and characterized the convention as consisting of "militant words, reactionary policies". In particular it com-plained of "the more or less conservative elements from the CB of RE" and "the wordy confusionists from the OBU".

A few months later, in March 1929, Tim Buck drafted *A Trade Union Thesis* for the upcoming sixth Convention of the Party. It dealt with the situation in the labor movement and proposed certain steps to be undertaken by the Communists. It mirrored a sense of frustration by the Party. While it had suc-ceeded in forming and leading a number of "militant industrial unions", such as the Mine Workers' Union of Canada, the Lum-ber Workers Industrial Union, The Needle Trade Workers In-dustrial Union and the Auto Workers Industrial Union, these unions "numerically ... are generally weak". A number of the other unions in the ACCL are "ultra-conservative, chauvinistic organizations", and there is "a clearly-defined tendency on part of the leadership of the ACCL, to introduce class collaboration as a basic policy". In the TLC and international unions there is "sharper persecution of Communists", and the bureaucracy of the AFL is "an agency of capitalism ... and of the United States Imperialism". Part of the blame for these conditions was laid at the door of ten "failures" of the party in its trade-union work, which, as listed, were mainly organizational weaknesses that if overcome could presumably increase the party's effectiveness in the labor movement. The main trade-union task for the Party as laid out in this thesis was:

Organization of the masses of workers in the unorganized industries into "Canadian" unions which by changing the relation of forces between "Canadian" and "International" unions will reduce the relative importance and destroy to a great extent the hegemony that the "Internationals" now have, by virtue of the lack of opposition.

But in the preconvention discussion at least one voice—an important one—was raised to suggest that thought be given to a new perspective, the creation of a "new revolutionary trade union centre". Sam Carr, just back from two years in the Lenin School in Moscow, wrote an article in *The Worker*, May 4, 1929, entitled "Why So Many Failures In The Industrial Work?":

My opinion is that while we will affiliate new unions to the ACCL and not form a new centre at present, we must understand that the reactionary leadership will sooner or later embark upon an expulsion policy against Communists and Left-wingers, and in general reach the condition of the AF of L (unless we succeed in completely changing the leadership and policies of the new congress in the near future, which is highly improbable). In such a case, the question of forming a new revolutionary centre in Canada may arise . . . At present, however, the immediate organization of a new centre is untimely and out of the question.

In an article two weeks later Tim Buck agreed with Carr, but then added:

To withdraw from the ACC of L now, and to set up a revolutionary centre would be contrary to all Leninist principles in trade union work. It would objectively strengthen the "International" bureaucrats and weaken the left-wing. It would divide the front against the AF of L imperialism and its support of American imperialist aims, and would leave the bureaucracy of the ACC of L entirely free to develop a policy of class collaboration patterned after the AF of L, if they so desired, as they assuredly would.

What Sam Carr had said, however, was different. With him the question of launching a new revolutionary trade union center was merely a question of timing, whereas with Buck it was a matter of "Leninist principles".

But when the Convention took place, two weeks after Buck's article had appeared, the objective had already become "the building of a revolutionary Canadian centre". The Central Executive Committee of the CPC announced this to the Convention in its reply to the political letter of the ECCI.

We accept entirely the line of the Communist International on our trade union work. Our objective in this field must be the building of a revolutionary Canadian centre, based on industrial unions and linked up with the world revolutionary trade union movement by affiliation to the RILU.

Before the end of the year this decision was implemented at an inaugural conference which launched the Workers' Unity League (WUL). This new organization was headed by Tom McEwen (then known as Ewen), who had just been elected industrial director of the Communist Party (replacing Tim Buck who became the Party's general secretary). The formation of the WUL was probably the most momentous decision the Communist Party undertook on the trade-union field throughout its history. By the time the WUL was dissolved six years later, it had established the basis for industrial unionism in Canada, and with it, the right of Communists to some share in the leadership of the Canadian trade-union movement.

Undoubtedly, this latter point had something to do with the decision to launch the "revolutionary trade union centre." While the Communists had helped establish the ACCL in 1926 and by 1929 had contributed a number of newly organized industrial unions to the new Congress, they felt that their leadership of these unions was coming under attack from the ACCL as it had in the TLC. But another factor had something to do with this decision. The Canadian Labour Party, which the Communists had long regarded as a transitional form of class political organization, had become nothing more than a party of Communist trade unionists. More and more the social-democrats had either deserted or boycotted this party. The Communist International in its 1929 letter urged Canadian Communists to abandon the Canadian Labour Party in favor of the direct assertion of the vanguard role of the Communist Party:

The Communist Party is still very weak and has yet to become a mass Party. This it can only do by penetrating deeper into the widest sections of the working class, by more and more emphasizing the independent role of the Party, neither screening it behind the Labor Party, or following a sectarian line of isolation from the working masses. In the present period the immediate task of the Party is not the building of a Labor Party. The major task before the Communist Party is to build a strong powerful Communist Party. If the foregoing measures are energetically carried out there will be no basis in future for a National Labor Party.

The character of the party's trade-union work was spelled out in straightforward and explicit language at the enlarged plenary session of the Communist Party's Central Committee in February 1931, and in the "Draft Statement" preparatory to the meeting which appeared in *The Worker*, January 3, 1931. The resolution on the Workers' Unity League adopted at this meeting stated:

The Plenum must once and for all dispel the misconception of many Comrades that the Workers' Unity League is only one of the various forms of trade union activity of the Party. It must be clearly understood that the WUL is the centre of all revolutionary trade union and economic work of the Party and the Left-wing.

Since it is obvious that all Party trade union work is to be conducted through the WUL, the Plenum decides that the present Industrial Departments be abolished, and that Party fractions in the WUL from centre to locals be the organ of the Party for the direction of trade union work.

With the outlawing of the Party in 1931 and the incarceration of its eight top leaders, the Workers' Unity League in addition to its trade-union functions became the main vehicle through which Communist campaigns on economic issues arising from the Depression were conducted. The WUL would combine industrial unions directly affiliated to it, plus those in the process of formation, "the revolutionary opposition groups" inside the reformist unions, and the National Unemployed Workers' Association. One of the issues that had come up was the opposition of J. B. McLachlan, mine workers' leader in Nova Scotia and President of the WUL, to having the same union setup as in Alberta. He felt that a certain amount of regionalism should be allowed, as this reflected the character of the country, and was in line with the miners' wishes. But the Party leadership strongly maintained the position it had taken with the OBU: there is but one working class in Canada and no concession could be made to any other approach. Tim Buck in his address to the Plenum (February, 1931) declared:

I insist we cannot have two policies for coal miners in Canada. We cannot have one policy in Alberta and one in Nova Scotia. If we were for the Mine Workers Union of Canada in Alberta, we ought to have it for both or neither . . . my criticism was not against changing the policy, but against the opportunistic method of changing the policy in pieces to suit the Nova Scotians and to leave the old policy in Alberta.

With little or no labor legislation in existence at the provincial level, the main way the WUL organized unions was to establish a base in a shop, mine, or mill and then declare a strike for union recognition and wage increases. Every strike was bitterly fought with a great deal of police violence and state repression used against the strikers.* The tone for this repressive atmosphere had been set by Prime Minister R. B. Bennett in a speech in 1932 when he vowed that he would stamp out "socialism, communism, dictatorship" with "the iron heel of ruthlessness". Yet, strikes were won, although more for wage increases than union recognition in spite of the depressed state of the economy. Tim Buck some years later put forward this claim:

The long established tradition of the AFL that "workers can't be organized in hard times" was shown to be false. The number of strikes increased. In all Canada there were 86 strikes in 1931 and the number increased steadily to 189 in 1934. Of the 189 in 1934 no less than 109 were fought under the leadership of the Workers' Unity League and of those, 84 were won. The only strikes won by the workers during the crisis years were led by the WUL.[2]

This assertion seems to have been substantiated in an estimate of the achievements of the WUL made by a leading historian of Canadian trade unions:

The most important accomplishments of the WUL were in the further spread of organization among the lumbermen of Port Arthur and Cochrane regions in Ontario and British Columbia among Western coal miners, the furniture workers of Kitchener, Stratford, and Quebec, the shoe workers of Toronto, Kitchener,

---

* See Stuart Jamieson, *Times of Trouble: Labour Unrest and Industrial Conflict In Canada, 1900-66* (Ottawa, 1968).

[2] Tim Buck, *Thirty Years, 1922-1952*, p. 96.

and London, the packinghouse workers of Western Ontario, the building trades and the coal and bread drivers of Toronto, Kitchener, and London, and finally among the population of the automobile, steel, and rubber industries, not yet touched by the CIO. Concerning the last group, it was communist leadership that gave the first fillip to industrial unionism among them in Canada.[3]

The WUL went beyond the confines of ordinary trade-union activities and was the umbrella for a host of other economic battles such as the unemployed workers' councils that were established in the major urban cities of Canada, the On-to-Ottawa trek of the single unemployed, and the petition campaign which won over 300,000 signatures for a National Non-Contributory Unemployment Insurance Bill.

But why did the Communists insist on calling the WUL the "revolutionary trade union centre?" What was "revolutionary" about its activity? After all, Lenin had called the trade unions in capitalist society the "most rudimentary class organizations" and declared that any attempt to try to invent "brand new, clean little workers' unions ... guiltless of bourgeois-democratic prejudices" was "foolish". In fact in November 1935, just after a decision by the Central Committee of the Party to dissolve the WUL, its chairman Tom Ewen put this trade-union center in a reformist rather than revolutionary frame of reference.

... the sky was never brighter for the realization of the aims and objects that caused us to form the Workers' Unity League almost six years ago. Better conditions, living wages and trade union unity were the objects we had in view when we held the first convention of the WUL in Montreal, Quebec. And we workers can get the living wages and union conditions that we are entitled to if we achieve trade union unity!

In other words, the aims and objects of the WUL were the same as those of other trade-union centers and could be accomplished within the existing society. Moreover, while the WUL at its inception was characterized by the Party as being "the centre of all revolutionary trade union and economic work of the Party", Ewen now denied as "poppycock" the allegation that the WUL was "a section of the Communist Party of Canada".

---

[3] H. A. Logan, *Trade Unions In Canada* (Toronto, 1948), p. 341.

The WUL was formed by a Party decision announced to its Sixth Convention in June 1929, and dissolved six years later by Party decision announced at the Ninth Plenum of the Communist Party of Canada, held in Toronto, November 1935. This was done in response to the decision of the Seventh Congress of the Communist International held earlier that year, which called for a massive change in Party policy from going it alone, to the "United Front Against Fascism". In his report to the Plenum, Stewart Smith, who had headed the Canadian delegation to the Communist International Congress, declared:

The revolutionary unions were formed solely because they were necessary under the given conditions to strengthen the working class, and if now, unity can be achieved then this is in line with the whole purpose and objectives of the revolutionary unions and the Communist Party.

Instructions were given at this Party Plenum to the WUL activists to begin immediately the process of merging their unions into the AFL:

And it is crystally clear that the entire situation in these industries (railroads, steel, metal, textile, mining and marine transport), as throughout the country demands that we be prepared to work for the merging of existing WUL and independent unions with the AF of L Unions as the next step in the fight for trade union unity in Canada. Why is this? Because those changes that we are speaking about go deeper within the AF of L at the present time than they do in the ACC of L and Catholic unions; and primarily because of the fact that the AF of L unions in Canada are the biggest section of the organized trade union movement, making up about 105,000 workers out of the 300,000 who are in trade unions . . . We are wholeheartedly in favour of building up the AF of L unions. And it is only if the Communists and progressives prove that they know how to build up and improve the trade unions that the workers will vote out bureaucrats and elect Communists and Progressives to office.

Thus the Communist policy had come full circle, from ending the secession of the OBU in favor of working within the AFL, to helping create the ACCL as a Canadian Centre opposed to the AFL, to setting up the WUL as a "revolutionary trade union centre" opposing both the ACCL and the AFL, and, to complete the circle, dissolving the WUL to join the AFL and opposing the ACCL and the Catholic unions. For the next three years, the policy of supporting the international unions of the AFL and TLC was given great emphasis. At the Eighth Dominion Convention of the Communist Party of Canada, held in October 1937, the resolution on trade-union work gave unequivocal support for this policy:

The interest of Canadian labor and the cause of democracy will be advanced if all the various trade unions that are now divided will unite under the banner of the Trades and Labor Congress, if in every city and town all the existing unions were banded together in one Trade and Labor Council . . .

. . . We call upon the leaders and members of the ACCL unions to make an end to their futile and narrow policy of isolated National Unionism and to unite in action with their brothers and sisters of the International Union movement.

It is interesting to note that certain leading individuals in the CCF, particularly in Ontario and British Columbia, began to worry about the headway being made by the Communists in trade unions, and the relative weakness of the CCF. In a letter to J. S. Woodsworth dated January 31, 1938, Herbert Orliffe, Ontario Provincial Secretary of the CCF, discussed this question in very explicit terms. The CCF in Ontario, according to Orliffe, was "static" and had been for some time. It needed "a shot in the arm" which could only be provided by attempting to get the trade-union movement to affiliate to the CCF. However, there were problems involved, the first being the division between the "National" and the "International" trade-union movement:

Unfortunately the International Trade Union representatives will have nothing to do with the National Trade Union locals as well as International Trade Union locals. It is an unfortunate situation, but it is so. If we are to change our constitution to provide for Trade Union affiliation (and I feel that in some form or other, it is, at this stage of CCF development in Ontario, essential to the existence of the CCF), then we must be prepared to choose between the two trade union movements, because, at the present moment, we cannot get both. If we must choose, I feel there can be no question of the choice. The weight is all in favour of the International Trade Union movement (by which I include both AF

of L, and CIO Unions): (1) because of its very great numerical
superiority over the National Trade Union movement and its very
much greater influence over the industrial workers of this country,
(2) because of the very fact of its internationalism — a position
much more in consonance with CCF principles than nationalism.

There was, however, an additional problem in Orliffe's view: how to affiliate those unions in which Communists were playing an active role. Openly-avowed Communists would present no problem since they could not join the CCF as they already belonged to a political party. But what would happen when Communists who were not known as such, would become members of the CCF as a result of the affiliation of their union locals? He left that problem to be discussed.

It is clear in spite of Orliffe's statement about CCF "principles" that neither the CCF nor the CP was really concerned over the principles involved in the contest between Nationalism and Internationalism in the trade-union movement, but rather about numbers.

The Communist Party did not develop any new approaches to its work among the trade unions, except during the period from 1943 to 1945 when, as the Labor Progressive Party (LPP), it campaigned for an all-out war effort on labor's part. In the first program adopted in 1943 the position of the LPP was made absolutely clear:

To permit the maximum effort of the workers to be devoted to
winning the war, the Labor Progressive Party urges the trade
unions to remain true to their voluntary wartime no-strike pledge,
and takes an active part in the fight for a Dominion Government
labor code which will assist the unions to carry out that pledge, in
order to allow uninterrupted war production and the avoidance of
strikes, lockouts and stoppages.

The logic of this position led to an advocacy of support to the "progressive" elements in the King Government and to alliances with Liberal Party supporters in the trade-union movement, particularly in the TLC where these supporters held the key executive posts. A leading member of the Party later called this

A complete betrayal of Marxism by the national leadership of the
LPP, . . . teaching the identity of interests of capital and labor,

(and) advocating Liberal-Labor coalition and . . . the practice of class collaboration.[4]

Tim Buck, in his first major postwar speech, delivered to the Second Convention, LPP, June 1946, admitted that the Canadian party had been influenced by the American party leader, Earl Browder, who had been expelled from the CP of the U.S.A. in 1945 for "revisionism".

It must be emphasized that our party work was detrimentally affected by the revisionism of Earl Browder. We gave wide circulation to the writings in which he put forward utopian perspectives of post-war economic and social development, denying the essential character of imperialism. Our own presentation of the post-war problems ahead of the people of Canada left room for the utterly erroneous impression that cyclical crisis can be avoided under capitalism.

"Browderism", as shown in a recent study,[5] was the policy of subordinating every party policy to the war effort and to securing the closest entente between the Soviet Union and the United States. This was certainly applied to the Canadian scene by Tim Buck and the party's political bureau, and it brought some immediate benefits, particularly in the Trades and Labour Congress where Liberal Party labor leaders collaborated with Communist trade unionists. But in this same speech, Tim Buck pointed to a deterioration already taking place in Soviet-Canadian relations in the wake of the espionage arrests. From that point on, the Party's concern in the trade-union field was to hold on "at all costs" to its hard-won positions in the labor movement. This battle is described elsewhere.[6] It is a testimony to the effectiveness of the Party's trade-union work that it was successful in holding on in many unions in the face of the most formidable attacks.

From the outset the approach that the Communists took towards trade-union activity was a sharp departure from that of the old socialist movement which had seen a division of labor between socialist parties and the trade unions. The socialist par-

---

[4] Fergus McKean, *Communism Versus Opportunism* (Vancouver, 1946), p. 237.

[5] Joseph R. Starobin, *American Communism In Crisis* (Cambridge, 1972).

[6] See I. M. Abella, *Nationalism, Communism, and Canadian Labour* (Toronto 1973), and Gad Horowitz, *Canadian Labour in Politics* (Toronto, 1968).

ties had regarded themselves as custodians of Marxism, the "true" working class ideology, whereas trade unions were the custodians of the immediate economic interests, in which Socialists *as individuals* would participate and excel. The Communist Party saw itself as the vanguard of both the ideological as well as the immediate economic interests of the working class. Consequently it had no inhibitions about intervening in *all* trade-union matters considering that as the Marxist-Leninist Party it was the repository of all that was best for the working class, both in its immediate as well as long-term aims. The Party thus became the organized "minority movement" in the trade unions, in the course of which two things happened. One was the tendency for the party's trade-union activity to concentrate on those unions which carried out party policy on trade-union questions, and thus in practice turn away from Lenin's advice that Communists must "work wherever the masses are to be found".

The other, and possibly the most important deficiency, became the lack of attention to ideological work among trade unionists. The Communists who won and were able to hold leading trade-union executive positions were accorded those offices not as revolutionaries but for their excellence in trade-union functions, which are, by their very nature in capitalist society, reformist. Where such officials ran as Communist candidates in federal, provincial, or municipal elections, they usually got very small votes*. It was a regular feature of Communist Party conventions and conferences to hear criticism of the Party's trade-union activists for their failure to recruit members of their unions into the Party or to sell them the Party's literature. The activists always accepted the criticism, and just as regularly continued to ignore the ideological aspect of party work, including their own development as Marxist-Leninists.

Yet the Party's long-standing "industrial concentration" policy was probably its most successful activity. Although it achieved less than what the Party hoped for, it pioneered two of

---

* One exception to this was J. B. McLachlan, miners' leader in Cape Breton, who contested that seat in the Federal elections of 1935 as a Communist Party candidate and received over 6,000 votes. He quit the Party the next year over its decision to dissolve the Mine Workers' Union and return to the United Mine Workers of America under John L. Lewis, who had done so much harm to the miners of Glace Bay and to McLachlan personally. Another was J. B. Salsberg who had been a leader in the needle trades unions prior to becoming a party functionary and was elected first to the Toronto City Council and then to the Ontario Legislature from the needle trades area in Toronto.

the most important themes in Canadian trade-union history: industrial unionism and the organization of the unorganized. As a result of this work the Communists have retained a base in the trade-union movement from which it was never possible to dislodge them, even at the height of the cold war.

Communism, Social-Democracy and Labor Political Action

The formation of the Third International was based on Lenin's firm resolve to draw a clear and sharp distinction between the two trends in international socialism: revolutionary communism and social-reformism. While the trends had begun to differentiate within the Second International, the experience of the war and above all, the Bolshevik revolution in Russia had made it imperative, according to Lenin, to "rupture" the socialist movement along these lines, and for the Communists to carry on ceaseless ideological warfare against social-reformism. This was stated explicitly in the "Conditions of Affiliation to the Communist International".

Parties desiring to affiliate to the Communist International must recognize the necessity of a complete and absolute rupture with reformism and the policy of the "Centre", and they must carry on propaganda in favour of this rupture among the broadest circle of party members.

This warfare would be not only of an ideological nature but should include basic organizational measures as well:

Every organization that wishes to affiliate to the Communist International must in a planned and systematic manner remove from all positions in the working class movement that are at all responsible (in the party organization, editorial board, trade unions, parliamentary fraction, cooperative societies, municipalities, etc) reformists and adherents of the "Centre" and put in them reliable Communists —and they must not be disturbed by the fact that in some cases it may, at first, be necessary to substitute rank-and-file workers for "experienced" leaders.

Lenin in his speech on the "Conditions" at the 1920 Congress of the CI, considered the reformists as "the principal social bulwark of the bourgeoisie" based on a privileged section of the working class which he called the "labor aristocracy":

No preparation, even preliminary, of the proletariat for the bourgeoisie is possible without an immediate, systematic, extensive and open struggle against this stratum . . . OPPORTUNISM is our principal enemy . . . opportunism in the upper ranks of the working class movements is not proletarian socialism, but bourgeois socialism . . . This is where our principal enemy is; and we must conquer this enemy. We must leave this congress with the firm determination to carry this struggle on to the very end in all parties. This is our main task.

This became the frame of reference for the Canadian Communists in attacking "social-reformism" or "social democracy". But this was not immediately perceived in Canada as "the main task". This was due primarily to the fact that, unlike the European countries, Canada as yet had no organized social democratic party in existence. There were provincial labor parties, a number of them belonging to the Canadian Labour Party to which the Communists were affiliated. Canadian Communists nourished the hope that through the Canadian Labour Party and through the independent work of the Communist Party, they might be able to circumvent a social democratic path for the Canadian labor movement. Their main attack at the outset was not against the social democrats but against the old Socialist Party which had refused to affiliate to the Third International, and the Socialist-led OBU which had refused to dissolve its organization and return to the AFL. Thus in the first federal election after the Party's formation in 1921, they fielded a candidate in North Winnipeg to oppose and defeat Socialist and OBU leader R. B. Russell, while supporting J. S. Woodsworth in Winnipeg Centre*. Woodsworth's comments on that situation at that time are interesting:

In North Winnipeg, "Bob" Russell was nominated by the Socialist Party of Canada. His personal popularity, notwithstanding the

---

* The results in Winnipeg North in the 1921 Federal Elections were: McMurray (Liberal)—3,743; Russell (Socialist)—3,190; Blake (Union Government)—3,042; Penner (Communist)—596.

*weakness of his party, would probably have carried him to over-
whelming victory, had it not been for the opposition of a small
Communist group, who insisted on affiliation with the Third International. Ironical, surely, that Russell, sent to penitentiary on the
charge of attempting to set up a Soviet Government in Canada
should go down at the hands of a Communist group.* [7]

At its Second Convention in 1923, the Workers' Party (later
the Communist Party) adopted a policy resolution on "The
United Front and the Canadian Labour Party", announcing its
intention to "join and strengthen the sections of the Labour
Party, wherever there are such, take the initiative on their creation where these are absent, and to bring about their greater co-
ordination throughout the country. . . ." It does not conceive of
the Canadian Labour Party as solely a parliamentary apparatus,
but

*. . . an organ of real action capable of reflecting whether on the
floor of the House, or on the street the spirit of such struggles as
those of the Winnipeg Strike or of the Nova Scotia and Alberta
coal miners. For a Labor Party that will show up the utter fraud of
capitalism, "democracy", and the realities of wage slavery! For a
labor party that will organize to carry out a proletarian program of
social reconstruction!*

But the Communist International had some misgivings about
the line of the Communist Party of Canada on the Canadian
Labour Party. These doubts were frankly stated and discussed in
the Draft Statement issued by the Central Executive Committee
(CEC) of the Party in preparation for the Party's Fourth Convention in 1925:

*The logical sequence of our work in the Labor Party, our criticism
of reformist leadership, our demand for a fighting policy, and our
attacks on all class collaboration schemes, coupled with the growing confidence of the workers in our party, has found us in some
sections of the Canadian Labour Party with the leadership in our
hands. A Communist was also elected President of the Dominion
Executive of the Labor Party.*

---

[7] J. S. Woodsworth, "The Labour Movement In The West" in *The Canadian Forum*,
April 1922.

This has given rise to misgivings, possibly in the Comintern itself, as to whether our leadership has been won at the expense of our communist principles. The question has been legitimately asked: "If the Canadian workers accept Communist leadership, why the Labor Party. Why not the Communist party only?"

The CEC defended itself against these misgivings, claiming that it had made no compromises with reformists to win those leading positions. But what was happening (and this was glossed over in the CEC's statement) was that many unions and groups had already withdrawn from the Canadian Labour Party, presumably under "social-democratic" influence. This withdrawal had given the Communists numerical predominance which was decisive in winning a number of key positions in the Canadian Labour Party, but misleading as an actual measure of Communist influence.

In January 1926, Spector had bad news to report about the decline of the Canadian Labour Party. In an article in *The Worker*, he reported on the expulsion of Communists from the Quebec section of the Canadian Labour Party, and the refusal of the Winnipeg Independent Labor Party to form a united front with the Canadian Labour Party in the federal general elections which had taken place a few months earlier. In an open letter to the Winnipeg Independent Labor Party, published in *The Worker*, November 14, 1925, on that occasion, the Communist Party blames the ILP for "the slow growth of the Canadian Labour Party in Winnipeg". And yet after complaining that the ILP would not cooperate with the Communist Party or the Canadian Labour Party, which in this letter the Communists admit they control, the statement goes on to declare:

The Communist Party of Canada is the Canadian section of the Communist International. The Communist Party will continue to expose in the interests of the workers, all the democratic illusions that are being fostered and nourished, by the disciples of evolutionary gradualness, not excepting the Winnipeg ILP ... Neither shall we countenance the voluntary handing over of leadership in the struggle to parliamentary reformists ... the history of the struggle of the workers is too full of bloody and treacherous betrayals not to mention the obvious preparation for further betrayals, to let mere sentiment and the fear of being [mis] understood even by sincere Workers, stand in the way of the Communists of Winnipeg or of Canada.

Thus it was obvious that the united front with the Winnipeg ILP (led by Woodsworth and Heaps) had to be on Communist terms and leadership.

It is significant to recall that earlier in 1925 the Communist Party had adopted a much different approach to a united front with the "progressive bourgeoisie" headed by Mackenzie King. So long as they were fighting for independence from Britain "the Communists of Canada will help them with all their might". Several times in the party's subsequent history, the Communists showed a far greater willingness to enter into a united front with King and the "progressive bourgeoisie" than with the social democrats who appear constantly as "the principal enemy".

An article by Maurice Spector on July 17, 1926, gives an oblique warning to J. S. Woodsworth that he will stop printing Woodsworth's weekly columns from the House of Commons in the Communist paper unless Woodsworth adopts a more Marxist phraseology. After listing a number of "glaring" examples of "middle-class phraseology" such as "people" instead of "workers", Spector said:

We could go on endlessly quoting similar passages. Mr. Woodsworth came into the Labor movement when he had already reached maturity, and in the school of social service, and the Church of that. But then there is still time to read. We suggest that he should begin. Get to understand the basic principles of Marxism, the language and the practice of the class struggle.

The Communist Party was obliged to step up its attack on social-democracy by the decisions of the Sixth Congress of the CI in 1928. Priority in the resolutions of this Congress was given to "the dangerous role" being played everywhere by social-democracy whose ideology was declared by this Congress to have "many points of contact with the ideology of fascism". On his return from the Congress, Jack MacDonald gave a report to an enlarged executive at which he declared:

The political orientation of the Sixth Congress is the intensification of the struggle against social democracy. But as emphasized by Bukharin*, the sharper methods of struggle against social democracy is not in any way identical with the abandonment of the United Front tactics, as some Canadians are inclined to think.

---

* N. Bukharin had replaced Zinoviev as the President of the CI.

The more sharply we come out against social democracy the more determinedly must we strive to capture the masses who follow the lead of the Social Democratic leadership. Our United Front tactics, however, must in most cases be applied from below.

A whole new tactical approach was placed before the Sixth Convention of the Party held in June 1929, by the ECCI, and was endorsed by the Central Executive Committee at the Convention:

We accept and endorse the line of the Comintern letter on the Canadian Labor Party, and agree that in the present period it is not the task of the Communist Party to build a Labor party, but, on the contrary our task is to combat the whole idea of a Federated Labor Party, as an integral part of the struggle to bring those working class organizations that are still affiliated to the CLP under the direct and open leadership of Local United Front movements organized from below on concrete issues. This means eventual liquidation of the CLP. This implies also a sharpening of the struggle against reformism in all forms . . .

The Convention report warned that the idea of a Federated Labor Party, from which the Communists would be excluded, was being pushed vigorously by the "reformists" and called on the Party to step up its efforts to head off this move by building up the Communist Party in the labor movement and by attacking all the leading reformists in the country. The report to the Convention given by MacDonald established the theme from which the Communists never looked back:

Woodsworth is one of the most dangerous elements in the working class. The fact is that he is the main representative of the bourgeoisie in the ranks of the working class, yet a large number of workers look upon him as a real champion of the workers.

The indictment against him was not so much for specific acts of an anti-working class nature, but mainly on ideology—his rejection of revolutionary socialism. He was also attacked for his refusal to join the Canadian Labour Party or to support it in any way. The criticism against him was also made in an international context, in which he was identified with the activities and statements of social democrats around the world. But the main motive behind this stepped-up attack was the apprehension in party ranks that since the Canadian Labour Party tactic had collapsed, a national social democratic party would emerge and command the support of labor.

When the founding convention of the CCF took place in July 1933, the Party's reaction was swift and predictable. It was expressed in a two-page critique written under the name of G. Pierce, a pseudonym for Stewart Smith, published in *The Worker*, July 29, 1933, and distributed as a reprint. This was followed in February 1934 with a full-scale analysis by Pierce published as a 218-page book, *Socialism and the CCF**. This was probably one of the most concentrated attacks on social reformism made by any Communist Party, and although it caused some embarrassment to the Party on subsequent occasions when a more united front tactic was called for, it has never been repudiated. In fact, in 1952 Tim Buck specifically endorsed the book, to put an end to speculation that because he had been in prison when it was written and published, it did not represent his views.[8]

The first part of the book is the standard exposition of the difference between reformism and revolution. Pierce states at the outset that the CCF is not Marxist, and since there is no other socialism, the use of the term "socialism" by the CCF is "deception". Pierce particularly takes umbrage at Woodsworth's statement that the CCF represents "a Canadian ... type of Socialism". But this is impossible according to Pierce because there is no such thing as a distinctive socialism since the class struggle is international. This only proves that "social reformism is nationalistic in scope and character". Pierce then attacks the three roots which according to Woodsworth have gone into this "Canadian Socialism": "American individualism, British traditions and Christian idealism". "American individualism" according to Pierce means "private property"; "British traditions are British Imperialism"; and Christian idealism means "religion". With these elements in it, "the CCF program can be obviously nothing else than an attempt to adapt the Canadian working class movement to the interests and institutions of Canadian Capital-

---

* In an interview in 1973, Stewart Smith states that the reason he wrote these attacks under a pseudonym was that he did not agree with them but was compelled to write along these lines as a party decision. He also asserts that he was a personal friend of Woodsworth's and it would have caused a rupture in their relations! (The interview is on tape at York University Archives, I. Abella, editor).

[8] Tim Buck, *Thirty Years*, p. 111.

ism". He ridicules the use of the term "Co-operative Commonwealth" as the name of the Party. "This term", he says, "is quite
meaningless", except that British imperialism has used the term
"commonwealth as a description of its colonial empire of imperialist exploitation". He apparently forgot or ignored the fact that
the term "Co-operative Commonwealth" was quite popular in
both of the early socialist parties in Canada, and was used by the
Social-Democratic Party of Canada, a Marxist organization, in
its platform to describe the society which the working class
would one day establish in Canada. It was also the title of a very
popular socialist work by Lawrence Gronlund published in the
United States in 1884 and widely sold in Canada.

In discussing the specific proposals made in the CCF program, Pierce describes the program as "the fusion" of "two main
currents" which are "liberal-laborism and the bourgeois revision
of Marxism". He then defines liberal-laborism as follows:

*The current of liberal-laborism and farm reformism is represented
by the main leaders of the CCF, Woodsworth, MacPhail, etc. The
reformist farmer organizations (United Farmers of Alberta, United
Farmers of Canada, United Farmers of Ontario), which represent
the class interests of the rich capitalist farmers and which constitute by far the largest section of the CCF are included in the
current liberal-laborism. In addition to these, the main "labor"
parties, such as The Independent Labor Party in Winnipeg, the
Canadian Labor Party in Alberta and Quebec, and others, are
influenced predominantly by liberal-laborism. Finally, the League
of Social Reconstruction, which consists mainly of petty-bourgeois
professional people and "intellectuals" is included in this current,
together with all the petty-bourgeois leaders of the CCF such as
Philpott, Reverend Bland, etc.*

Having established by this method that the main thing about
the CCF is "liberal-laborism", he continues to attack this current
throughout the rest of the book. Yet from 1936 to 1938 and from
1943 to 1945, the Communist Party itself became the advocate of
"liberal-laborism": it used exactly that term to describe its tactical approach during those periods! Pierce further accuses the CCF
of flirting with Social Credit by including in its program "socialization of finance". He then attacks Major Douglas's "A plus B
theorem" as though the doctrine had actually been incorporated
in the CCF program. He attacks the CCF for trying to create the
illusion that higher wages can bring about a rise in the standard of

living. "To speak of 'a constant rising standard of living' is cheap and unadulterated deception and demagogy. The only way in which the workers today can prevent the persistent reduction of their wages is by the most determined struggle and class organization".

Pierce cannot find one positive thing to say about the CCF. Even its demand for the repeal of Section 98 of the Criminal Code he finds "hypocritical". In his treatment of the history of the socialist movement in Canada, he is contemptuous of the role of reformists and particularly of Woodsworth:

In Canada, the social reformists headed the wave of strike struggles after the war in order to lead the strikes to defeat and to diffuse their propaganda of class peace among the masses. The great general strike in Winnipeg, in which the masses of workers displayed the greatest heroism, was the occasion for the infusion into the working class movement of a whole series of capitalist leaders and the commencement of a concerted drive of social reformism to spread defeatism among the workers, to preach class peace, to conduct propaganda against strikes, and develop systematically the social-reformist propaganda of "the peaceful, parliamentary transformation of Capitalism into Socialism".

Yet this critique of the program and roots of the CCF, however comprehensive and devastating, is not the main feature of this book. What stood out was the assertion that there is a kinship between reformism and fascism, and that in fact, social reformism in general and the Canadian social democrats in particular, are "social fascists", helping the "fascization" of the Canadian state. Chapter 5 is entitled "The Role of Social Reformism as the Twin of Fascism", and Pierce takes this as his theme for the second half of the book.

In order to establish the "link" between reformism and fascism, Pierce asserts first the fundamental identity of the Canadian state and the German "fascist dictatorship":

As a matter of fact, there is no fundamental difference between the capitalist democracy of Canada and the Fascist Dictatorship of Germany.

THEY ARE BOTH DICTATORSHIPS OF THE SAME RULING CLASS, THE CAPITALIST CLASS. The ruling class changes the form of its state in accordance with its requirements in striving to maintain its rule and crush the revolutionary forces of the working class and toiling farmers.

His argument then seeks to show that social-reformism and fascism are two alternate methods decided upon by the capitalists to bolster their rule:

Understanding these facts, the community of ideas *between the social-fascism of the CCF and Fascism becomes plain. Both fascism and social-fascism represent ideological super-structures of decaying monopoly capitalism. For this reason they intertwine and coincide in all fundamental respects. Monopoly, decaying capitalism is incapable of producing new lasting ideas; what it produces is a retrograde ideology, covered with a screen of deceptive demagogy. Fascism and social-fascism, both growing up as a modern screen of decaying capitalism, adopt common ideas for deceiving the masses, growing out of religions, idealist philosophy, the denial of the class struggle, the theory of "the classless state", and the theory of curing capitalism without abolishing capital.*

It would be incorrect, however, according to Pierce, "to conclude from all these facts that Fascism and Social-Fascism are identical". They "play different tactical roles which complement and facilitate each other". The CCF was formed "to fill the role of confusing, splitting, and demoralizing the ranks of the workers in these struggles, by means of parliamentary promises". But this role must be vigorously exposed by the Communists:

We have seen the real meaning of the CCF promise of Socialism. The CCF promise of "Socialism" is a hoax. It is a fallacy and a lie. It is monopoly capitalism covered with deceitful words. It is a fraud, an outgrowth of decaying, degenerating capitalism.

After unfolding page after page of this polemic, full of invective, slander, and hyperbole, in which no misdeed is too gross for the new party (which had just been formed six months prior to the publication of this book and presumably only a few months prior to Pierce's writing it), the author draws the only conclusion possible: the CCF must be destroyed.

The question of whether capitalism can succeed in establishing a Fascist dictatorship and whether it can succeed in herding the masses to war is the question of whether or not the social-reformist

*leaders can be isolated from the masses and this main social sup-
port of capitalist rule destroyed, i.e., whether or not Communism
wins the majority of the working class for the revolutionary way
out of the crisis.*

*Either the masses will desert the CCF and take up revolutionary
struggle, or if the CCF's influence remains strong enough to hold
the masses in passivity, the masses will be crushed under the
Fascist iron heel, until the Communists succeed in re-organizing
the forces of the proletariat and preparing the Proletarian revolution.*

Even after having pronounced this apocalyptic judgement,
Pierce has one further conclusion or refinement to suggest. Quoting from Stalin, he states that within the general struggle to
destroy the CCF, "it is essential to concentrate on struggle
against the so-called 'left' wing of social democracy". Pierce
names some of the "left" elements within the CCF against whom
special attacks should be concentrated, and they are in the main
those who consider themselves Marxists: "Irvine, MacInnis, Pritchard".*

Of course, Pierce did not originate the concept of "social-
fascism". It emanated from the Communist International and
more particularly from Stalin. During the so-called "third period" marking the end of partial capitalist stabilization and the
approach of economic crisis in the capitalist world, it was Stalin's
judgement that the chances of revolution would be revived, particularly in Germany, and therefore the main "strategic and
tactical" line had to be an all-out assault on social democracy in
order for the Communists to win hegemony over the proletarian
movement. By 1932 it had already become apparent to many
outside the Communist movement that this line was making it
possible for German fascism to gain headway, while the Communists and Socialists were fighting each other ferociously. Trotsky made this comment about the term "social-fascist" three
months prior to the German elections which brought Hitler to
power:

---

* William Irvine, M.P., never considered himself a Marxist. He was a minister of the
social gospel who joined Woodsworth in advocating a form of Christian Socialism.
Angus MacInnis and William Pritchard were long-time members of the Socialist
Party of Canada which was Marxist. MacInnis, Pritchard and W. W. Lefeaux
brought the British Columbia section of the Socialist Party of Canada into the CCF
in 1933, and remained a strong Marxist element within the CCF of BC, for some
time.

... At first it could appear as a pretentious, blustery but harmless stupidity. Subsequent events have shown what a pernicious influence the Stalinist theory actually exercised on the entire development of the Communist International.

Pierce applied the theory of "social-fascism" to every facet of CCF program and activity. In the end he effectively destroyed any single point of contact there might have been for some cooperative activities between the two parties or their members. The book combined a theoretical analysis of the roots of social democracy and its ideology with an assault on the integrity and sincerity of social democrats. It made no distinction whatever between immediate and long-term goals.

The Communist Party through this work had declared war on the CCF. It never rid itself of the stated aim of destroying the CCF, and especially its left wing, nor did it ever repudiate the serious charges it levelled against Woodsworth and the main CCF leadership. It did, however, modify its tactical approach from time to time.

The first modification came less than two years later in the aftermath of the Seventh Congress of the Communist International, held in 1935, and which according to Stewart Smith, who had represented Canada, "re-shaped the tactical line of the Communist Parties", and projected the idea of "a united front against fascism". Stewart Smith's report to the Canadian Central Committee in November 1935 on the results of the Congress was somewhat tentative in his proposals for reshaping "the tactical line" of the Canadian party but did present a new objective with respect to the CCF:

The central aim of the united front confronting our party, the working class and all progressive people is the question of how the CCF, the trade unions, the farmer organizations and the Communist movement can be brought together into a broad united front party.

It could be a federated labor-farmer party to which the Communist Party would affiliate while "retaining our freedom of independent action".

He listed a whole series of "immediate issues" on which "the CCF and the Communist Party have common ground", as proof of how easy it would be to join forces formally. All the issues which he listed in this category he had explicitly rejected in his book two years earlier. In fact there was no mention of the book in his report. This could possibly be explained by Stewart Smith's constant reference to the change as being merely "tactical" and thus involving no fundamental change of a strategic or theoretical character.

The first explicit reference by the Party to Pierce's (Smith's) book in the post-Seventh Congress period came in 1939 in a pamphlet written by Leslie Morris entitled *The Story of Tim Buck's Party 1922-1939*. Referring directly to Pierce's book, Morris said this:

*Particularly did the book condemn the statement of Mr. Woodsworth that a "Canadian" type of "Socialism" was possible and that we could escape the results of capitalism. Happily, since that time Mr. Woodsworth has seemingly abandoned any such theory.**

The basic criticism of the CCF program as a self-styled "Socialist" program remains. What the Communist Party in 1932 failed to see sufficiently was the need then, as now, for sharply differentiating between the "Socialist" program drawn up by Mr. Woodsworth and a group of intellectuals with little experience in, or knowledge of the throbbing labor movement, and the tremendous significance of the CCF as a mass movement embracing hundreds of thousands of supporters whose fundamental desires are for democracy and for socialism—desires of a piece with those which inspire the members of the Communist Party. In the condition of today this fundamental characteristic of the CCF is of transcending importance.

Nevertheless, in spite of the failure to correct or repudiate the theory of social-fascism, the Communists did initiate and take part in many "united front" activities in which some very prominent CCFers, including T. C. Douglas, participated.[9] And while Woodsworth in particular remained adamant about having any formal relations with the Communists, *de facto* their activities during the period (1932-39) did complement each other. The Communists initiated or conducted what they called "extra-parliamentary activities" such as the nationwide petition for Unem-

---

* It is not quite clear what theory Woodsworth was supposed to have abandoned—the Canadian Socialism or the possibility of escaping the results of Capitalism; or possibly Morris considered that both of his assertions about Woodsworth constituted one theory.

[9] Walter Young, *The Anatomy of A Party* (Toronto), p. 262.

ployment Insurance, another for the repeal of Section 98, the On-to-Ottawa trek, the relief struggles, and others. The CCF parliamentary spokesmen fought these issues out in the legislative bodies. This similarity in issues and solutions was remarked upon by at least one long-time CCF foe of the Communists, Angus MacInnis, M.P. After returning to Ottawa from a speaking tour of the Maritimes in 1935, MacInnis wrote to a friend in Vancouver as follows:

Tim Buck was following us on a speaking tour of the Maritimes. I do not mean to say that he was deliberately following us, but that was how it happened. From the press reports of his meetings I could not see that he was saying anything different from what we were saying.

This similarity became even more apparent on the two municipal bodies, Winnipeg and Toronto, to which Communists had been elected, and in the Manitoba Legislature where the Communist Provincial leader had been elected in 1936. A witness to this cooperation on the Winnipeg City Council was Stanley Knowles, who, referring to the Communist Alderman Jacob Penner, said this:

... he was an awfully good alderman. He attended to his meetings thoroughly—every problem that had to be coped with in Ward Three.... You couldn't disagree with the things that he opposed and worked for in the Council, and we found ourselves voting with him most of the time. He either voted with us or we were voting with him.[10]

But the main area of contact between CCFers and Communists was the trade-union movement and this became the arena for a bitter, long-lasting conflict between the two parties. This was especially the case in the new CIO unions which were being built in Canada and in which CCF and Communist trade unions began a fierce struggle to win leadership. Although a number of issues were contested between the two, the main conflict revolved more and more around the question of independent political action, by which was meant a trade-union political stance outside and away from the two old parties. This was the contin-

---

[10] Quoted in A. B. McKillop, *Citizen and Socialist: The Ethos of Political Winnipeg (1919-35)*, unpublished M. A. Thesis, University of Manitoba, 1970, p. 167.

uation under new conditions of the debates in the prewar socialist movement in Canada which had resulted in the creation of
the Canadian Labour Party.

Now with the achievement of one of labor's chief goals—the
building of industrial unionism and the consequent organization
of hundreds of thousands of previously unorganized workers—
the question of labor breaking politically with capitalist parties
became once again an important and practical goal. This was
particularly so because the Hepburn Government in Ontario,
which had been elected in 1934 on a pro-labor platform, had
thrown the whole weight of the provincial government against
the CIO.

For the CCF the solution was clear: its leaders insisted that
the CCF should be labor's political arm. Their program was
attuned to labor's immediate needs, they said, and its socialist
aims were sufficently moderate to appeal to the widest section of
politically conscious workers. The Ontario section, and David
Lewis, national secretary, began also to emphasize this from
another point of view: that the CCF, if it was going to be
successful, had to effect a marriage with the labor movement.

For the Communists the issue was much more complex.
Their party could never hope to become, at least in the foreseea-
ble future, the political arm of labor. Yet they shared in the
desire to see the labor movement as independent of the two
capitalist parties. They looked for a form of labor political action
which would include them. They therefore opposed trade-union
endorsement of the CCF and proposed instead a joint Commun-
ist-CCF arrangement whereby Communist candidates could con-
ceivably be supported in certain ridings, and in any event, Communists would have a say in determining labor's electoral platform. Tim Buck formulated this quite explicitly at the Eighth
Dominion Congress of the Communist Party in 1937:

*Labor unity through a united front of the Communist Party and
CCF and a united trade union movement would establish the
working class base for people's unity and the militant spearhead of
a people's front which would smash reaction and make our Canada
a land of democratic people's progress.*

But this was rejected by the CCF and there followed interne-
cine warfare inside the trade unions and the central labor bodies.
It was, of course, mixed up with other trade-union issues, but
this was the core question of that whole struggle. It was the

confrontation of two inflexible strategies, with the trade unions as the battleground.

In 1943 the CCF won an important victory when the annual convention of the CCL endorsed the CCF as "the political arm of labor" and recommended to all its unions that "they affiliate with the CCF". This was a basic turning point for the CCF in its efforts to effect an alliance with labor, although there still lay ahead a number of years of bitter conflict with the Communists over what the latter termed "too partisan" an approach. The *Canadian Tribune*, in its issue of October 16, 1943, made it clear that the Communists would insist on their right to be elected as union representatives to CCF Councils and Conventions if unions they led were to affiliate to the CCF.

But the Communists had more success in the Trades and Labour Congress. A new alliance had begun to develop there between the Liberal Party supporters and the Communists, and one of its first fruits was in the establishment by the TLC, also in 1943, of political action committees in which the specific kind of political action was to be left to the locals to decide. This Liberal-Communist alliance in the TLC and to some extent in certain unions of the CCL coincided with a new burst of support which the Communists had extended to Mackenzie King in his prosecution of the war effort. The official party position on this was announced in a Canadian Press dispatch of May 29, 1944:

The Labor-Progressive Party will strive to elect a Liberal-Labor coalition Government in the next election it was revealed in a statement of policy issued by the National Executive of the Party following a three-day Conference here with all provincial leaders. The statement said: "It is the considered opinion of the Labor Progressive Party that only the coalition of Liberal, Labor, and farm forces can lead Canada to full co-operation in the United Nations along the lines charted by the historic joint declaration of Churchill, Roosevelt, and Stalin at Teheran last December. "The Liberals have worked to maintain the unity of Canada. They represent those of the Capitalists who understand that they can and must co-operate with Labor and farmers for Victory and great post-war advances".
Criticizing the CCF the statement said: "the CCF leaders cynically spurn and reject the national unity policy. Instead of standing for a practical policy of immediate social progress, they take refuge in radical sounding phrases about Socialism".

Whereas in the Pierce book of 1934, the CCF was accused of

advocating "liberal-laborism" and downgrading socialism, the Communists in 1944 adopted liberal-laborism and critized the CCF for *not* downgrading socialism. This may well be explained on historical and dialectical considerations of "time, place, and circumstance", which is precisely how the Communist Party did explain it. But to others, including some members of the Party, it seemed another example of the Party's pragmatism, or, to use a Party term, "opportunism". But the Party changed its position again almost immediately after the war, and at its first postwar convention, in June 1946, attacked Mackenzie King for reneging on his war-time promises, and criticized the CCF for having "failed to come forward in a consistent effort to arouse the people against Mackenzie King's reversal of policy".

The alliance between Communists and Liberals in the TLC evaporated in the very first chill of the cold war. The drive to oust Communists from leading positions then took on the character of a crusade, in which the Liberals in the TLC, the CCF in the CCL, and the international officers of both the AFL and CIO cooperated.

In the end, the main body of the trade-union movement, after merging in 1956, joined forces with the CCF to create a new political instrument for the labor movement outside the two old parties.

The culmination of this bitter struggle in the trade-union movement coincided with the fierce debate that broke out within the LPP as a result of the Twentieth Congress of the CPSU.

A minority of the leadership of the Party attacked important aspects of past party policy including the attitude to the CCF. The minority position on the CCF was stated by an amendment to the main policy resolution at the sixth Convention of the Labor-Progressive Party, April 1957:

Right from the beginning we have made grave errors in our relations with the CCF. Borrowing Stalin's erroneous phrase, we labelled CCF leaders as "social fascists". Instead of seeing the CCF as another socialist trend in Canadian life and CCF supporters as socialist-minded workers with whom we should have the closest relations, we have been in a state of continuous battle with the CCF which has only played into the hands of its right-wing leaders who have sought to isolate us from their followers. [11]

---

[11] For a comprehensive description of this inner Party debate see Douglas Rowland, *The Communist Party In the Post Stalin Era*, unpublished M.A. Thesis (1968). University of Manitoba.

This position was overwhelmingly defeated at the Convention as "revisionist". Yet the Party's problem in estimating its relationship with social-democracy has remained. It was relatively easy to absorb Lenin's theoretical critique of social-democracy as an ideology, but it was much more difficult to relate the ideological critique to the working out of viable practical relationships with a social-democratic party that had the support of the vast majority of class-conscious workers (class-conscious as defined in its most general form: those workers who have ceased to support the old capitalist parties). The Communist Party made a grievous error in so quickly rejecting the notion of "Canadian Socialism", as advanced by Woodsworth. Certainly as Marxist-Leninists, Communists rejected his concept of socialism on fundamental grounds. But was it necessary to include the concept of "Canadian" in the denunciation? It will be recalled that on the status-of-Canada question in 1929 Buck had insisted, against the Comintern, on the necessity of studying the Canadian peculiarities. Surely he could have done that in regard to the CCF, for in fact there were certain important Canadian peculiarities in the program and structure of the CCF. For one thing, it had a large farm component in its ranks at the foundation, which, because of its roots in Western agrarian radicalism and because of the heavy impact of the Depression on the Western economy, was one of the prime sources of militancy in the CCF. Thus one of the errors which the Communists made was to accept the general Marxist conception of the conservatism of the petty-bourgeoisie, without taking cognizance of their immediate capacity for radicalism. Concretely this expressed itself in a wrong analysis of the Western farmer (see below). But the Canadian party's unremitting hostility to the CCF was based primarily on the Communist International and on Stalin's perception of international social-democracy, which the Communist Party of Canada accepted entirely and applied automatically to the CCF.

Other Ideological and Political Themes

Reference has already been made to the lack of a detailed Marxist study of Canadian political economy to illuminate the political problems which the Communist Party of Canada had to grapple with. But in 1923 *The Worker* carried a series of five articles by H. M. Bartholomew which examined in detail the corporate structure of Canada. The theme for this series, entitled *Capitalist Dictatorship in Canada*, was outlined in the first article:

... this spectacular rise of Canadian capitalism has been accompanied by land grabbing, wholesale expropriation, corruption of legislatures, on a scale which beggars description. It is a tale of tyranny striding along in seven league boots.

The result has been a concentration of wealth and a concentration of power such as few countries can rival. By the very laws inherent in capitalist production itself, "one Capitalist always kills many" (Marx), and the net result is an accumulation of wealth and power in the hands of a small group of financiers. Thus we find that fifteen men control assets in excess of $4,295,000,000 or considerably more than the whole national debt of Canada.

It was an updated version of Gustavus Myers' *History of Canadian Wealth (1914)*, with a voluminous array of facts, names, and figures, which confirmed that the monopolistic development which Myers had noted had progressed further. No other study of this kind was done by the socialist movement until 1935, when Watt Hugh McCollum's *Who Owns Canada?*, a CCF publication, appeared. It is not clear whether Bartholomew made his study before or after reading Lenin's *Imperialism* because the English translation of that book had only just become available. But in any event he graphically demonstrated that Canadian capitalism, through mergers and combinations, had reached the state of monopoly capitalism as defined by Lenin. This series has never been referred to in any of Buck's histories of the Communist Party of Canada, nor does it appear on any curriculum of party schools on Marxism-Leninism.

The Communist Party position on what it called "the agrarian question" started out as an attempt to differentiate the various strata which it perceived to exist among the farmers of the West. In its first resolution on *The Workers Party and the Farmers* in 1922, the Central Executive Committee made this analysis:

Because the Workers' Party understands that the common enemy of both the farmers and the industrial workers is CAPITALISM, it will try to foster and co-operate with any tendencies in the farmer's movement toward a clear recognition that the industrial workers and the farmer have interests in common against capitalism.
We recognize, however, that our common interests as workers are shared chiefly by the lower, middle-class farmer, the poor farmer,

and the agricultural laborer, and that the class of wealthy farmers possess capitalistic ideas and ambitions which make it our enemy.

From that it concluded that the Progressive Party was led primarily by the wealthy farmers but that "the small and middle-class farmers of the West are becoming disgusted with their present leadership", and that serious divisions would appear between "those who already want to go back to the Liberal Party and those who do not. . . . Sooner or later an organized left-wing will arise which will produce a split in the movement between the small farmers and the ones of the United Grain Growers Limited type".

But when the predicted split did take place and the left wing formed the "Ginger Group" allied to Woodsworth, Heaps and Irvine, the Party was not too pleased. It attacked this alliance regularly.

The Communist International, in its letter to the Party in 1929, insisted on a more Marxist approach to the farm question, "to rally the poor farmers to the struggle against the rich farmers". A new formulation resulted which held that the provincial governments of the West belong "to the rich farmers". The CEC of the Communist Party further responded to the criticism of the Communist International as follows:

The CEC, CP of C accept the line of the CI letter on the Agrarian question. Our policy until now in the agrarian field has been based upon the conflict between agrarian capital and industrial and finance capital rather than upon the class struggle on the farm, sharpening class relation on the basis of mechanization and rationalization. This has led to an underestimate of the importance of organizing agricultural workers and poor farmers against the rich farmers as well as against big capital.

With this kind of analysis, Communist farmers were directed to leave the "farm reformist organizations" and build the Farmers Unity League (FUL) whose chief aim would be to try and "bring about the dissolution of these organizations". This was changed after the Seventh Congress of the Communist International but even then, as the Party's agrarian director insisted, "this did not call for any radical changes in our basic economic program as applied to the farmers". The Party's inability to analyse the nature and ideology of the independent commodity producer, who was for such a long time the main factor in Western politics, remained chronic. It was reflected in the Party's impact on the farmers' movement, which was probably less pronounced than in any other field.

From its inception the Communist Party advocated the repeal of the British North America Act. In the Party's view it was a British imposition, a symbol and instrument of Canada's colonial status, with no redeeming features at all. In particular it wanted the abolition of the Senate and the post of Governor-General, and the clear unequivocal assignment to the federal government of the powers to deal with labor, health, welfare, and unemployment insurance. It regarded the division of powers at Confederation as a deliberate dodge to obstruct social legislation. It regarded the provincial governments as being usually in the hands of reactionary interests opposing the Central Government. These views, which had received spasmodic treatment in the Party's literature, were brought into focus in its submission to the Royal Commission on Dominion-Provincial Relations in 1938. Internal free trade, it said, and central control of external trade were the main achievements of Confederation, but economic disunity as reflected in the division of powers remained. "National unification was incomplete."

The divisions left by Confederation have become the strongholds of reactionary finance in their fight against the program of reform and democracy demanded by the Canadian people. The setting of the province against the nation, the part against the whole, has the primary object today of paralyzing all efforts to achieve social legislation and a re-organization of taxation to compel the rich to pay their share to meet the costs of the crisis . . .

. . . The forces responsible for these developments in Ontario and Quebec are the centre around which a new reactionary political combination of forces is being gathered in the Dominion of Canada. It is the centre of all opposition to complete national unification of Canada and is fostering separatist movements and propaganda, which ultimately hold the danger of the provincial dismemberment of the nation.

A new approach by the Party to the western provinces was introduced. Now they are no longer considered to be ruled by the rich farmers acting as agents of the financial oligarchy. Instead they are seen as victims of this oligarchy:

Long exploitation by the East left them no reserves to face their problems with. The resulting responsibilities of the provincial governments are far beyond their revenue . . . the proposals of the

Western provinces are in fact the opposite of sectional. In the main, and in general form, they coincide with the interests of the people of the nation.

The Communist Party brief proposed "that all social legislation shall be assumed by the Dominion Government", this to include unemployment insurance and relief, health insurance, crop insurance, minimum national standards of education, housing, mothers' allowances, old age pensions, aid to youth, maximum hours for labor, minimum wages, working conditions, enforcement of labor's rights, Dominion control over companies, agricultural prices. The people of Quebec would endorse such centralization because they would see that it represents the means to establish economic and social equality, while still having provincial control over cultural matters. This should be guaranteed by a Dominion Bill of Rights.

The rationale behind this submission is as much political as it is economic, although the politics are more implicit than explicit. The Brief did not answer the obvious question as to what guarantees there were that the Central Government would serve the interests of the people, with such extraordinary increase in its powers, any more than the "reactionary" provinces. The answer to that was given by Tim Buck in his address to the Eighth Dominion Congress of the Party in October 1937, almost a year before the presentation of the Brief.

According to Buck, "around Bennett, Beatty, Meighen, Duplessis, Drew and other representatives of ultra-reactionary finance capital, a coalition is taking form on the basis of a program of defense of the interests of monopoly capital". On the other hand, Mackenzie King vacillates but is under increasing pressure from the reform Liberals who "are beginning to take the first steps toward rallying the Liberal ranks around genuine liberal principles".

The real program of the Tories—as distinct from their demagogy—is based definitely upon the interests of monopoly capital. The political position of the reform Liberals makes co-operation between them and the progressive farmers and the Labor movement a logical development. The ability of the reform liberals to gain the support of the main body of Liberal opinion and thereby isolate the top reactionaries depends in large measure upon the political strength developed by the trade union movement and the farmers' organizations.

Thus we have the interests of monopoly capital being defended by the Tories, utilizing their base in the central provinces, and the forces of liberalism centering around the Dominion Government headed by King, resisting the attacks by the monopolists, in the interests of reform and "peoples' rights". The problem as seen by Buck is to work with "reform Liberals" to bolster up the vacillating Mackenzie King and thus to defeat monopoly capital. Seen in this light, the Party's submission to the Rowell-Sirois Commission is based on reform liberalism, and on supporting the reform liberals in the King Cabinet. In the same speech Buck asserted that "there is a strong current of opinion even among the Conservatives which looks for democratic progress". The evidence for this was seen in the "New Democracy" movement launched by W. D. Herridge, Bennett's brother-in-law, who had served under Bennett as Canadian ambassador to Washington.

This conception of a united front with "progressives" in the Conservative and Liberal parties was actively promoted by the Party from the Eighth Congress to the outbreak of World War II. In a pamphlet *The Horse and The Jockey*, published in 1938, Stewart Smith, who edited the Party's Brief to the Royal Commission, declared:

Let the hesitating progressives of the King Government and the Old Line Parties come forward fearlessly and let the Trade Unionists and the Farmers' Organizations step to the forefront. Then there will be no doubt of an overwhelming victory in the next Federal Election—a victory that will start Canada on the road of democratic revival and true national unity.

On March 1, 1938, the *Vancouver News-Herald* carried a British United Press dispatch reporting a speech by a leading Canadian Communist:

Vote Liberal, Says Communist
Communists should give support to the King Liberal Government in the forthcoming Dominion Elections and fend off the fascism which would result from the Conservative Party gaining power, said Norman Freed, Executive Secretary of the Communist Party of Canada in a public address Tuesday night.

"Because the King Government had supported progressive policies,

because it was susceptible to mass pressure, it was preferable to the Manion-Drew group"...

... Though he would like to see J. S. Woodsworth or Tim Buck as Prime Minister of Canada, such a course was not possible now, the speaker said. "The sane alternative was to re-elect the King Government to prevent fascism in Canada". *

Following this concept of the united front, the Communist Party offered its support to W. D. Herridge who had already linked up with Alberta Social Credit to represent it nationally. At the same time, the Party criticized the CCF for taking a negative view of Herridge. This adoption of liberalism as an ally of the Party submerged a few months later with the outbreak of the war and the subsequent banning of the Party for opposing it. When the Party reappeared in 1943 as the Labor Progressive Party supporting the war, it was more than ever convinced of the necessity to form links with liberalism. Even after the war, when the Party felt that Mackenzie King had departed from liberalism, Buck called on all "Canadians who desire genuinely liberal policies", to support the Labor Progressive Party in its postwar proposals, which were in fact a continuation of the proposals contained in its submission to the Royal Commission in 1938.

The most consistent activity which the Party carried on throughout its entire history was educating its members in Marxist theory. No member could enter the Party without at some point being exposed to classes, lectures, and literature of this kind. There were branch or unit classes, city or district schools, national schools, and for particularly prominent leaders, the two-year Lenin School in Moscow.* Except for the top schools, most of the classes limited the reading of Marx and Engels to *Wage-Labor and Capital, Value Price and Profit, The Communist Manifesto, Socialism: Utopian and Scientific.* The works of Lenin that were usually studied were *Imperialism* and *The State and Revolution.* But more and more the classes were preoccupied with Stalin's works, *The Foundations of Leninism, Dialectical and His-*

---

* Walter Young in *Anatomy of a Party* refers to this item, though he dates it incorrectly as 1939. He reports that a CCF M.P. wrote to Buck asking for an explanation. Buck replied "that Freed had been misquoted but, in any case, better King than Manion..." (W. Young, p. 268).

* This was interrupted by the war and was not revived until the sixties. To take the place of the Lenin school was a three-month national school mostly for full-time party functionaries.

torical Materialism and the *History of the CPSU (B)*. As early as 1935 a 59-page mimeographed "Educational Course" was put out for winter study in every Party unit which stated:

. . . the course will be based on one pamphlet alone: "The Foundations of Leninism" by J. Stalin. Every Party member must buy a copy of this pamphlet which he must read and study himself and which will be collectively studied and discussed during the course.*

Starting with Ryerson's *1837, The Birth of Canadian Democracy* (1937), and *French Canada* (1943), the Communist Party turned its attention to Marxist studies of Canadian history. In 1946 a Committee was established to work on an overall "Peoples' History of Canada". Ryerson presided over this Committee and from this research came his two books: *The Founding of Canada* (1960) and *Unequal Union* (1968). Ryerson in an article answering the "revisionists" during the Party debate in 1956-57, criticized himself for "a rather idealized treatment of the bourgeois democrats Lafontaine and Baldwin". He blamed this on "liberalism" and stated that he came to see this better as a result of the upsurge of "right-wing revisionism" that he saw manifest in the post-Stalin debate. He was referring to his book *French Canada* and one inferred from this that such "liberalism" would not be present in his future works. The Party was not able, in the period being discussed, to put out a political economy of Canada but it did produce later an updated analysis of the nature of Canadian capitalism in 1962: *Anatomy of Big Business* by Libbie and Frank Park.*

Underlying much of the united front activity in the thirties was the Party's perception of the rise of fascism in the world and of the need to subordinate everything to meet and defeat this threat, internationally as well as in Canada. This became the pervasive theme of all its activities particularly after the Seventh Congress of the CI in 1935. However, it had formed the League

---

* During that same period the CCF in Vancouver was conducting classes at the Elks Hall under the direction of W. W. Lefeaux, a pioneer of Marxism in Canada. His course was based on a systematic chapter-by-chapter study of Karl Marx, *Capital* Vol. I. (outlines provided by Mrs. Lefeaux, Vancouver, July 1974).

* Two small works which appeared in the thirties were obviously influenced by Marxist historiography and political economy. They were F. H. Underhill, *The Conception of the National Interest* (1935) and Leo Warshaw, *Forces Leading To A Centralized Confederation* (1938). Unfortunately these and other Marxist works by Canadian academics cannot be dealt with in this volume, but these works, to my knowledge, mark the first attempt by non-Communists to use Marxism as an analytical tool in the study of Canadian history.

Against War and Fascism a year before this Congress, and this body became its main vehicle for mounting campaigns in support of collective security and the League of Nations, and aid to the Spanish Republic. It was the work of the Communists that resulted in the formation of the Canadian Youth Congress in 1937, which brought together a wide-ranging number of youth organizations in English Canada, including the youth wings of the Conservative, Liberal, CCF, and Communist Parties. The Party exposed through its press and publications the existence of fascist groups in Canada and in a few isolated cases even engaged in physical combat with these groups. All these activities won an estimable reputation for the CPC for its strong anti-fascist stance. However, neither the Communist Party nor its supporters were prepared for the sudden announcement of the Soviet-German Non-Aggression Pact in 1939, which brought to an end this phase of the Party's activity.

Summary and Conclusions

The Communist Party of Canada emerged out of the socialist movement which had been present and growing in Canada since 1890. It allied itself to Leninism, to the Communist International which Lenin founded, and to the Soviet Union which it regarded as the universal model of Marxist strategy and tactics for a proletarian revolution. Its founders thought they saw in Lenin's works and in the Russian Revolution the answer to many problems which had plagued the Canadian socialist movement, and they sought, with Comintern guidance and direction, to apply these answers to the Canadian setting.

They made a big effort to make Marxism relevant to Canadian problems and they certainly overcame the abstract and universal nature of the old socialist movement's propaganda and agitation. But though they sought to approach every major problem with a theoretical dissertation and analysis, how much of it was Marxism and how much just plain pragmatism is open to question. Certainly theory and tactics were often confounded, and the ephemeral nature of many of their "party lines", the frequent oscillation and even reversal of them, suggest that theory was in many instances subordinated to the needs of the day.

The Party was founded at a time when the Communist International thought that revolutions in capitalist countries were imminent, and consequently the emphasis of party activity must be revolutionary in word and deed. But ·as the prospect of revolution receded, the Communist Party took up the battle on immediate issues which were reformist rather than revolutionary and in the course of that, could not disentangle itself from the contradiction or tension between its revolutionary aims and its immediate goals. It often was to the right of the CCF. Certainly its solutions to immediate questions, if separated from revolutionary rhetoric, were very similar to those of the CCF and even, on many occasions, to those of the Liberals.

The Communist Party was very much influenced by the prevailing trends in Canadian political thought. Certainly the position on Canada's so-called "colonial status" was admittedly influenced by "bourgeois" Canadian nationalists. The Party was frequently influenced by Mackenzie King, whom they regarded as a representative of "the progressive bourgeoisie". On three occasions the Party called for unity behind King: in 1925-6 on the issue of Canadian independence, in 1937-9 on the issue of constitutional and social reform, and in 1943-5 on the support to an all-out war effort. There is no evidence that King ever reciprocated, although he was not altogether oblivious of them.

The Communists found it easier to advocate unity with Liberals than with the CCF. They saw the CCF as their historic foe and rival for the leadership of the working class. Instead of seeing *social democracy* as a historically inevitable trend among the workers, they saw *social-democrats* as "misleaders" and "betrayers". They were thus unable to come up with a coherent and consistent method of relating to the CCF.

The fears that many socialists had expressed about the role that the Communist International would play in the internal affairs of the Canadian Party were in many respects justified. The direction which the Communist International gave the Communist Party of Canada on very specific questions was often wrong. But there is only one recorded instance when party leaders resisted the Comintern's advice, and that was Tim Buck's early position on U.S. domination of Canada. Buck was probably more correct on that issue, but he was forced to back down under pressure from the Communist International, as was his colleague Stewart Smith. The dependence of the Canadian Party on the Communist International, which had become Stalin's personal political instrument, posed a serious question to non-Communist socialists about the credibility of Communist demands for the independence of Canada and of the trade unions.

The Communist Party was, however, at all times to be taken seriously even when it was small in numbers and in influence. For the whole period from 1921 to 1957 it represented Marxism in Canada. It dominated Marxist thought in Canada during those years. Since then, in the wake of the Stalin exposures, new trends in Marxist thought have come up in Canada outside the ranks or influence of the CP, but the Party remains an important wing of the Marxist movement.

The greatest impact of the Communist Party on Canadian society was during the thirties when no other organized force was prepared to give expression to the discontent of the Depression and to initiate imaginative, militant, and effective extra-parliamentary activity on a whole host of domestic and foreign policy questions. Its activities helped the CCF in parliament, for its parliamentary groups took up these questions and fought for them in the various legislative bodies across the country. Its work played a big role in undermining Bennett's political support. Its participation in cultural activity undoubtedly influenced a number of left-wing writers and artists. It won adherents or "sympathizers" for the first time in the Canadian academic community. Its members took an active and leading part in building the trade-union movement and were partly responsible for making this period the most momentous in Canadian labor history. It took the initiative in organizing anti-fascist activity and propaganda.

Yet the problems which confronted this movement were never resolved. In the first place many problems were of an objective character. While liberal and radical Canadians were prepared to accept the militant type of activity which the Party epitomized, especially during the Depression, they were not prepared to accept a revolutionary solution.

The subjective difficulties, however, were of a different order, and were mainly rooted in the dependence of the Party on leadership from the Communist International and the Soviet Party. Certainly the Party's fortunes rose and fell like a barometer as the Canadian perceptions of the Soviet Union oscillated. But the oscillations in party theory, and tactics based on this direction, were on the whole harmful to the Party and to its image among non-Communist socialists, who might otherwise have been the closest allies of the Communist Party of Canada.

CHAPTER SIX

ROOTS AND SOURCES OF CANADIAN SOCIAL DEMOCRACY

Agrarian Radicalism

The development of Canadian society after Confederation produced fissures and conflicts which by the end of the First World War seemed to challenge its very foundations. Authoritarian Toryism, the dominant ideology of the ruling élite, by alienating important sections of the Canadian people—labor, farmers, and French Canadians—undermined the ideological basis of social order, and opened the floodgates to a rapid rise of radicalism.

This was, in part, an international phenomenon. The impact of the bloodiest war in history had shaken European capitalism to its roots, and produced a revolutionary wave in which the working class, because of its importance in most European countries, and because of its ideological and political development during the previous hundred years, took the lead. Socialism appeared to have greater strength than ever, with Communism as the new variant of Marxist socialism emerging as the main revolutionary ideology of the twentieth century.

While labor was an important element in the postwar unrest in Canada, it was not the main one. It was the farmers' revolt in

171

Nova Scotia, New Brunswick, Ontario, Manitoba, Saskatchewan, and Alberta that had the greatest impact on Canadian politics at that time. A statistical gauge of this was the provincial elections* from 1919 to 1922 where the number of agrarian radicals elected exceeded labor representatives, and especially in the federal elections of 1921 in which the farmers' party obtained 64 seats while labor elected 2. Although the causes of this upsurge were different as between farmers and labor, their radicalism interacted, their target was the same, and they both undermined permanently the two-party system by their massive entry into parliamentary politics as independent groups. It was this interaction that ultimately determined the character and ideological outlook of Canadian social-democracy.

Although the farmers' revolt affected six out of the nine provinces (excluding Quebec, British Columbia, and Prince Edward Island) it was strongest, most militant and longest-lasting in the Prairie Provinces for reasons that have been amply demonstrated elsewhere.[1]

Writing of its origins and genesis, Paul Sharp characterized this movement as follows:

In the decade before 1914 a general democratic ferment on the Canadian prairies intensified agrarian discontent. During these years Western Canadian farmers joined the crusade for greater democracy which was sweeping through North America. The protest against the concentration of wealth and political power in the hands of a capitalistic plutocracy thus spread into the latest frontier area on the continent.[2]

The farmers' movement was, according to Sharp, "a struggle against monopolism" or as a popular book called it, "the Revolt in Canada against the New Feudalism". An essay in *The Grain Growers' Guide* in June 1913 asked the question "Who Owns Canada?" and came up with the answer that "forty-two men controlled one-third of the wealth of Canada . . .". Gustavus Myers's book *History of Canadian Wealth*, which appeared the

---

* Ontario 1919: Farmers 43, Labor 11 (formed Farmers-Labor Government), Nova Scotia 1920: Farmers 7 and Labor 5; New Brunswick 1920: Farmers 10, Labor 0; Manitoba 1920: Farmers 12, Labor 11; Saskatchewan 1921: Farmers 12, Labor 0; Alberta 1921: Farmers 38, Labor 2.

[1] In C. B. Macpherson, *Democracy In Alberta* (Toronto, 1962), and in W. L. Morton, *The Progressive Party In Canada* (Toronto, 1950).

[2] Paul F. Sharp, *Agrarian Revolt In Western Canada* (New York, 1971), p. 54.

next year, confirmed that analysis. This book was given wide prominence in the farmers' press, and was studied in the farm organizations:

The rapid concentration of wealth in Canada is no mere fancy. Already, it is estimated, less than fifty men control $4,000,000,000, or more than one-third of Canada's material wealth as expressed in railways, banks, factories, mines, land and other properties and resources.[3]

The targets of the radical farmers' movement were already clear: railroads, banks, the Canadian Manufacturers' Association, and their friends and supporters in government. The means by which these giants of finance had fastened control over the country were likewise identified: high tariffs, bounties, government subventions of all kinds to business, the financial and credit manipulations of the banks, graft and corruption of the political parties, and uncontrolled land speculation. From these evils the solutions proposed were straightforward. As promulgated in the Farmers' Platform of 1916, in conventions of the various provincial farmers' organizations, and in the speeches and writings of the recognized farm leaders, the most popular proposals were free trade and the elimination of most tariffs; sharply graduated income, inheritance, and profit taxes; single tax on land; nationalization of railroads, telegraphs, and express companies; government control of credit and currency, and anti-combines legislation. The ideologists most often quoted in the farmers' press were Henry George, Edward Porritt, Thorstein Veblen, Gustavus Myers; in the twenties, Major C. H. Douglas was added to the list. There were strong moral overtones in the Canadian farmers' movement, with many of the farm leaders prominent in temperance causes, the Moral and Social Reform Council (circa 1907), and church organizations. There was, of course, the strong element of rural democracy, which included demands for electoral reform, for proportional representation, abolition of the senate, removal of all voting restrictions, full equality for women*, abolition of the party system, and alteration of the rules of responsible government through direct legis-

---

[3] Gustavus Myers, *History of Canadian Wealth* (Toronto, 1973), p. i.

* The farmers' movements were probably the first to elect women to legislative bodies in Canada: Louise C. McKinney to the Alberta Legislature in 1917 and Agnes McPhail to the House of Commons in 1921.

lation, referendum, and recall.

Agrarian radicalism in the main was populist. It was against the evils of capitalism, but not against capitalism itself. Its chief enemy was the monopoly form of capitalism which it regarded as an aberration of the principles of competitive and free-trade capitalism. As landowners, proprietors of their own means of production, and petty producers, they had a *petit-bourgeois* outlook, as has been shown by Macpherson. What has to be further elaborated is how this outlook influenced the character of Canadian social-democracy which began as a working-class movement, largely Marxist oriented, but changed in some important particulars.

Because some of the main studies on Canadian agrarian radicalism have been done by Americans, emphasis has been given to the American model of populism and its influence on Canada. While there undoubtedly has been American influence, its scope has been exaggerated. The conditions to which Canadian agrarian radicalism responded were indigenous, although there were similarities with the United States. The attempt to establish American-based farm organizations like the Patrons of Husbandry, the Patrons of Industry, and the Non-Partisan League flourished for a period before being replaced by uniquely Canadian movements. The failure of the populist and labor-based socialist movements in the United States to merge or form alliances stands out in contrast to the Canadian development, and counts as one of the factors that explains the failure of American social democracy and the relative success of the Canadian form.

Many of the founders of the CCF, who had been members of the Socialist or Labour parties, had been looking at the British model as the one to adapt to Canadian society. The Canadian Labour Party founded in 1917 by the TLC, and the provincial Independent Labor Party organizations, were so conceived. But what was established in 1933 was not the British model. It was, according to the presidential address of J. S. Woodsworth, "A Canadian ... distinctive type of Socialism".

One of the factors that explains this change, according to Woodsworth, was the realization that Canada, unlike Britain, was "not predominantly industrial", and consequently "a labor party could not, unaided, hope to obtain power".

But probably as important was the actual state of the organized labor movement in Canada during the twenties. It was small and divided, with three major centers—the TLC, the ACCL, and

CCCL—and in the first period of the thirties, a fourth: the WUL. The majority of trade unionists belonged to the craft unions of the AFL-TLC which were relatively conservative, and more and more under the influence of the anti-political stand and legacy of Samuel Gompers. Industrial unionism, which was to bring a more militant and political working class into the ranks of organized labor (as had been the case in Britain in the latter part of the nineteenth century), had not yet taken hold. Perhaps if the OBU had succeeded, when it came on the scene in 1919, to build genuine mass unions, the climate would have been more favorable to a British-type labor party.

An additional factor that complicated the prospects for such a party was the refusal of Woodsworth and many of his colleagues to join the Canadian Labour Party because the Communists were already occupying important executive positions in it. Instead they kept the ILP of Manitoba unaffiliated to the CLP.

In contrast to the political weakness of labor, the farmers had surged forward to become an important factor in Canadian politics and particularly in Canadian radicalism. Both Woodsworth and William Irvine had worked with the farmers in the Non-Partisan League*. Irvine in 1920 published his famous book *The Farmers in Politics* in which he associated himself completely with the official political position of the UFA and its president, Henry Wise Wood, in replacing the concept of class conflict with that of "group government". When Woodsworth and Irvine constituted the new "labor group" in the House of Commons in 1922, they began to develop a very close relationship with the more radical of the farmers' representatives and through them with the farmers' organizations.

Sharp describes the cooperation between the "rising labor movement in the growing cities of the West" and especially during the war years "in support of direct legislation, the single tax, a graduated income tax and other reforms". He claims, however, that this cooperation received a blow due to the opposition of many farmers to the "extreme radicalism and violence of the famous Winnipeg Strike in 1919". Certainly some farm spokesmen like the editor of *The Grain Growers' Guide* did condemn the strike, as did some farm organizations, particularly in

---

* William Irvine became the first secretary of the NPL in 1917, and J. S. Woodsworth served as secretary of the Alberta League for a short period in 1918. Woodsworth had written several articles for *The Grain Growers' Guide* in 1915 and 1916.

Manitoba. Some of this was undoubtedly due to the fact that the RNWMP and the Winnipeg Citizens' Committee mounted a considerable propaganda campaign against the Strike directed to the farm movement, whereas the Strike Committee practically ignored that field altogether.

Yet the extent of farmers' hostility to the Strike is exaggerated. In the Ontario provincial elections of October 1919, there was close collaboration between the UFO and the ILP of Ontario, a body which unequivocally endorsed the Winnipeg Strike. Even more resounding was the fact that in the Manitoba elections in 1920, every one of the seven labor candidates running in rural areas was elected, together with four strike leaders elected in the Winnipeg constituency. J. S. Woodsworth never ceased in the House of Commons to extol the strike and to express pride in his own role in it. This did not seem to weaken his relations with the radical farm leaders, particularly those who later formed the "Ginger Group" under his leadership.

Woodsworth's attitude to the farm movement was quite different from that of many of the socialist and labor groups, particularly the Marxist. An examination of the socialist publications from 1904 to 1921 shows that the Socialist Party of Canada, the Social-Democratic Party, and the Socialist Party of North America paid little attention to agrarian questions. A Socialist Party of Canada pamphlet of 1914 endeavors "to use the Marxian Theory of Value as a means of unravelling some of the vexing problems that confront the farmers". The author's main theme is to convince the farmer that he is actually a "wage worker" expending a certain amount of unpaid labor-power every day which is appropriated by the capitalist class, almost exactly as occurs to a propertyless proletarian selling his labor-power to a factory owner. Irvine's book *The Farmers in Politics* was commented upon by the *Western Clarion* organ of the Socialist Party of Canada, but in a caustic and somewhat savage manner. As mentioned in the previous chapter, the Workers' Party and later the Communist Party worked out a farm policy which projected a concept of class struggle in the countryside with the poor farmers and farm laborers fighting the "middle and rich" farmers, under the leadership of the Workers' Party.

The divergence in political paths for socialists which was taking place at this time was, in some measure, between those who felt that a socialist party must be strictly proletarian in ideology and composition, and those who were more inclined to the concept of a workers' and farmers' party with an ideology acceptable to both. This divergence encompassed more than a Communist—non-Communist split. The advocates of a proletarian party included many Marxists and laborists who had rejected the Communist Party and International, and who eventually joined the CCF, but held fast to their ideas of what kind of party it should be.*

From the period of the war almost up to the formation of the CCF, the intellectuals were still notably inconspicuous in radical movements and in expressing support for radical ideas. An attempt made by Professor R. M. MacIver of the University of Toronto to launch a movement of social reconstruction in 1917 misfired. He sent out an appeal to various Canadian organizations to establish the "National Problems Club" which would be united under a Central Committee with the avowed purpose of

bringing East and West, French-speaking and English-speaking Canada, agricultural Canada and Industrial Canada to the understanding of each other's problems . . . in the great work of the welding of a nation, which is the foundation of all true national life.

There was little response to that letter or to his follow-up, and two years later MacIver, in a book titled *Labour In The Changing World*, struck a very different note:

Anyone who today speaks of the essential identity of interest between capital and labor is convicted thereby of either simplicity or hypocrisy . . .

For how can there be identity of interest between two parties one of which seeks to diminish what the other seeks to augment, to one which accrues all of the joint product that it can withhold from the other.

However, there is no record of any further activity of this nature by MacIver.

At least two academics were dismissed from their university

---

* In a biography of A. A. Heaps, who joined Woodsworth in 1925 as an M.P. representing the Winnipeg ILP, Leo Heaps writes, "Heaps advocated a Canadian Labour Party that would represent the legitimate aspirations of labour. But the CCF did not listen to Heaps. Instead it took a wrong turn in the thirties. . . . " L. Heaps: *The Rebel in the House*, p. 117.

posts during this period for their radical views. These men, both of whom were particularly close to the farmers' movements, were the Reverend Salem Bland of Wesley College (dismissed in 1917) and Professor L. A. Wood* of the University of Western Ontario (dismissed in 1923).

It cannot be said with any certainty that repression, or the fear of it, was the cause of the non-involvement of members of the intellectual community in radical activities. It must have been, however, an inhibiting factor. There certainly was strong propaganda directed against the radicals and particularly against Woodsworth. An official 1920 publication of the Department of Labour which was widely circulated pictured Woodsworth as one of the members, conscious or not, of the "Russian Soviet Propaganda System in North America", as were Russell, Ivens and A. E. Smith. In 1925 James Mavor, Professor Emeritus at the University of Toronto, published an attack on the public ownership of Ontario Hydro, which he likened to Lenin's teachings, and in which he labelled as the three most insidious forces in Canada the Methodist Church, the entire trade-union movement, and the Communist Party (in that order).[4]

The Social Gospel

But whatever the reasons, the absence of intellectuals in Canadian radical movements up to this period was not duplicated in other countries. By contrast, however, Canadian radicalism attracted to it and was greatly influenced by an outstanding group of former Protestant ministers, particularly in Western Canada: Salem Bland, J. S. Woodsworth, William Ivens, William Irvine, A. E. Smith, and Henry Wise Wood. All of these clergymen were alienated in one form or another from the official church. Bland was dismissed from Wesley College in 1917 by the Methodist Church which controlled it. Woodsworth, uneasy from the start about his role as a minister, finally withdrew from the ministry in 1918. William Ivens was removed from his pastorate at a

---

* He was in the process of finishing his seminal work *A History of Farmers' Movements in Canada*, and he had been proposed as a "labor-progressive" candidate in the federal elections.

[4] James Mavor, *Niagara In Politics* (New York, 1925).

Winnipeg Church and promptly founded the Labor Church. William Irvine was forced to leave his Presbyterian charge and then became a Unitarian minister but only for a brief period. A. E. Smith resigned over opposition within the church to his role in the General Strike. Wood, although trained in a theological college, never took up preaching.

These men were all participants in one form or another of the Social Gospel movement which has been described in detail elsewhere.[5] Their participation in the radical and reform movements had its main impact *after* they left the church, and the implication that the Social Gospel movement had anything more than a very tenuous and nostalgic connection with religion, may be an exaggeration. Their speeches and writings contained very little reference to religion, except perhaps Bland's *The New Christianity* which in any event was more social than gospel. The Labor Church, headed by Ivens, described itself in its membership cards as "independent and creedless". Woodsworth's own attitude to religion was summed up by an article which he wrote for the *Toronto Star Weekly* in 1925 and which he reprinted in the booklet "Following the Gleam" (Ottawa, 1926):

Religion for me was nice and clear-cut. I could outline the scheme of salvation more clearly than I could analyze a sentence. Now my religion is not only less dogmatic, but it is less definite, less certain. Many might say that it is no religion at all. For me the change means emerging from the confines of a stuffy room into the sweet, pure air of God's out-of-doors.

One case cited in Richard Allen's *The Social Passion* as evidence of a religious expression is highly dubious:

During the same years, Winnipeg Social Democrats had shown evidence of desiring a religious form of expression. In December 1916, a Socialist Sunday School was created "to impart the idealistic and religious conceptions of our noble cause . . . that the kingdom of love and happiness must be set up here on this earth, based on just social and economic conditions.[6]

The directors of the Socialist Sunday School, Jacob Penner, John Queen, and Charles C. Manning, were not religious. The

---

[5] Richard Allen, *The Social Passion* (Toronto, 1971).

[6] R. Allen, *The Social Passion*, p. 83.

Sunday school idea was intended to provide an alternative activity for the children of Winnipeg socialists, in order to keep them from the religious Sunday schools.

The upsurge of radicalism in the West embraced primarily the working class of the bourgeoning cities and the prairie farmers. Its main impact on the Western community beyond these groups was on the reform-minded clergy, who by identifying with this Western radicalism broke with the Church. One of the main roles which these ex-ministers fulfilled was in providing ideological and organizational links between radical labor and the farmers.

Woodsworth had already made these links before his resignation from the ministry. So had Bland and Irvine. From the time of his resignation in 1918, Woodsworth identified himself more completely than ever with the labor movement. He joined the International Longshoremen's Association in Vancouver, helped found the Federated Labor Party of British Columbia, ran under its banners in a provincial election, was one of the principal speakers at their Sunday night forums, and joined the Manitoba Independent Labor Party on his return to Winnipeg in 1921. This became and remained his political power base until the formation of the CCF in 1933.

Woodsworth in this period began to emerge as the ideologue of Canadian social democracy. His perceptions of the class structure of Canada, and the political implications of this analysis, were contained in a series of articles he wrote from 1918 to 1920, and which were published in the *Western Labour News*.

While some of his conclusions were put forward tentatively, his purpose in writing these articles was definite and clear:

The writer has recently been living in British Columbia and Alberta. Through the Western Labor News he would send a word of greeting to friends and former associates in Winnipeg. Among the scattered loggers and settlers up the coast, among the farmers in Alberta, a new movement is arising. It is expressing itself in various organizations, but it is broader and deeper than any organization. It is the spirit of the new day—a passion for justice—a reaching out toward new ideals of brotherhood.

He believed that the time had arrived for a new party but that it would be "too much to expect" that this could be a Labour Party:

Now that the old parties have joined forces in a Union Government it would seem that the democrats have a splendid opportunity to develop a genuine people's party in which farmers, industrial workers, returned soldiers and progressives could all find a place.

But it would be "a long and severe" fight to bring such a party into being and into power.

We fight not against abstract "capitalism" but against capitalism in league with militarism, with Imperialism, with protection, with authoritarianism in religion and education, with subsidized press and soporifics and palliatives in the form of amusements and "welfare" provisions.

It will be difficult also, he said, because of the regionalism of Canadian society. "Nova Scotia has little in common with Ontario, or the Prairie Provinces with British Columbia".... "Further we have not a common language"..., "...the Montreal Labor Council conducts its business in both English and French...", "...all through Western Canada the majority of our non-English immigrants, who in reality hold the balance of power are unable to read an English newspaper".

Each group maintains its own identity, the lingual, religions, national ties are stronger than those of class interests.

Yet in spite of the pessimistic note, the spirit of the article was one of confidence. "Men are thinking—thinking as never before...out of it all a new civilization is being born—a new religion is arising". Woodsworth detailed further difficulties a new party would have to face. "Nationally" Canada "has not yet achieved her independence...and is...under the shadow of Great Britain...." "On the other hand Canada is commercially and industrially tied up to her big neighbour to the South". Labor is organized in international unions and "it would be difficult to bring on a general strike on, say, conscription, with Mr. Gompers at the head of the AF of L".

He returns to the question of the heterogeneity of the population, which seems to trouble him:

What sympathy has the French Canadian habitant with the trade unionist of Toronto, the miners in Sydney with the fisherman of

British Columbia, or even the prairie farmers with the fruit growers of the Okanagan? No sooner is an industry organized, than European foreigners or Orientals are introduced and the organization slows up . . .

But if Labor is to be victorious—or rather victorious in the near future, the various groups of workers must be in some way drawn together . . .

This will be made easier, he says, if we "review the forces in the field", and examine the class structure of Canada, not from the European model, but looking at the particulars of Canadian society:

As a matter of fact we have no aristocracy and hence no true bourgeois class. Our farmers, though not peasants, are not land-lords. Up to recently there has been a constant passing from one class to another . . .

The most important bulwark of the new movement would be "the industrial workers—the distinctive product of capitalism and the class that feels most directly the evils of the system. . . . But in Canada, at least, Labor would have a poor chance of a speedy victory if she stood alone. Fortunately allies are coming to the rescue". The returning veteran "drawn largely from the ranks of labor, disillusioned and broadened by their experiences at the front . . . " would be a significant "ally" of the working class. "The farmers form a third group" according to Woodsworth. In outlining the importance of this group in any new radical party, he felt called upon to answer arguments put up by "our scientific friends"—meaning Marxists—who claim that the farmers are not class conscious, and in fact should be considered as part of the bourgeoisie:

The mischief is that the city worker does not understand the position of the farmer any more than the farmer understands the position of the city worker. They speak a different language. They have a different mentality. They run up against the capitalism system from a different angle. But fundamentally the interests of the farmer and the industrial worker are one. They will come to recognize this most clearly as they find themselves fighting a common foe. The farmer, like the miner, the factory worker or the logger is a producer.

It is true that he is not a wage earner, but, as the trek from country to city shows, he is not economically as well off as the wage earner. Nominally, he owns the tools of production, in reality he is anything but independent. The mortgage company often owns the land, the banks, the manufacturers and the railroads have the farmer at their mercy. The costs of production and the prices of his products are fixed by forces over which he has no control. Under such conditions, the old individualism is breaking down and the farmer is organizing industrially and politically.

Finally he includes "the little business group" as a potential ally because they "are almost as much the victims of the system as the industrial workers". He says that all this parallels the approach of the British Labour Party, and even of the Bolsheviks for "in Russia the government is a coalition of workers, peasants, and soldiers". But at the same time he rejects Marxist doctrine, although not completely:

The creed of the Federated Labor Party* is remarkable not merely for what it says, but also for what it does not say. There is no mention of "surplus value" of "materialistic interpretation of history" of "class conscious wage slaves" and the other well-worn phrases so familiar to us all. The Labor Party leaves the "scientific orthodox" group and the revisionist groups to fight out their theories, but takes the great underlying principle stressed by Marx, viz., the collective ownership and democratic control of the means of wealth production. Men may differ widely in theory and yet unite to fight a common foe.

In two articles written in the immediate aftermath of the Winnipeg General Strike (and published in the *Western Labour News*), Woodsworth enumerated the salient features he considered necessary for "the new social order". The first set consists of ten points for the economic transformation of Canada: "socialization" of railways, telegraphs, express companies, elevators, and "other public services of transportation and communication"; "socialization" of mines, timber limits, fisheries, water power, electric power, and "other national resources socially operated", "socialization" of banks and insurance companies, state organi-

---

* When he wrote this article, Woodsworth was still living in British Columbia, where he was one of the leaders of the FLP, which had been organized by the B.C. Federation of Labor earlier that year.

zation of distribution of food products and raw materials; taking over existing munitions works and producing in them supplies for public works; the "progressive socialization" of "manufacturing establishments and commercial institutions"; the "expropriation" of unused lands; compensation for present users of socialized or expropriated property; the raising of public revenues through land tax, steeply graduated income tax, confiscation of large private estates at the death of their owners; and joint administration-worker control of socialized industries.

In the next article he advanced a five-point program for the "Provision for Social Welfare". These included free medical and hospital service; free compulsory education to sixteen, with more emphasis on vocational and scientific training; social insurance covering unemployment, accident, and old age; highest possible standards of living; and full equality for women including the idea that the state should pay mothers and housewives for their labor. He summed up the social welfare part of this program with a phrase that later became the slogan of The Independent Labor Party: "Property rights have had precedence over human rights. The position must be reversed."

These two articles are the most forthright statements that Woodsworth ever made in favor of a straight socialist program. They contain some of the planks in the 1917 platform of the Non-Partisan League with which he was chiefly associated in 1918. But they go further, and, significantly, change the term "nationalization", which the NPL used, to "socialization". They seem to represent a shift from the position of his 1918 article in which he favored moderation of working-class demands in order to appeal to the natural allies of the working class. The fact that these articles appeared immediately after the General Strike may have something to do with the heightened note of radicalism and passionate advocacy. We know from his subsequent references to the Winnipeg General Strike that Woodsworth was greatly inspired and elevated by it, and this feeling lasted all his life.

He does not discuss in these articles the path to power or the means by which this platform would be implemented. It is clear, however, from everything he had said up till then that he takes it for granted that the platform would be implemented by parliamentary means. Yet from several other references it seems that he had a much broader view of this question than some historians attribute to him.

Woodsworth understood that the struggle for working-class demands cannot be limited to electoral battles nor to trade unions either. In one of the 1918 articles already referred to, he briefly refers to this question:

Then again some of the old controversies are dying down. "Should we use the industrial or the political weapon?" We find answers using both to good advantage. It is well to attack the enemy on both fronts and sometimes a flank attack is more effective than any frontal attack. The organized workers, on the other hand, have advocated one big union. Now, in the most natural way possible, the units of organized labor fall into line in a general strike.

In an article in the *Western Labour News* which he wrote during the Strike and which was cited in the Crown's indictment against him as "seditious libel", Woodsworth stated that the "peaceable" transformation of society, which he favors, does not depend on the foes of capitalism:

Whether the radical changes that are inevitable may be brought about peaceably, largely depends on the good sense of the Canadian businessmen who now largely control both the industry and Government of the country. We confess the prospects are not overly bright.

In answer to a Conservative M.P. who in 1927 attacked him in the House of Commons for having made this statement, Woodsworth reiterated this position and inserted the above quotation into the official record.

In an account in the *Lethbridge Herald*, July 12, 1919, of his speech to the Lethbridge Trades and Labor Council on the Winnipeg General Strike, he is reported to have "declared that the only way Labor can get what it wants is 'to in some way get control of the military and courts of Canada' ".

Nevertheless it is incontestable that as between the Russian path and the British path Woodsworth favored the latter. Yet he was not firmly convinced of the British path either, but for other reasons. He ultimately felt that the class composition of the progressive forces in Canada was different and that a Labour Party was not suitable to Canadian politics. The dramatic emergence of the Progressive Party in the Federal Elections of 1921 and the victories of farm parties in Ontario and Alberta confirmed this opinion. While the federal Progressive Party was not the new movement he had advocated in his 1918 articles, because it did not include Labor, he continued to hold the perspective of a broad "peoples'" rather than a labor party. He utilized his election to the House of Commons to carry on work towards that end, particularly among the farmer M.P.'s.

Describing the situation at this time of Meighen's accession to the post of Prime Minister, replacing Borden, the *Toronto Star* of August 14, 1920, editorialized as follows:

The new Prime Minister is a Tory through and through and he has sent out his call to all who are like-minded with himself. They will respond. We shall now have under his leadership of his party, a clear-cut line drawn between Toryism and Liberalism in the country.

It is the impulse of Toryism to dig in, to entrench and take a defensive position, resisting change and reform. The ruling impulse of true liberalism is to seek a battle of movement, and press forward, un-afraid of change and determined upon reform.

. . . New groups have arisen in the country. These new groups have been thrown off, have broken away in politics, because of the too great Conservatism of the political leadership the country has had. It should be the aim of Liberalism to attract to itself these groups and marshal a general progressive movement for the betterment of the country and the people who dwell in it.

Yet when the new Parliament convened in 1922, it soon became clear that the appeal of the Liberals to the "new groups" was not the only appeal that would be heard by the farmer M.P.'s during that and subsequent sessions.

Mackenzie King might have been more successful in courting the Progressives had it not been for the presence of the new "labor group" which, with only two members, began to address a strong appeal to the farmers, with a brand of socialism and radicalism which was attractive to many of them. Thus in the next three Parliaments the struggle was not solely between the Tories and Liberals, but between the Liberals and Labour for the support of the farmers. In the course of this the socialism of Woodsworth moderated somewhat under the influence of the farm groups and also to some extent from the labor-agrarian radicalism of his colleague William Irvine.

Woodsworth's approach to his role as M.P. obliged him to do what had not been done in the Canadian socialist movement up to then: to study the particulars of the Canadian political environment and to concretize socialist ideas in relation to fundamental problems of Canadian political thought: nationalism, independence, constitutional questions, and French Canada. As dealt with in the previous chapters, the other main section of the Canadian socialist movement—the Communists—began at this time to do the same and although they studied Canadian questions within the framework of a Marxist analysis, it is interesting to note the similarities between their conclusions and Woodsworth's.

A Radical Political Economy

At the outset Woodsworth confronted questions of political economy: the nature of Canadian capitalism and its relationship to government, capital investment (foreign and domestic), and the class structure of Canadian society. In effect, he took up a tradition of radical social analysis that had originated with the farmers' movement.

Besides works of a general social criticism, such as Henry George's *Progress and Poverty*, which were widely distributed in Canada by the agrarian radicals, they produced or circulated four major works specifically about Canada: Edward Porritt: *Sixty Years of Protection in Canada* (1907); Edward Porritt: *The Revolt in Canada Against the New Feudalism* (1911); *Who Owns Canada? (The Grain Growers' Guide* 1913); and Gustavus Myers: *History of Canadian Wealth* (1914).

The first three were concentrated attacks on what the farmers labelled "the Triple Alliance" of "Railway, Banking and Manufacturing interests", an "Alliance" which "owes its wealth and power in a very large degree to favors which have been conferred upon it by parliaments and legislatures".* Myers's book, in addition, was a historical treatment of capital accumulation in Canada beginning with the era of French rule, and bearing the imprint of Marxism in many of its interpretations.

While all these books were polemical, they contained serious analyses of the Canadian economy; all concluded that, as a result of the special relationship between Canadian government and business interests, Canada had become a highly monopo-

---

* The use of this terminology to describe the farmers' enemies had become frequent in *The Grain Growers' Guide*.

lized society. *The Grain Growers' Guide* opened its study on June 25, 1913, with the following declaration:

Those who believe that Canada is a truly democratic country, and that her people are free and independent men and women will find cause to reconsider their attitude after studying the article, Who Owns Canada? *which is published in this issue. The startling fact is there revealed that 42 men, by their positions as officers and directors of the leading corporations and business institutions of this country, control more than one-third of the total wealth possessed by the nation.*

It named the men, detailed their control of major financial and industrial concerns worth $4,000,000,000, and then declared:

It is doubtful if ever before in the history of the world there has been such a concentration of the control of wealth in the hands of a few as exists in Canada today.

However devastating the critique of Canadian capitalist society was in these works, the proposals that were advanced seemed weak and mild by contrast. Porritt's second book proposed "a tariff revision" and a removal of "the hold" of "the New Feudalism" on "the Government at Ottawa" in order to establish "effective democracy".

The Grain Growers' Guide proposed free trade, tax on unimproved land, lower freight and interest rates, and "Direct Legislation, the Initiative, Referendum and Recall" which it described as "the most powerful weapon that can be placed in the hands of the people to right their wrongs . . . ."

In view of the farmers' concern for social analysis, it indeed seems strange that the Marxian Socialists ignored this, and outside of a few references to Myers's book, never undertook a Marxist study of Canadian society, and did not use one when it was provided ready-made for them.

But Woodsworth did. He took up Myers's book in his first budget speech of May 29, 1922, and quoted a whole passage from it (although he did not mention the source of that quotation). He gave a synopsis of the history of Canadian capital based on the book and this led him into an attack on the continued concessions being given by the governments to railroad builders, manufacturers, and banks, the old "Triple Alliance." He took note of two new factors that had been added.

One was the great riches made by the Canadian capitalists through profiteering during the war, and the other, the increased penetration and control of important sectors of the Canadian economy by U.S. capital.

Woodsworth had dealt with the role of U.S. capital in his maiden speech and although he was one of the first to bring out some of the salient features that are so conspicuous today, he did not seem especially perturbed about this development nor about the trend it presaged:

I take it that our economic future in this country is inextricably bound up with that of the United States. We may maintain our own political identity but economically we are bound to have the very closest relations with the great country to the south of us. It is many years since Goldwin Smith pointed out that the natural lines on this continent run North and South. Artificial lines have been run East and West, and along these artificial lines we have built our trade boundaries. That makes it very difficult to pass freely across those boundaries. We must recognize that although we differ in a very important sense economically from the United States—in that we are a debtor nation while they are a creditor nation—at the same time the ties between us are so intimate that we cannot hope to prosper unless they also prosper.

He considered U.S. investment as a fact which did not alter the class structure nor the nature of the political struggle in Canada:

From my standpoint—and I think I can speak for a very large number of the common people of this country—it does not make very much difference whether the money is held by some great corporation in this country or outside . . .

He considered that the movement for Canadian autonomy had to be waged against British control, not American.

A key element in Woodsworth's social criticism was his constant emphasis on poverty, unemployment, and exploitation of labor. Although he considered all of these endemic to the capitalist system, he also felt that parliament could and should take measures to alleviate these conditions.

He became the recognized spokesman of organized labor in the House of Commons during this period. Particularly dramatic and effective was his role in Parliament during the continuing struggle of the Cape Breton miners and Sydney steelworkers between 1922 and 1925, which was highlighted by the deployment of federal troops and the arrest and conviction of the popular union leader J. B. McLachlan. He filled many pages of Hansard with speeches on the plight of the workers, condemned BESCO, the company involved, and fought for the release of McLachlan. On his release, McLachlan, who was a Communist, wrote to "Comrade Woodsworth" to acknowledge his role:

My main purpose in writing you is to thank you for all you did for me while I was in jail, for all the meetings you addressed, for the petitions and resolutions you had the workers all over the country send in to the Department on my behalf.

He supported the farmers' demands for tariff revisions and advocated amendments to the Bank Act to curtail the credit and eliminate the currency function of the chartered banks. He supported the demands of the Western provinces for their right to tax unused lands, to reclaim ownership of their natural resources, and to tax mineral leases held by the CPR and Hudson's Bay Company in these provinces.

Many of these questions were new to Woodsworth, but were pressed upon him by contact with the farmers' movement in Parliament, for whom these concerns were central. Speaking in the 1923 debate on amending the Bank Act, Woodsworth explained to the workers why these should be their concerns as well:

Labour is not consciously and definitely interested in this question but generally takes the attitude that all these questions belong to the capitalists, that all this is part of the present system which they desire to see superseded. I urge, however, that when we touch the financial system we touch every nerve centre of our present system. We understand its operations a little better . . . It is obvious we cannot hope to get much through this House. The most we can do is protest. Let me say, as has been said elsewhere, that either we as a people must own and democratically control these great financial institutions, or they will absolutely own and control us.

By taking up these questions of concern to the farmers and becoming knowledgeable about them, he began to emerge as a spokesman for the more radical wing of the Progressive Party in parliament, foreshadowing the eventual split, when the majority of the Progressives returned to the Liberal fold, and the rest joined labor representatives in forming the "Ginger Group". By that time Woodsworth was definitely regarded as the leader of all the radicals in the House of Commons, not just of labour.

He did seem at odds, however, with the other member of the original two-man labor group, William Irvine, who became the chief advocate in Canada of Major C. H. Douglas's Social Credit theories, and made them a central theme throughout his first term as M.P. Yet Woodsworth never publicly disassociated himself from Irvine over these theories, except perhaps by omitting reference to them in his own speeches and writings.

Irvine was a significant figure in the left-wing constellation of that period. He personified both ideologically and organizationally the links between the farmers' movement and labor. His book *The Farmers in Politics*, published in 1920, was an important addition to the literature of radical social criticism in Canada. It continued the main themes of the previous publications mentioned above, but added the political and economical developments of the war:

On the coming to power of the Union Government, parliament was virtually done away with, its place being taken by orders-in-council. Here was class legislation, the most flagrant and brazen ever perpetrated. Kaiserism made its abode in Ottawa—where it still flourishes. The iron heel of censorship was placed on the neck of every protestor. Literature in opposition to plutocratic class rule was banned, and the worst features of the inquisition were not to be too bad to be resurrected and brought to Canada to do service in the interest of a class tyranny of the most shameful kind.

He dealt with the war profiteering and the consequent national debt which became a constant issue in the twenties:

The working class, including the farmers, is living now far below the standard of life of 1914; the country is obliged to shoulder enormous debts unscrupulously incurred under the cover of war; the profiteers have made a sum approximately equal to that of the swollen national debt . . .

He took up again the charge that a handful of men controlled the economic and political life of Canada:

. . . Roughly speaking about five percent of our population has,

through organization made the laws which the other ninety-five percent had to obey. The exploitation of the natural resources and the exploitation of labor, have served to produce twenty-three money kings who control the whole arterial system of Canadian commercial life. These kings of commerce and industry are the commanders of the political parties. They dictate the policies, and they make the laws and they do both in the sole interests of property rights and business.

But the main purpose of his book was to plead the cause of "group government" by which he meant the abolition of the party system, and the inauguration of a system of representation by economic groups: "farmers, laborers, manufacturers and all other groups" who will then be compelled "to co-operate to make a commonwealth of happiness". He criticized "syndicalism, Bolshevism, Marxism" but praised "guild socialism", which he called a "group system". He rejected Marx's "two-class theory of society" which he said did not encompass all the various divisions in society, such as those between "sick and healthy, wise and foolish, and others".

Irvine's participation in the House of Commons during his first term in the self-described role as the labor group ("I wish to state that the honourable member for Centre Winnipeg [Mr. Woodsworth] is leader of the Labor Group—and I am the group") was not in too close consonance with that of his "leader". His constant themes were "group government" and "social credit", terms which were conspicuously absent from Woodsworth's speeches. One observer in a study of Irvine suggests the following:

Whether Irvine completely lost his socialist beliefs during this period is unknown, but the lack of any reference to socialism in his speeches and writings during the period suggests that for a few years socialism was of little interest to him.[7]

The suggestion is wrongly placed. Irvine had not adopted socialism when he entered Parliament in 1921. It was owing to the close association with Woodsworth in Parliament, particularly during his second term beginning in 1926*, and especially

---

[7] J. E. Hart, *William Irvine and Radical Politics In Canada*, unpublished Ph. D. Thesis, University of Guelph, 1972, p. 96.

* He was defeated in 1925 and returned in 1926.

under the impact of the Depression, that he adopted socialism. But by then, the farmers of Alberta, who influenced Irvine greatly, had regained some of that "bitterness of feeling against Capital" which he claimed in *The Farmers in Politics* they had lost. But he held on to his ideas of social credit, again probably under the influence of the Alberta farmers, and succeeded in inserting a version of it in the Regina Manifesto.

As stated above, Woodsworth was the representative in the House of the Independent Labor Party of Manitoba which had been formed in 1921. He was also associated with the Federated Labor Party of B.C., which he had helped found in 1918. He was present at the foundation of the British Columbia Independent Labor Party in January 1926. The British Columbia Independent Labor Party "Platform and Manifesto" was identical with the FLP "Platform and Manifesto". It was a Marxist-oriented document, bearing significant resemblance to the platforms of the Socialist Party of Canada and the Social-Democratic Party. It reflected the radical tradition of British Columbia socialism and was quite different from the *Manifesto of the Independent Labor Party of Manitoba*. The B.C. document was primarily a programmatic and theoretical statement of fundamental aims, a disquisition on the inherent evils of capitalist society "which can be removed only by a change in our economic system. For this reason we do not put forward any lengthy list of immediate aims". *The Manitoba Manifesto*, on the other hand, opened with two short paragraphs stating in very general terms that it has "in view a complete change in our present economic and social system", followed by fourteen detailed immediate aims. There was no mention of socialism, that being replaced by the phrase "Co-operative Commonwealth". The catalogue of immediate aims itself was couched in much more moderate terms than Woodsworth's article in the *Western Labour News* just two years earlier. "Public ownership and democratic operation of public utilities; and as soon as possible of essential large scale industry", and "the nationalization of the banking system" replaced the long list of sections of the economy which Woodsworth proposed to "socialize". Woodsworth's demand then for the "socialization of *banks* and insurance agencies" was now changed to "the nationalization of the *banking system*" [my italics]. Here again the program reflected the people and groups that formed the various sections of the Manitoba ILP. Fred Dixon, a "single-taxer," not a Socialist, was one of the prime founders of the ILP merging his own Dominion Labor Party into the new group, and doubtless his views played a major part in formulating the party's platform.

It must be pointed out that although Woodsworth was becoming more and more the ideologist of all these disparate trends, he was in no position to bring about a uniformity of ideas, let alone of tactics, nor did he try. In an article in the *Western Labour News* of October 11, 1918, he explicitly stated his approach with the declaration that "Men may differ widely in theory and yet unite to fight a common foe".

However, the perception of what or who is the "common foe" is largely determined by "theory" and this was reflected in the groups coming together to form the CCF. Some held the foe to be the capitalist system, others the financial system and the land system, and still others the evils of the monopolies, but not capitalism itself. These differences were already evident in the speeches of the self-constituted CCF group in the House of Commons, February 1 and 2, 1933*, when the House debated a resolution by Woodsworth calling for the immediate "setting up of a Co-operative Commonwealth" to solve the "present depression".

Two of the farm representatives, Agnes Macphail and G. G. Coote, concentrated their attack on the banks and the financial system. They both advanced the view that the main measures needed to alleviate the Depression were for the government to take over the control of credit and the issuance of currency from the private banks and to inject "new money to finance new wealth". Angus MacInnis gave a lecture in Marxian economics and criticized his farm colleagues for placing the blame on the banks for what was essentially the failure of the entire capitalist system. William Irvine, while stressing the need "to socialize the credit system of Canada, which represents 96 percent of all the money distributed throughout the country" declared that the next fight in Canada will be between "capitalism and Socialism".

But the difference took a subordinate position to the Depression, which at this time was at its worst. The Depression became in fact that "common foe" that made it possible for groups that differed "widely in theory" "to unite to fight" under one banner. This is reflected in the Regina Manifesto which combined a long-term programmatic declaration, eclectic in character, with

---

* This was in the period between the formal establishment of the CCF in Calgary, August 1932, and the first convention (which adopted a constitution and a program) in Regina, July 1933. Eight members of the House, four from the ILP's and four from the farm groups, formed a CCF caucus in the House of Commons.

an "Emergency Programme" to fight "unemployment and the widespread suffering it has caused".

The Regina Manifesto

A comparison of the Regina Manifesto with the various socialist platforms which antedated it shows a considerable change in concept, terminology, and class orientation. The Manifesto also shows a greater concreteness in the manner in which it dealt with Canadian problems, doubtless the legacy of the ten years of parliamentary experience which the new movement inherited at its foundation, as well as the greater emphasis it put on social reforms.

The Regina Manifesto is the program of "a federation of farmers, labor and socialist organizations" whereas all the previous socialist parties had declared themselves to be working class.

The alliance between farm and labor groups was reflected in the Regina Manifesto in the amount of attention given to farm demands, and to a recognition of the place of agriculture in Canadian society. None of the socialist party platforms had paid any attention at all to farm demands or the role of agriculture. Except for a plank in the 1902 platform of the Ontario Socialist League (OSL), which called for "a national currency and government banking system" (and was dropped two years later when the OSL merged with the Socialist Party of Canada), there was no further mention of the socialization of finance until the Regina Manifesto. The Manifesto gave it great prominence because this had become by then a major demand of the Canadian farmers.

The Regina Manifesto not only rejected violence as a means of social change but stated that the CCF seeks "to achieve its ends solely by constitutional methods". Except for the Workers' Party which explicitly opted for "the conquest of political power ... [by] the establishment of the working class dictatorship", there was considerable ambiguity in the socialist and labor parties as to how they envisaged the attainment of "a new social order". The CCF was the first to spell out that the path must be "solely ... constitutional". The declaration of intent to uphold constitutional means to achieve socialist ends defines that this is unmistakably a social democratic movement and program in which the means take precedence over the ends.

The socialist parties and even some of the ILP platforms dealt with immediate demands as being of secondary concern. The Social-Democratic Party "will support any measure that will tend to better conditions under capitalism" but only "as a means of preparing the minds of the working class for the inauguration of the Co-operative Commonwealth". "The Federated Labor Party as a socialist party holds that the difficulties which the working class is laboring under can only be removed by a change in our economic system. For this reason we do not put forward any lengthy list of immediate aims." The Workers' Party saw "the fight for the immediate needs of the workers" ... "a force for the abolition of capitalism" and therefore supported immediate demands for that purpose, but did not list any.

In the Regina Manifesto, however, the CCF listed in some detail fourteen immediate reforms which it described as constituting "a far-reaching re-construction of our economic and political institutions". It is true that the concluding paragraph which refers to "eradicating capitalism" implied that these fourteen planks do not equal the eradication of capitalism. But it moved the fight for immediate demands into a primary rather than a secondary position, and it tended to resolve in that way the ambivalence of the socialist groups on the status of immediate demands. Thus some twenty years later this concluding paragraph itself could be "eradicated" without doing violence to the main character of the CCF and its practice during those years.

Many of the socialists at the founding convention fought to keep the formulations and tone of the CCF program in line with what they considered to be Marxist principles. In the end, however, the Regina Manifesto was adopted, albeit with some concessions to them. Within a few years most of the non-Communist socialist groups and individuals had been absorbed into the CCF on the basis of the Regina Manifesto, even though some still had reservations.* The culmination of this process finalized the split in the Canadian Socialist movement which had been developing since the Russian Revolution. All Socialists in the CCF, whether they agreed with the Regina Manifesto or had

---

* Not untypical was a letter sent by Angus McInnis, M.P., on May 11, 1933, to Robert Skinner: "Now as to the CCF nosing out the Socialist Party, I am not particularly concerned. What we need is a revolutionary party. The name does not matter. As you say, we'll have to control the CCF."

reservations, were committed to an organization whose reformist character had by then been clearly established.

But this did not mean that Marxism had no further role to play in the CCF. It figured largely in a study done by the Saskatchewan CCF Research Bureau in 1934 using the same title that the farmers had used in their 1913 study: *Who Owns Canada?* The preface admitted to its Marxist character, but obliquely:

In spite of feeble and tortuous essays written to prove that the classic interpretation of the capitalist economic system and its tendencies written in London, sixty-eight years ago is outmoded and all wrong, the developments of the first thirty-four years of the 20th Century have merely piled up mountains of facts which verify that interpretation and dot the "i's" and cross the "t's" of the statements made therein.*

The central theme of the work is stated on the first page:

One hundred great corporations dominate Canadian industry! Fifty Canadian "big shots" hold within their hands the fate of these great corporations and many more, and through these companies they control the lives and fates, not only of ten million Canadians, but also of millions of Brazilians, Mexicans, Spaniards, and Frenchmen.

Some of those listed were on the original 1913 farmers' list or were their descendants. But the corporations through which these men exercised their control were largely the same, only their assets had greatly increased. Altogether this *Who Owns Canada?* was much more detailed and analytical than its predecessor. (No mention is made of the original!) One of the central conclusions confirms the original when it comments on the degree of concentration in Canada's corporate structure:

Corporations in the United States of America may be more numerous and larger than those in this country, but Canada is way ahead of its bigger neighbour when it comes to concentration of control.

---

* This reference recalls the publication in the 1880s of H. M. Hyndman's *England for All* using many of Marx's ideas which the author "acknowledged" by stating in his preface that he was "indebted to the work of a great writer and original thinker". This irritated Marx and soured his relations with Hyndman. (Marx-Engels Correspondence, p. 397).

The book ends with a strong argument against those who believe it possible "to regulate and temper Capitalism" through "a planned economy", through a return to "pure" Capitalism, or through Social Credit:

As long as private monopoly ownership of the means of production, distribution and exchange exists, no government, whether Liberal, Conservative, or Labor, can control it, but the "Fifty Big Shots" no matter who they are at the moment, will control the government.

Shortly after this pamphlet was issued, a much more elaborate and detailed study of Canadian society was published by the Research Committee of the League for Social Reconstruction: *Social Planning for Canada (1935)*, the result of three years of study and discussion by seven academics, who were among the first of a number of eminent scholars who associated themselves publicly with the CCF during the thirties. According to a contemporary critique of the LSR this work

was the most systematic and important statement of Canadian socialism that had yet been made; it may be so still.[8]

Woodsworth in his foreword to the book explained its significance. It was a break with previous Socialist literature in Canada which "has been scarce", "too abstract" or dealt too much with Soviet Russia, Great Britain, Vienna, the Scandinavian countries "under conditions which differ widely from those existing in Canada".

The authors of this book drew on many theoretical sources to buttress their analysis of the Canadian economy. On the Marxist left they acknowledge a debt to Lenin, Engels, Strachey, and Palme Dutt, but oddly enough do not mention Marx. Yet it is clear that much of it is based on Marxist economics, even if, according to Horn, "Marxism entered the LSR analysis of society . . . indirectly and in diluted form through books by British or American authors who were to varying degrees influenced by Marxism".[9]

Much of the Canadian material in the book underscored a

---

[8] M. S. D. Horn, *The League for Social Reconstruction: Socialism and Nationalism In Canada, 1931-1945*, unpublished Ph. D. Thesis, University of Toronto, 1969, p. 72.

[9] Horn, *The League for Social Reconstruction*, p. 267.

constant theme of radical social criticism up until then: "In few capitalist countries does the state play a larger part in the functioning of the economy."

The "aid and service" given to industry and finance by the successive governments of Canada, federal and provincial, have led to the creation of an economy dominated by monopolistic control built up through the "predatory activities" of "big business". Big business has been able to avoid social welfare measures through skillfully using "the doctrine of provincial rights" to play province against federal authority and vice versa. The CCF, on the other hand, in order to transform society, would have to amend the constitution to ensure greater powers to the central government while preserving "the cultural and racial rights of minorities".

The cosy relationship between government and business, according to the book, was reflected in the nature of the Canadian state and in its constitutional and judicial features which express that relationship:

The State sides with the class whose interest is in vested property rights in insisting that order is of higher social value than justice.

The book dealt at some length with a relatively new theme in radical literature, the large-scale growth of foreign, mainly U.S., investment, and its dominance in certain key sectors of the Canadian economy:

That foreigners control this or that particular industry will trouble none but those earnest patriots who in defiance of all the evidence persist in believing that the Canadian capitalist is a different kind of being from the foreigner, that the one is a philanthropist, the other a robber and a cheat...

... From the socialist point of view, however, the most serious disadvantage of the large foreign investment in Canada is that even when we socialize industry it will be difficult to rid ourselves of the annual tribute to the foreign investor.

... even a socialist Canada will probably have to give preferential treatment to the foreign investor.

While there is much trenchant criticism of the capitalist system and its endemic contradictions, there was some considerable ambivalence in the book as to whether the entire capitalist system is to be "eradicated" or just some features of it. For instance, in one place the authors say:

Some of these troubles as we have seen are of natural origin. But most of them are the legacy of an unplanned, haphazard expansion by and for private enterprise: Waste and exploitation in the boom, debt and dislocation in the depression.

If unplanned, capitalism has brought us to this pass, the sensible thing to do is to substitute a plan.

Yet the importance of this work was not in its projections of the path to a Socialist Canada, which merely elaborated on the Regina Manifesto, but in its carefully documented analysis of Canadian political economy: dealing with class structure, historical development, and the nature of the Canadian state. It, and the pamphlet *Who Owns Canada?*, provided the Canadian left with a concrete political economy brought up to date. The Communist Party was still indulging in abstract Marxism without a political economy of its own, and when the CP did begin to change in this respect with its brief to the Rowell-Sirois Commission (1938), it did not improve upon what the CCF had already done. In fact, there is much in the CP's brief that was obviously derived from the political economy of the CCF and the LSR.

The publication of *Social Planning for Canada* led to a more detailed Marxist interpretation of Canadian history, the tone of which was set by F. H. Underhill in a paper presented in 1935 to the Canadian Political Science Association. In it Underhill attacked the "tendency... of the modern bourgeois liberal mind ... to concentrate attention upon the political forms in which a society is organized instead of upon the economic forces which lie behind them...."[10] This leads Canadian liberal thinkers to regard the present crisis as "a crisis of federalism" instead of seeing it as "a crisis of capitalism". The nub of Underhill's thesis was stated in the following passages:

The essential work of the Fathers of Confederation was to weld the scattered British possessions in North America into a unity within which Canadian capitalism could expand and consolidate its power, to provide for the Capitalist entrepreneurs of Montreal and

---

[10] Frank H. Underhill, "The Conception of A National Interest", *In Search of Canadian Liberalism* (Toronto, 1975).

Toronto a half-continent in which they could realize their dreams and ambitions. The dynamic drive which brought Confederation about had its centre in Montreal among the railway and banking magnates who were dreaming of new fields to conquer.

... it was inevitable that during this period national interest should be interpreted primarily in terms of the interests of this industrial-financial group which was steadily emerging into a position of economic dominance ... The conflict of interests is accompanied by a conflict of ideas; and the two generations since Confederation not merely in the victory of industrial and financial capitalism but in the imposition of its ideology upon our society as a whole ...

Underhill is quoted in later years by one historian as stating that "he had never read Marx",[11] and by another as saying that "he never read any Marx except the Communist Manifesto".[12] Horn claims that Underhill's economic interpretation came mainly from Charles A. Beard, who did use a Marxist interpretation of history, and who is referred to in Underhill's paper on "The Conception of The National Interest".

Yet whether directly or indirectly acquired, Underhill and his colleagues in the LSR did bring a Marxist interpretation to bear on problems of Canadian history and economy. Later Marxist works by others elaborated on these themes, but did not differ in their essential interpretative framework.

Creighton wrote about this period and acknowledged the impact of Marxism on Canadian historiography, but in sarcastic terms:

The popularity of Marxian economic interpretation of history is one of the most interesting features of the 1930's and of the early 1940's. [This was due to ...] ... the depression, and the economic and social distress which it had caused, and the political protest movements which it had helped to inspire. Of course, most of the professional economists—and especially Innis—refused to accept the simplified Marxian version of historical determinism which the circumstances of the movement made so popular, but these timid academic scruples did not deter those party historians, party economists, and party scientists who made up that superbly confident body, the League for Social Reconstruction, and who were recog-

[11] Walter Young, *The Anatomy of A Party*, p. 54.

[12] Horn, *The League for Social Reconstruction*, p. 267.

nized respectfully at the time as the "brains trust" of the co-operative Commonwealth Federation.[13]

Thus while the Regina Manifesto in fact rejected Marxism as a guide to political action, it did not reject it as a critique of capitalist society. In fact, the academics who joined the movement and helped write the Manifesto, elevated the status of Marxism by using it as one of their tools for the analysis of Canadian conditions. As Creighton points out, Marxism became more popular in that period because of the severity of the economic crisis, and the emergence of the LSR was due, in part, to that situation.

Marxism was never legislated out of the CCF, it was merely absorbed. This was particularly true in British Columbia where the Socialist Party of Canada, and the ILP, both Marxist, were the original groups that composed the B.C. section of the CCF. Wallis W. Lefeaux, who became first president of the CCF in British Columbia, was an accomplished Marxist and continued to give popular lectures on Marxist political economy under CCF auspices for many years. He was elected to the B.C. legislature in 1941 and became the financial critic of the CCF legislative group. Many of his speeches on the budget were like treatises on Marxist economics. Angus MacInnis, who came out of the B.C. Socialist movement, considered himself "a real Marxian Socialist" for many years after the foundation of the CCF.

The eclectic nature of the Regina Manifesto reflected the viewpoints of the diverse groups and trends that united around it. It was not surprising that the differences expressed at the founding convention of the CCF should surface again, as indeed they did on many subsequent occasions throughout the life of the party. What may appear ironic is that most of these eruptions were provoked by the left, which although it had expressed major reservations over the Regina Manifesto at the beginning, found itself defending this document against attacks from the right. The moderates were never happy with the first and last paragraphs of the Manifesto which they felt were put in as a concession to the "doctrinaire" socialists, particularly those from B.C. These attacks on the Manifesto reached their apex in 1956 when the Winnipeg Declaration replaced the Regina Manifesto, eliminating the offending paragraphs.

Woodsworth tended to occupy a middle position, often criti-

---

[13] Donald Creighton, *Towards the Discovery of Canada*, p. 36-7.

cized from opposite extremes. He was condemned, for instance, when he ordered the suspension of the Ontario Provincial Council of the CCF in 1934 for cooperating with the Communists. But he was also suspect in the eyes of some others, particularly those who wanted a closer relationship with the trade-union movement and who felt that Woodsworth was himself too doctrinaire, and even too radical, to satisfy the trade union leaders.

Evidently A. A. Heaps, M.P., was one of those, according to his son's biography of him:

The major political difference between the two was that for Woodsworth every capitalist was suspect as a wicked exploiter of labor. He seemed unaware that men could come from a background of wealth and still possess a sensitivity and a troubled conscience towards the ills of mankind. Heaps could genuinely befriend and respect Bennett, while Woodsworth was intellectually unable to do so.[14]

But much of the debate inside the CCF was esoteric. As a result of the Regina Manifesto, the work of its parliamentary representatives, the public statements of its leaders, the literature it issued, and its activities during the depression, the CCF created a public image which persisted. It moved into and occupied the left wing of the Canadian ideological spectrum, and was regarded as the embodiment of the idea of Canadian socialism which henceforth became identified with public ownership and nationalization on a wide scale. This image was never materially affected by the sophisticated exchanges regularly taking place among CCF activists as to how far and how fast the party should move.

The establishment of the CCF on the basis of a radical social criticism was aided by the action and ideological performance of the two major parties. Bennett and his "iron heel of ruthlessness" revived the authoritarian Toryism that had appeared to be in decline during the twenties. When he tried to move from there to liberal, even radical, reformism, he lacked credibility. Even his own party neither believed nor supported this shift. Mackenzie King, on the other hand, who had espoused liberal reformism in 1919, for a variety of reasons failed to move against the effects and conditions of the Depression. Consequently, unlike socialist parties in the United States, where Roosevelt's New Deal became the embodiment of radicalism and thus

---

[14] Leo Heaps, *The Rebel in the House* (London, 1970), p. 118.

undercut the support the American Socialists had or might have gained, the CCF was seen by many Canadians to be the main fighter in legislative bodies against the Depression, and against the system itself.

Canadian Autonomy and the BNA Act

Woodsworth was a Canadian nationalist, although this aspect of his political thought did not emerge strongly until after he was elected to the House of Commons. This was the period when, in the wake of the war, the question of Canada's relationship with Britain came to the fore in a new way. What had been a major current in French Canada now was becoming important in English Canada. Mackenzie King took the lead in bringing about a new definition of the British connection to make Canada self-governing in major respects. Woodsworth supported this and coupled it with proposals for the revision of the BNA Act, first merely to patriate it, and later to give the federal government authority to legislate on labor and social matters. He also regularly advanced the demand for the abolition of the Senate.

In presenting his case, which he expanded upon and developed from year to year, Woodsworth drew upon the writings of J. S. Ewart, long-time advocate of Canadian independence, J. W. Dafoe, who was for autonomy within the British Commonwealth, and Clifford Sifton, even though Woodsworth said he was "not a very great admirer" of some of Sifton's other policies.

But Woodsworth's nationalism was not coterminous with that of the constitutionalists. His nationalism springs in the first place from his socialist convictions, anti-imperialist and anti-capitalist. The main theoretical source of his anti-imperialism was the English economist J. A. Hobson whose work *Imperialism*, published in 1902, had influenced a whole generation of economists and political theorists, including Lenin. In a speech on February 2, 1923, in the House of Commons, Woodsworth quoted Hobson's definition of imperialism:

Imperialism is the endeavour of the controllers of industry to broaden the channel for the flow of the surplus wealth by seeking foreign markets and foreign investments to take off the goods and capital they cannot sell at home ... It is not too much to say that the modern foreign policy of Great Britain is primarily a struggle for profitable markets of investment to a larger extent each year. Great Britain is becoming a nation living on tribute from abroad and the classes who enjoy the tribute have an ever increasing incentive to employ the public policy, the public purse, and the public force to extend the field of their private investments.

Woodsworth learned from Hobson that imperialism inevitably leads to war and since Britain was the leading imperialist power, wars involving Britain were likewise inevitable. Therefore, Canada must declare her freedom from British foreign policy and from future military entanglements. Without that freedom, Canada will either be involved automatically or "tricked" into participation.

I say, frankly that this country was tricked as other countries were with regard to the real causes of the last war ... We were deceived as to the causes of the War, we were deceived during the war as to the real aims of the allies ...

He returned to the attack on British imperialism in a 1925 debate on voting supply for military training in Canada:

In addition to the military preparedness which we have, and what I might call psychological preparedness. We maintain the attitude of boosting our own. We have our own song Britannia Rules the Waves—*and I am not at all sure it is much preferable to* Germany Over All—*They both exhibit the same spirit, the same desire to dominate, but of course as a Britisher I suppose I naturally would like to think of the British dominating. It is hard to get out of one's skin. But at the same time, I say to both of them: this is a spirit that will never witness peace. ...*

He linked imperialism with racism and rebuffed an interruption by the Minister of Defence who accused Woodsworth of "verging very nearly to a statement of disloyalty ... by his comparison of the British Anthem to the German". Woodsworth repeated his statement and defied the Minister to take whatever steps he wanted against him.

A revealing insight into Woodsworth's thinking along these lines is contained in an article in *The Canadian Forum* of April 1926. He was contributing to a series of articles launched by the magazine seeking a broad consensus for a new political movement. In his reply Woodsworth said he could not "do better than append the Manifesto of the Independent Labor Party". But the version which Woodsworth appends contains fifteen points, while the 1921 and 1925 versions have only fourteen points. The extra one which appears in Woodsworth's article as point fourteen is "Opposition to all encroachments of Capitalist Imperialism".[15]

A few months after the article appeared, Woodsworth produced a little pamphlet called "Following the Gleam" in which he appends the Independent Labor Party Manifesto, but here it has the original fourteen points. I have not been able to find any explanation for this discrepancy, but it is likely that this additional point is Woodsworth's own, and not that of the Party which he was then representing in Parliament.

In 1927 he once again drew upon Hobson, whom he described as "a recognized authority", to buttress his argument for Canadian autonomy. He quoted Hobson as saying, "Imperialism is a depraved choice of national life, inspired by self-seeking interests which appeal to the lusts of quantitative acquisitiveness and forceful domination". He pointed to the danger of Canadians living abroad being regarded as British subjects in British spheres of influence and getting involved in British conflicts there and, "then there will be an outcry all over this country and a demand that we must save Canadian lives".

Woodsworth was in fact continuing a position which had found strong support in the farm movement prior to the outbreak of the war, and, in a different form, had been expressed in the socialist and labor movements as well.

The *Weekly Sun*, journal of the Ontario farmers, and *The Grain Growers' Guide* prior to World War I, contain many strong articles of an anti-imperialist character. The *Sun's* editor, W. L. Smith, was an ardent anti-imperialist who said in 1909 that "the spirit of aggression as expressed in preparation for War is quite as strong in evidence in Great Britain as in Germany. . . ." He foresaw that "Canada stands to lose through imperialist war, by the loss of autonomy, by the discord which certainly would be created in our diverse elements and by the crushing burdens that would be imposed by military expenditures. . . ."

In a letter sent to Laurier that same year, W. C. Good, later president of the United Farmers of Ontario (UFO), expressed

---

[15] J. S. Woodsworth, M.P., "Grandsons of Confederation", *The Canadian Forum*, April 1926, p. 207.

what he felt were the views of the farmers:

I merely wish to express upon you as strongly as I could and in view of the fact that there is a strong feeling against the naval programme among the farmers, and that the question has never yet been brought before the electorate and that therefore definite action should be postponed until the matter has been pronounced upon by the people . . .

In a forceful article entitled "Canada and the Empire" written for the *Farmers' Magazine* and reprinted in *The Grain Growers' Guide* on February 19, 1913, E. C. Drury, then Vice-president of the Canadian Council of Agriculture, wrote on the naval program:

This is a new thing so far as Canada is concerned. Never before in her history has it ever been hinted that she was under any obligation, moral or otherwise, to assist in any way in maintaining the armed forces of the Empire, or rather of Great Britain, since there is no such thing as an Imperial Force . . .

Once we participate in the naval defence of the Empire, it appears that we stand pledged, to support Britain in all her wars—a virtual tribute, since we can have no real say in the making of peace and war—or to withhold our support at the peril of severing our connection.

In its issue of February 3, 1914, *The Grain Growers' Guide* gave the official results of a referendum it had conducted asking eleven questions, the eleventh of which follows:

Do you believe that Canada instead of spending millions for naval armament (either British or Canada) should devote her energies and spend millions, if necessary towards the establishment of universal peace and disarmament and the settlement of international disputes by arbitration?

The results were 6055 yes, 493 no, and 255 undecided. A month later the *Guide* ran in three consecutive issues a summary of J. S. Ewart's articles under the title *The Kingdom of Canada*.

In the issue of August 5, 1914, obviously printed just before Canada became involved in the war, the *Guide* printed this message on its front cover:

THE DEMON OF WAR

*The war demon is abroad in Europe and thousands of men are
engaged in the slaughter of their fellow men. Those who ordered
the war will be comfortably located far beyond the danger zone but
homes will be desolated, crops destroyed, children orphaned, fathers
and sons killed and maimed, wives and mothers left to mourn their
dead and rear their families alone. Is Canada to be forced blindly
and needlessly into this horrible struggle?*

Evidently the answer to that question came before the next
issue, because on that front cover, an entirely opposite message
was emblazoned. Now it was "BRITISH IDEALS MUST
TRIUMPH . . . British civilization and British manhood is now
on trial. . . . In self-defence we must do our utmost in the struggle
in which Britishers everywhere are now engaged". One is hard
put to explain such a sharp and sudden turn, but several explanations could be argued: sentimentality towards Britain, and the
fact that the first wave of patriotic fervor was gripping the
nation. Later, the farmers' support for the war was based on
other considerations, the chief of which, according to W. L.
Morton, was the prosperity it brought the farmers (at least in the
first period):

*The war also pulled the Canadian economy out of the slump which
had begun in 1913 and had become severe by 1914. By 1915, a war
boom was under way which was also a wheat boom and a land
boom of the same kind as that of 1896-1911.*[16]

Yet the attitude of the radical farm movement towards the
British connection and for Canadian autonomy was only temporarily suspended. The anti-war policy began to grow again as a
result of war profiteering and graft (which were regularly featured in the farmers' press), inflation, and the conscription of
farmers' sons. The earlier themes of anti-imperialism and anti-
militarism were revived in the postwar period and became part
of Woodsworth's arsenal of arguments in the debates over Canadian autonomy in the House of Commons.

Canadian socialists did not hesitate at all in their firm and
immediate response against the war. They saw it as an imperial-

---

[16] W. L. Morton, *The Progressive Party In Canada*, p. 40.

ist emanation and a threat to the working class. More and more they were the source in the Trades and Labour Congress and in the local unions of bitter opposition to war-time policies of the Government and "big business". It was the socialists particularly who headed up the anti-conscription movements in the TLC and in English-Canada generally.[17] The war and all its political and social consequences in Canada played a decisive role in radicalizing the labor movement and in deepening the perception of imperialism as a special set of iniquities visited upon the working class by capitalism.

Woodsworth had associated himself with the anti-war sentiments of labor and farm groups. He did so first as a pacifist. He had been dismissed in 1916 from his position of Director of the Bureau of Social Research for opposing registration and in a letter to the *Free Press* he outlined the reasons for this opposition:

This registration is no mere census. It seems to look in the direction of a measure of conscription. As some of us cannot consciously engage in military service, we are bound to resist what—if the war continues—will inevitably lead to forced service.

In his resignation from the Ministry in 1918, he added a new ground for opposing the war:

The war had gone on now for four years. As far back as 1906, I had been led to realize something of the horror and futility and wickedness of War. When the proposals were being made for Canada to assist in the naval defence of the Empire, I spoke and wrote against such a policy. Since the sudden outbreak of the war, there has been little opportunity to protest against the curtailment of our liberties which is going on under the pressure of military necessity and the passions of war.

According to my understanding of economics and sociology, the war is the inevitable outcome of the existing social organization with its undemocratic forms of government, and competitive system of industry. For me, it is ignorance, or a closed mind, or camouflage, or hypocrisy, to solemnly assert that a murder in Serbia or the invasion of Belgium, or the glaring injustice and horrible outrage are the cause of War.

---

[17] See Martin Robin, *Radical Politics and Canadian Labour*, p. 119-77

Thus for Woodsworth war had become part of the capitalist system, to be resisted and fought on those grounds as well as on pacifist grounds. However, this was not expressed in any specific programmatic demand until the appearance of the Manifesto of the Manitoba Independent Labor Party in 1921, which contained a clause declaring "opposition to all forms of militarism, abolition of Secret Commitments, the development of a Democratic League of Peoples".

But it was after his election to Parliament that all these currents came together in Woodsworth's long and consistent advocacy of Canadian autonomy. In this he was supported by Irvine and many members of the farm groups, such as Agnes MacPhail, W. C. Good, E. J. Garland, Henry Spencer, and others. But it was Woodsworth who gave the lead on this question to the radical progressives.

While giving support to actions by Mackenzie King in asserting Canada's autonomy with regard to foreign policy commitments, Woodsworth went further by linking up the question of Canadian autonomy with the need to amend the BNA Act. In 1924, he introduced the first of a series of motions dealing in one form or another with the need to make the Constitution a Canadian Act, capable of being amended by "the governing powers of Canada". The passage of such a declaration, he said,

. . . means simply that Canada regards herself as grown up and that, being in that position she believes that she has the right to full self-determination and to the fullest measure of home-rule.

While Woodsworth's first motion along these lines was merely a formal declaration of intent, he made it clear that with such powers, Canada ought then to amend the Constitution to give the federal government the right to legislate on such things as labor matters, hours of work, and unemployment, and to reform or abolish the Senate. In presenting his case in that fashion Woodsworth ran into opposition from the French-Canadian members, who made it clear that they could not support any move that would transfer additional powers to the federal government or would give the federal government any rights to amend the constitution without a formula involving provincial consent. In this debate Mackenzie King disassociated himself from any suggestion in Woodsworth's speech and motion that Canada would not support Britain in future troubles. He explained that his position was only "that the responsibility and the extent of it will be determined by this Parliament . . . ."

In 1927, Woodsworth took up the attack again, this time calling for a "special select committee" of the House "to consider what amendments might be made in the British North America Act which, while conserving the principles of Confederation, would enable us more adequately to cope with the complicated problems which now confront Canada". He made it clear in a special plea to the French-Canadian members that what he had in mind by "conserving the principles of Confederation" was "a document . . . which would adequately guarantee the rights of all minorities". He directed an especially strong attack on "the reactionary character" of the Senate, and then proceeded to read into the record a document purporting to show that "fifty members of the Senate control and direct the economic life of Canada. That is to say that fifty Senators are directors of 334 commercial and financial institutions".

But this new motion which sought to give greater recognition to the fears of French Canadians was no more successful than before in winning their support. For Woodsworth would not budge from his position that greater centralism was indispensable for social legislation and hence a key principle for socialists. This was expressed in even stronger terms in the Regina Manifesto, which is understandable in the midst of the conditions of the Depression. But what is hard to understand, in view of Woodsworth's close contact with French-Canadian members of Parliament, especially Bourassa, is the failure of the Manifesto to even mention the word French-Canadian. They are included as one of Canada's many unnamed "racial and religious" minorities. There is not the slightest recognition that they occupy any special place as a nation or a national community, let alone the currently popular term "one of Canada's two founding races".

The Regina Manifesto on constitutional matters embodied the main lines of the position worked out by Woodsworth and the Ginger Group in Parliament during the twenties. It is interesting to note that when the Communist Party of Canada began to take up the question of the status of Canada, with the publication of Tim Buck's article *Canada and the British Empire*, in March 1925, it used much of the same material and argumentation as Woodsworth had developed up to that date. The main difference was that while Woodsworth called for the amendment of the British North America Act, the Communists called for "its repeal", and where Woodsworth advocated greater autonomy for Canada, Buck called for "complete independence from Downing Street".

There was also revealed a similar ambivalence to Mackenzie King, who while regarded as a capitalist spokesman, was nevertheless supported by both Buck and Woodsworth for his assertion of Canadian autonomy, and was regarded by them as a representative of the more enlightened and progressive sections of Canadian capitalism.

Both Woodsworth and Buck saw the increasing penetration of American capital into Canada, but neither of them saw this as being as great a problem as the continuation of the colonial or semicolonial relations between Britain and Canada. Buck in his article on this question and his subsequent historical writings on this period, credits a number of "bourgeois" spokesmen like Ewart, Sifton, Dafoe, Bourassa, as influencing the Communist position, but he never mentions Woodsworth. About the closest he comes to such a mention was in 1970 when he wrote as though the Canadian Communists had pioneered the demand for a change in Canada's status and that "our demand was acclaimed by many people, particularly among middle-class radicals".[18] Since the documents show that Woodsworth's first statements on this question antedate Buck's, it would be correct to say, using Buck's own terminology, that in fact "middle-class radicals" influenced the Communist position, rather than the opposite.

This was likewise true on the broader issues of the Constitution and on the question of the status of French Canada. The Communist Party submission to the Rowell-Sirois Commission in 1938 basically follows the approach to the BNA Act worked out by Woodsworth in the twenties, in the Regina Manifesto in 1933, and in the LSR publication of 1935 *Social Planning for Canada*. The concept of French-Canadian rights as being "minority rights" concerned only with religious and cultural questions, which was the Communist Party's position in its brief, was originated by Woodsworth and subsequently taken over by the CCF. It was not until 1943 with the publication of Stanley B. Ryerson's *French Canada* that the Communist Party developed its own independent position on French Canada.

The position of the CCF on constitutional questions was one of great importance in the development of Canadian social-democratic ideology. It combined anti-imperialist and anti-capitalist themes from the traditions of the farm and labor movements of English Canada with the social and economic demands

---

[18] Tim Buck, *Lenin and Canada* (Toronto, 1970), p. 72.

of socialism. In working out this mix, the role of Woodsworth and his colleagues in Parliament was crucial. This position was worked out by the time the CCF was formed and certainly well in advance of the entry of the academics into the socialist movement. This is not to belittle the contribution they made, but it was by way of deepening and refining the CCF's positions on important Canadian questions. It was indeed Woodsworth who developed the main outlines of this program.

Labor, Social-Democracy and Communism

The CCF was a merger between labor, farmer-labor, and farmer groups, together with the first significant influx of intellectuals to associate themselves publicly with the socialist movement in Canada. The labor groups were mainly labor-political organizations, such as the Independent Labor Party, sections of the Canadian Labour Party, and the remnants of the Socialist Party of Canada, particularly from British Columbia. There were no trade unions affiliated to the CCF although there had been such affiliations to the Canadian Labour Party. Local unions could affiliate to the CCF but few, if any, did. National unions could not join as there was no provision in the CCF constitution for this. The party at its outset did not seriously discuss linking up formally with the trade-union movement. Certainly Woodsworth, Irvine, Heaps, and MacInnis, representing labor groups in the House of Commons prior to the founding of the CCF, established a national reputation for their advocacy of labor causes in Parliament. They became indeed the unofficial parliamentary spokesmen for labor in Canada. Most of the main leaders of the Winnipeg General Strike joined the CCF at its inception: Woodsworth, Heaps, Queen, Ivens, Pritchard, Bray.* The parliamentary groups of the CCF always enjoyed close contact with trade-union officers at all levels including those who were members or supporters of the Liberal or Conservative Parties. But in the first number of years after the foundation of the CCF, trade unionists were not prominent as members of the CCF nor conspicuous as party supporters in elections.

---

* Russell joined sometime in the fifties. Johns remained out of politics and Dixon had died in 1931.

The trade-union movement was then weak, its numbers considerably reduced as a result of the mass layoffs and continued large-scale unemployment. By 1933 the organized labor movement dropped to between 12% and 15% of the labor force. The LSR in its book *Social Planning For Canada* made these observations of the labor movement in that period.

The unskilled in all industries are largely unorganized. The only industries in which trade unions are really powerful are railways, printing, building, clothing, skilled metal-work, and musical entertainment. . . . Moreover, the unionists are divided among themselves. In Quebec 26,894, more than half the total for that province, are [unions] completely controlled by the Roman Catholic hierarchy . . . [these unions are] . . . anti-militant, anti-class conscious and anti-socialist . . . 55,120 Canadian workers belong to "national" unions affiliated with all Canadian Congress of labor . . . a disproportionate amount of time and energy has been consumed in criticism and conflict between the All-Canadian and the American-affiliated Trade and Labor Congress groups. The smallest but most active group of unionists is the Workers' Unity League (21,253 members in affiliated unions) . . . Communist in its sympathies . . . Their militancy at a time when most orthodox unions are in a state of coma has nearly doubled their membership in a year . . . Most of the organized workers (167,720 or 58%) belong to the "international" unions . . . its leaders (in Canada) have been to say the least exceedingly cautious and its rank and file are not yet an effective political force, nor do they exert a unified influence on the labor market as a whole.

Moreover, the CCF did not have a thought-out or co-ordinated approach to trade unions outside of being in favor of them or expecting to get their votes. In the meantime, as the above passage indicates, the Communists were busy organizing the unorganized and gaining important footholds in those industries which were later to provide the basis for the industrial unionism that began to take root in Canada in 1936.

The success of the CIO in Canada changed significantly the strength and élan of the labor movement, and brought significant changes in the labor strategies of the CCF and Communists. The Communist Party of Canada dissolved the Workers' Unity League and moved into important positions in the new unions. Those forces in the CCF, particularly in Ontario, who had felt for some time that it should tie up with the trade unions in some kind of labor party, now pressed forward to try to make this the strategy of the CCF. As Orliffe's letter to Woodsworth* shows, they also considered it necessary to move in this direction in order to circumvent the Communists, whose new status in the trade unions represented a distinct threat to the CCF. Woodsworth was less than enthusiastic about the policy, but Lewis, Coldwell, MacInnis, Orliffe and others began to concentrate their efforts in this direction, regardless of Woodsworth. It is not clear why Woodsworth was unenthusiastic, but he appeared to view with distaste the kind of struggle which this policy entailed.

Yet the struggle between the CCF and the Communists which erupted in the CIO Unions was but the continuation of a conflict between the Communists and Socialists in the twenties, especially in the Canadian Labour Party, and between the CCF and the Communists almost from the day that the CCF was formed. The Communists adopted the line of the Comintern which regarded social democracy as the "last social basis of capitalism" and thereby the principal ideological enemy of communism. Under Stalin's direction, this was translated into a fight against social-democrats, and the Canadian Communists had from the late twenties regarded Woodsworth as their main target.

Woodsworth's attitude to the Communists became more hostile and rigid as their attacks on him increased. There was some truth to a statement he made in a letter he wrote in 1931 to his erstwhile colleague in the Methodist Church, Rev. A. E. Smith, who had become a leading Communist:

For old times sake I regret very much indeed that we should have apparently drifted so far apart. I must say that throughout the years I have tried my best to co-operate with you, and with the group with which you are working, but after the report of the Labor Defence League, which you signed, and after the scurrilous attacks in "The Worker" it has seemed to me impossible to work closely with those who persistently denounce us as enemies of the working class.

He repeated this idea in subsequent letters to Becky Buhay (May 20, 1933) and Sam Carr (April 10, 1935). He disapproved very strongly of David Lewis's withdrawal of a CCF candidate in a Toronto Provincial Riding so as not to take votes away from

---

* Orliffe to Woodsworth, January 31, 1938, quoted in Chapter V.

J. B. Salsberg, the Communist candidate.

There is very little if any factual truth in the accusations made by the Communist Party against the CCF and Woodsworth. Abella provides evidence that as the struggle within the CIO was joined both sides engaged in practices that to say the least were questionable.[19] But a victory for the CCF and a defeat for the Communists in that arena was inevitable, and by the time that was decided, the CCF had become the political arm of an important section of the trade-union movement, and the Communists were effectively removed as a serious threat to the CCF.

The main factor that made it possible for the CCF to win commanding heights in the CIO, and to become its political arm in 1943, was not the battle with the Communists, although that was important, but the attempt of the Hepburn Government to smash the CIO. The workers responded by electing thirty-four CCF members to the Provincial Parliament in 1943, thus establishing the CCF as a viable third party in Ontario. This was the "missing link" of support that the CCF had needed to complement its existing strength in the West.

Summary

The CCF was the inheritor of several radical strands in the political history of English Canada. It represented the legacy of the main elements of the Socialist and Labour Parties that started at the turn of the century, and which in twenty years had established socialism as a force in the Canadian labor movement. It also inherited some of the traditions of the radical farmers who in that same period began their "revolt against the new feudalism" which they carried into the twenties. From a thematic point of view, the CCF took over the anti-monopoly and anti-imperialist sentiments which had existed in both labor and farm movements. It also embodied the social reform traditions of the trade unions and, in the persons of some of its main leaders, it inherited the concerns of the Social Gospel.

Much discussion has taken place about the origins of Canadian socialism with special reference to its British roots and, in

---

[19] Abella, *Nationalism, Communism, and Canadian Labour.*

the case of its populist wing, to its American antecedents. That discussion is important as to its beginnings, but the CCF became a viable and important political force when it became Canadian, when it overcame the tendency of the early socialists to make abstract and doctrinaire pronouncements and began to study Canadian history, political economy, and constitutional law, into which it infused a socialist ideology.

But while there was no integrated theoretical rigor in the socialism of the CCF, its programs, its literature, and its parliamentary positions did have cohesion and discernible principles. This in fact is one of the criticisms that some contemporary historians level at the founders of the CCF, particularly at Woodsworth, when they assert that he "resisted all efforts to achieve rapid party growth through ideological compromise".[20] The tenor of this current social-democratic revisionism is to assert that Woodsworth was too much an "idealist" and not enough of a practical politician, with the further suggestion that this contributed to the lack of electoral success of the CCF.

At every stage, the character of social democracy and the kind of leaders it produces reflect fairly accurately the level of class consciousness which the radical section of the working class and middle class has attained. It represents the spontaneous striving of these people towards a form of socialism. The radicalism of the twenties and thirties produced leaders and programs that suited those times. Because it was in these two decades that social democracy finally emerged as the main ideology of anti-capitalist and anti-imperialist opinion in English Canada, the public perception of the CCF (and its successor, the NDP) still retains an image of social democracy based on those conditions. This may and indeed does cause embarrassment among some of the present leadership, but it is part of the roots of the CCF-NDP and cannot be obliterated. In fact, it is a source of strength of the social democratic ideology that explains in part why social democracy continues to exist and grow in spite of all the concessions and reforms made by liberals in response to labor demands. In other words, although reformism is the main aspect of social democratic practice, it is its anti-capitalist roots that give it the firm place it occupies in the Canadian ideological spectrum.

---

[20] S. M. Lipset, quoted in K. McNaught, *A Prophet In Politics* (Toronto, 1963), p. 267.

CHAPTER SEVEN

NEW SOCIALIST THEMES IN THE SIXTIES AND SEVENTIES

Socialism experienced an upsurge in Canada beginning in the sixties and continuing up to the present. The socialism of this period developed alongside the existing socialist movements but had many distinctive features in its themes, its sources, and in the composition of its advocates and supporters. Its most spectacular growth was in Quebec where, for the first time in Canadian history, a significant socialist movement took root among the French Canadians. This has had a considerable impact on the Quebec social and political environment. In English Canada, a new socialism also emerged, mainly among young intellectuals, particularly students and academics, who have produced some original theoretical applications of socialist theory to Canadian society and by so doing have already made an important contribution to Canadian political thought.

According to one early assessment of this upsurge, "it is above all the national question which has led to a revitalized Canadian socialism, and which is now the leading item on its agenda".[1] In Quebec it was the Quiet Revolution and the new

---

[1] Gerald L. Caplan and James R. Laxer, "Perspectives on Un-American Traditions in Canada", Ian Lumsden ed., *Close The 49th Parallel, etc. The Americanization of Canada* (Toronto, 1970), p. 310.

Quebec nationalism that gave socialism its impetus in this period. In English Canada it was a new national consciousness that arose in the wake of the crisis of U.S. imperialism, and the perceived threat of U.S. domination of Canada, that produced as one of its consequences the radicalization of the youth movement and, out of that, the growth of a new socialist variant.

There were, as well, new developments within Canadian social-democracy, chiefly the change from the CCF to a more labor-based NDP. In Quebec it was an indigenous social democratic party, the Parti Québécois (PQ), that emerged as the main radical and nationalist party in that province.

The Communist Party of Canada, which had been the first political party to raise the national question, was unable to attract the radical youth who were turning to Marxism through their perception of this issue. As a result of the revelations about Stalin, and the failure of the CPC to break with the rigid orthodoxy of the Soviet Communist party, the radical youth formed their own Marxist groups and parties outside of and often opposed to the Communist Party. They are providing the intellectual input into socialist thought that was missing in the early days of socialism in Canada.

The Quiet Revolution and the Growth of the Socialist Idea in Quebec

---

The "Quiet Revolution" has been variously interpreted and defined but there is general agreement that following the defeat of the Union Nationale in 1960, Quebec society experienced a series of sweeping changes in its political, economic, and social institutions, and above all in the ideological themes that expressed and stimulated peoples' behavior on the major issues.

The ideological monolith that was Quebec for over one hundred years, and which had been effectively described by Pierre Trudeau in his "Quebec on the Eve of the Asbestos Strike"*, shattered under the first impact of the Quiet Revolution. Ideas that had been interdicted by the Church and by the

---

* Pierre E. Trudeau, ed., *The Asbestos Strike* (Toronto, 1974).

conservative and reactionary politicians who had the support of the Church began to flourish. This was most dramatically seen in the upsurge in socialist thought, which previously had never commanded much support from French Canadians. Those in the past who defied the Church to become socialists had found themselves small minorities in English-dominated movements such as the Communist Party and the CCF. Neither of these two movements had ever felt comfortable with French-Canadian nationalism, which they regarded as essentially reactionary and as a diversion from the struggle for socialism which, in their view, had to be conducted on a Canada-wide basis, under centralized leadership.

The first new socialist organization to appear in this period combined socialism with nationalism. It was *L'Action socialiste pour l'indépendance du Québec* (ASIQ) founded in September 1960 by a group which published *La Revue Socialiste*, a magazine whose masthead proclaimed the slogan: "Pour l'indépendance absolue du Québec et la libération prolétarienne-nationale des Canadiens français". This was in fact one of the first separatist organizations in contemporary Quebec. It was organized by people who had been sometime members or supporters of the Parti Social-Démocratique (the provincial extension of the CCF) or of the Communist Party of Canada. They were able to reconcile what had been two different conceptions of socialism, through a common acceptance of nationalist goals.

The main theme in this periodical had been the concept of "décolonisation". Quebec, it was stated, is a colony and therefore the models for the Quebec socialists should be the third-world revolutions: Algeria, Cuba, China, Vietnam. The ideologists they looked up to, in addition to Marx and Lenin, were Fanon, Castro, Guevara, Mao, Ho Chi Minh.

The slogan of "décolonisation", which was directed mainly at targets outside of French-Canadian society, was coupled with the slogan of "laicisme" directed inwards. This time, anti-clericalism was not the formidable spectre it had once been in Quebec's history. The main elements pushing the Quiet Revolution were breaking down the ramparts of Quebec traditionalism. The Church itself was undergoing changes in this regard, so that in a certain sense the socialists were pushing on an open door on this question. Nevertheless, the diminution of the ideological role of the Catholic hierarchy in Quebec society was one of the factors that made it easier for the socialist idea to grow in these new conditions.

The merging of socialism with nationalism led in the direction of separatism and in particular to a concept of a path of socialism distinctive to Quebec. In a strong attack on what he called the Anglo-Saxon chauvinism of the CCF, and by implication of all Anglophone socialists, Raoul Roy set out a series of propositions which excluded, in advance, any joint efforts of French and English towards a common socialist goal:

It is not English Canada which is going to give us liberation. Either we are going to win it ourselves by our own battles or we are going to remain slaves.[2]

He rejected any concessions to what he called alternately "pan-Canadianism" or "pan-Saxonism". To him the cultural aspects of language, common history, and national oppression were of equal importance to the orthodox Marxist view of class versus class.

This approach to Quebec socialism was taken up by some of the Marxist groups which succeeded the ASIQ. One of the most significant was the group around the periodical *Parti pris* which was published from 1963 to 1968. They acknowledged the ideological debt they owed to Raoul Roy.

Nous devons à Roy l'usage des thèmes des décolonisation et de révolution.[3]

Marcel Rioux, a leading socialist scholar, gives this evaluation of the significance of *Parti pris*:

Of all the publications of the left during this period, it indeed appears that Parti pris *has had the biggest audience and the greatest impact on Quebec society.*[4]

One of the characteristics of this group was the age of its members. According to Rioux all of them were in their twenties when they founded the magazine in 1963. They were new to socialism, with no ties to the old left. They were intellectuals, the majority of them university students or graduates, the most con-

---

[2] Raoul Roy in *La Revue Socialiste* (été 1960), p. 27.

[3] Paul Chamberland in *Parti pris*, Vol. 2, no. 1, September 1964, p. 22.

[4] Marcel Rioux, "Remarques sur le phénomène *Parti Pris*", Joseph Bonenfant ed., *Index de Parti pris* (1963-1968) (Sherbrooke, 1975), p. 6.

spicuous of whom were Jean-Marc Piotte, Paul Chamberland, Gabriel Gagnon, and Pierre Maheu. According to a study made for the Royal Commission on Bilingualism and Biculturalism their magazine had a circulation of 3500, 60 per cent of which were university students, 20 to 30 per cent professionals, civil servants or intellectuals, and 10 per cent workers.[5]

While accepting Roy's thesis on decolonization, they drew different conclusions for what they called "the strategic perspective," which was outlined in a manifesto published September 1964.[6]

The struggle for independence is seen here as a "two-front" process in which the ultimate issue will be between, "on the one side capital and the bourgeoisie, whose profound interests are the same, whether Québécois, Canadian, or Yankee. On the other side are the popular classes, more and more dissatisfied with their lot but without a real class consciousness, and the elements of a revolutionary left which has not yet succeeded in linking up with these popular classes.... With this deepening, the struggle for national liberation at last falls into a total perspective. Independence formerly regarded as an end, is seen now as a prelude, a necessary step in a revolutionary struggle which both surpasses it and amplifies it".[7]

The Manifesto saw the situation as encouraging: the colonial power at Ottawa is "considerably weakened", the very existence of Confederation is "problematical". Inside Quebec those who were ruling on behalf of the colonial power—the clergy, the federalist ideologues, the old petty bourgeoisie—are all "in decline". This is not due to the rise of popular actions but to the new national bourgeoisie which, in seeking to build a state which serves their interests, destroys the "traditional social order" and creates conditions for an increase in the industrial proletariat.[8]

As the establishment of the bourgeois social order represents relative progress and as the winning of independence is a prelude to the revolutionary struggle, we are, in spite of ourselves, the objective allies of the national bourgeoisie in this first phase of the struggle and we must support them and push them forward in their reforms.

---

[5] Quoted in Sheelagh and Henry Milner, *The Decolonization of Quebec* (Toronto 1973), p. 183.

[6] *Parti pris*, Vol. 2, no. 1, Septembre 1969, p. 2-17.

[7] *Ibid.*, pp. 11-12 (my translation – N.P.).

[8] *Ibid.*, pp. 13-14.

But we must have no illusions: the progress registered on this front is due above all to the rising strength of the new bourgeoisie . . . it would be a total lack of initiative on our part if we would rely on them, it would be to become a rear guard. Our momentary alliance with the bourgeoisie is only a tactical one, and our principal efforts must be elsewhere.[9]

In order to fight the "true battle" which is on the "second front" against the social and economic content of colonialism,

We have to create a genuine peoples' party, revolutionary and socialist, to create it with the support and energy of the masses themselves. It will be a long and arduous task, but it is the only path that can lead to revolution.[10]

In the Manifesto *Parti pris* undertook to organize the new party and to provide through its columns the research, popular education, and even organizational instructions which were necessary in this direction. It closed with an exhortation to follow the examples of Africa, Asia, "and soon South America".

A second manifesto issued a year later[11] introduces a new proposal for immediate action. It asks its readers to take part in a "mouvement de Libération Populaire" (MLP), which in fact had already been in existence for several months and had participated in numerous demonstrations and public assemblies. "It is not yet the revolutionary party needed to make the revolution", but a transitional body "that will train militants to create such a party". The bulk of the manifesto is an analysis of class structure in Quebec, a description of alienation caused by colonialism, a discussion of the various types of revolutionary action that could be undertaken by a revolutionary party, and a fairly detailed elaboration of the tasks of the MLP.

The discussion in the Manifesto of the possible activities of a revolutionary party was clearly a response by the editors to a debate that was going on over the question of peaceful means of struggle or violent, clandestine or open, armed struggle or guerilla warfare. This debate had been precipitated by the growth of the Front pour la libération du Québec (FLQ), some of whose activists were close to *Parti pris*. In the Manifesto and in an

---

[9] *Ibid.*

[10] *Ibid.*, pp. 14-15.

[11] Manifeste 1965-66 du Mouvement de Libération Populaire et de la Revue *Parti pris* Vol. 3, no. 1-2, August-September 1965, pp. 2-41.

article in the same issue by Jean-Marc Piotte,[12] the majority of the *Parti pris* group rejected the idea of violence, terrorism, a clandestine organization and an underground press. It is not called for, according to Piotte, because all the conditions are favorable to open public activity and organization. The activities which are projected for the MLP consist of agitation, propaganda, political education of its members, and training of cadres capable of carrying the ideas of the movement into other groups. In another article Leandré Bergeron gives an outline of the kind of education members will receive: political, economic, social history of Quebec; socialist theory: the Utopians, Marx, Jaures, Lenin, French and Italian Marxism; socialism in practice in Yugoslavia, Israel, Algeria, Sweden, China, Russia, England; and the way to organize a socialist party.[13]

This debate continued in *Parti pris* throughout its six-year existence. The editors maintained a consistent position on two main questions: a rejection (which was always on tactical grounds, never on grounds of principle) of violence and of clandestine activity; and secondly a strong insistence that for Quebec, independence and socialism were inseparable. In an editorial in the January-February 1967 issue, *Parti pris* vigorously upheld the latter position:

Independence and socialism are unquestionably inseparable: besides the experience of several among us shows this clearly: some have come to socialism as a result of understanding the question of colonization and others have been led to work for independence through a social awareness. . . . There is no common strategy possible between socialist independentists and socialist anti-independentists inside the same party.[14]

What this argument involved above all was the relationship that should exist between the socialist movement or parties and the non-socialist separatist parties which were developing at the time. This particular editorial had to do with the Rassemblement pour l'indépendance nationale (RIN), which most of the *Parti pris* editors regarded as a left-wing group which the socialists

---

[12] Jean-Marc Piotte, "Où allons-nous?" in *Parti pris* August-September, 1965, pp. 64-85.

[13] *Ibid.*, p. 101.

[14] "L'indépendance au plus vite" in *Parti pris* January-February 1967, p. 3, (my translation—N.P.)

should support.[15] This was opposed by many of the contributors and supporters of *Parti pris* and the argument became particularly sharp and bitter in 1968 when René Lévesque was in the process of linking up with the existing separatist parties to form the Parti Québécois. The inability of the leading group within the *Parti pris* to resolve those differences resulted in the closing of the periodical in the summer of 1968.

In writing about the *Parti pris* Marcel Rioux said that in its short life, this periodical contributed greatly to the development of radical thought and action in Quebec.

(It has) . . . prepared the way to the politicization of the trade unions, to numerous political action movements and to an independentist party of social democratic character but which has a good number of socialists in its ranks. . . . The three pivots of reflection and analysis undertaken by Parti pris *have been the building of socialism, the politics of decolonization and the de-clericalism of Quebec. If the building of socialism is a universal objective, the other two are more specifically Québecois.* Parti pris *succeeded in tying all three together in an ideology adapted to the Quebec situation.*[16]

Parti pris, which started publication in October 1963, was followed by another magazine, *Socialisme 64*, launched in May 1964. This magazine has appeared in 24 numbers since then, the last one coming out in May 1974. Issue number 20, covering the months April, May, June 1970, announced a change in name to *Socialisme Québécois* and at the same time changed its outlook to an explicitly Marxist-Leninist view. Like the *Parti pris*, *Socialisme 64* and *Socialisme Québécois* have had an important impact on socialist thought in Quebec, reflecting and influencing the debates and conflicts within the developing socialist movement there. Marcel Rioux, one of the first editors, stated that discussions had gone on in 1963 about starting a socialist periodical with the group that a few months later founded Parti pris, but that no agreement was reached and eventually two separate magazines were published.[17] It is not quite clear what these differences were except for a remark which Rioux made, indi-

---

[15] The RIN led by Pierre Bourgault fielded candidates in the 1966 provincial elections and received 6% of the overall vote, with fairly high percentages in working-class ridings in Montreal.

[16] Marcel Rioux, "Remarques sur le phénomène *Parti Pris*," p. 8 (my translation – N.P.)

[17] Rioux, *ibid.*, p. 6.

cating that *Socialisme* would be directed at the Confederation of National Trade Unions (CNTU) and at the Quebec Federation of Labor (QFL) to try to make the labor movement socialist, and that this was considered as a more "precise option" than what the editors of *Parti pris* had in mind for their publication. Like the *Parti pris*, however, the new magazine subscribed to the nationalist view of socialism, which held that Quebec was a colony and therefore had to gain national liberation on the road to socialism. But *Socialisme 64* in its first issue modified the third-world syndrome as applied to Quebec:

French Canada walks a tight rope, swinging between the two types of societies and nations to which it belongs. From the socio-economic point of view, it is a developed country which takes part in an advanced capitalist economy and which therefore knows all the advantages as well as the problems of this kind of society. On the other hand it shared, and still does, with certain economically underdeveloped countries, the fact of being dominated politically, if not actually colonized. This is the uniqueness of Quebec and also its ambiguity. Having developed economically in symbiosis with the English-Canadians, and having attained a standard of living comparable to most advanced states, it still has the desire for national liberation which it has never won. Can it have the two simultaneously? . . . Only the socialists choose both options and they are the only ones to raise this challenge. [18]

Socialisme, unlike *Parti pris*, opened its pages to "all socialist tendencies". While it held the socialist concept of the unity of thought and action to be valid, it was satisfied to have its editors participate in socialist and radical movements or parties according to their personal and individual choices. [19] This gave the magazine an eclectic character with the main weight tending to a radical social-democratic rather than a revolutionary socialist position.

This changed when a new group, many of them formerly associated with *Parti pris*, took over editorial direction of the magazine in 1970, giving it a new name, *Socialisme Québécois*, and a new policy. In an editorial statement the new group denounced the "eclecticisme" of the past. This would be replaced by a policy of accepting only those contributions based on "the

[18] *Socialisme 64*, Vol. no. 1, p. 8.

[19] *Socialisme 65*, numéro 6, printemps 1965, p. 10.

principles of Marxism-Leninism, which alone are capable of forming a theory and political practice applicable to the realities of Quebec."[20]

The main tactical problem facing Marxist-Leninists in Quebec, according to this editorial, was that of defining their position towards the Parti Québécois. It saw the correct policy to be somewhere between the unconditional support given the PQ by some members of the Quebec left, and the opposite approach which could find no points of contact between the revolutionary left and the PQ.

But instead of the balanced approach forecast, the magazine's main concern was to criticize and attack the PQ. The tone of the criticism became strident and the position of the magazine became quite similar to the hostility which the old Marxist left had displayed towards every form of social democracy. This was typified by a vehement attack on Pierre Vallières by Gilles Bourque for joining the PQ,[21] and especially for his theoretical explanation of this move.[22] Bourque's article was so full of sarcasm and invective that in the next issue (which appeared two years later) Stanley Ryerson (like Bourque, a member of the editorial board) was constrained to publish a protest against "le ton employé dans son article".[23] The main burden of Bourque's attack was that the PQ was a party of a section of the national bourgeoisie and therefore could not be trusted to carry out essential changes in the structure of Quebec society. To suggest, as Vallières did, that the working class ought to support the PQ, would only delay the realization of a genuine working-class party based on a class-conscious proletariat.

In an article in Nos. 21-22 (April 1971), Luc Racine and Roche Denis saw the main weakness of the socialist movement in Quebec in the sixties to be its adoption of "bourgeois nationalism" and "l'appui tactique" which meant supporting bourgeois or petty-bourgeois parties as the first step in a two-stage struggle for socialism. This, said Racine and Denis, led to a whole number of related errors and shortcomings, chief among which was the failure to present a serious analysis of Quebec's economy

---

[20] *Socialisme Québécois*, avril, mai, juin, 1970, No. 20, p. 2.

[21] Gilles Bourque, "En Réponse à Pierre Vallières", *Socialisme Québécois* No. 23, 1972, pp. 125-138.

[22] These explanations were first written as articles in *Le Devoir* and *Québec Presse* and later expanded into a book *L'urgence de choisir* (1972).

[23] Stanley B. Ryerson, "nos débats difficiles" in *Socialisme Québecois* no. 24, 1974, p. 79.

and class structure, because the socialists looked at the Quebec nation mainly in cultural terms:

But Marxism is unthinkable without a critique of political economy and without a complete rupture with all the nationalist mixtures that one can imagine.[24]

Many of the editors and contributors to *Socialisme Québécois* had been participants in the socialist movements of the sixties and had played key roles in formulating the ideas of socialist nationalism which they were now repudiating. Yet this self-criticism does not tell the whole story. The ideological explosion which came as part of the Quiet Revolution was an all-pervasive *national* outburst that affected every segment of Quebec society, albeit in different ways. As Léon Dion said, socialism made its first major inroads in Quebec as part of this explosion because it took on a national identity which previous socialist movements there had woefully lacked.[25] The first new socialist organization in this period, L'Action socialiste pour l'indépendance du Québec (ASIQ), was at the same time one of the first separatist movements to appear in the Quiet Revolution. *Parti pris* inherited the ideas of the ASIQ and tried to build a mass separatist movement under socialist leadership. When that failed, it tried to work through the Rassemblement pour l'indépendance nationale (RIN) and did have some success. But the launching of the Parti Québécois (PQ), which quickly became the main separatist movement, seemed to invalidate this tactic, as there was little if any room for a revolutionary or even radical socialist point of view in this party.

Nevertheless it is incontestable that during the sixties the merging of socialism with nationalism popularized both ideas in Quebec, and helped radicalize a section of the population, particularly the students, academics and the activists in the labor movement.

The ideas of socialism had long been excluded from Quebec universities. This changed during the Quiet Revolution, and the study of socialism became very popular on the campuses. Marcel Rioux, himself a socialist who had been unable to teach in Quebec during the Duplessis regime, describes this development.

---

[24] *Socialisme Québécois* No. 23, 1972 pp. 7-8.

[25] Léon Dion, *Nationalismes et politique au Québec* (Montreal 1975), pp. 85-128.

In the space of three or four years among a good number of Quebec intellectuals, particularly the youngest, there took place a pronounced break with the interpretative framework of the past decades. Around 1963 the Dean of the Faculty of Social Science at the University of Laval remarked that the author most frequently quoted with approval at a colloquium on the social science, and whose name was scarcely known or mentioned in the past, had been Marx.[26]

The demand for Marxist courses and instructors grew during this period, particularly at the new provincial university, University of Quebec, but also at the University of Laval and the University of Montreal, which had been under clerical domination and direction prior to 1960.

The radicalization of the Quebec labor movement was an outstanding feature of the Quiet Revolution. This process had begun during the war, and the big turning point in labor militancy dates from the Asbestos Strike of 1949. Many Quebec specialists believe that the Quiet Revolution began with that epic struggle. At any rate there is substantial agreement for the proposition that the labor movement was an important component in bringing about the new Quebec. The adoption of the new labor code in 1964, the changes in 1965 which gave public service employees and teachers the right to strike, the deconfessionalization of the Catholic syndicates, the unification of the TLC and CCL unions, and the organization of a province-wide teachers' union—all contributed to the rapid growth of the trade-union movement. In fact during the ten years from 1960-1970, the rate of growth of Quebec trade unions was almost double that in English Canada. This growth in numbers and in militancy was accompanied by ideological changes within the labor movement, and certainly among the trade-union activists. Writing in 1974, Marcel Rioux had this to say:

Thus in the course of the two last decades, the trade union movements of Quebec have passed from a position of class collaboration, to a position of class struggle, from a federalist position to a position generally pro-independentist, and in a most significant way, from a pro-capitalist to a socialist position.[27]

---

[26] Marcel Rioux, "Remarques sur le phénomène *Parti Pris*," p. 7.

[27] Marcel Rioux, *Les Québécois* (Paris, 1974), p. 168.

Rioux was referring here to the manifestoes which the three trade union centrals, the CSN, the FTQ, and CEQ had adopted in 1971.* These manifestoes, drawn up and adopted separately, called for the workers to get rid of capitalism in favor of social-ism.[28] They laid the basis for a Common Front which led to the historic General Strike of May, 1972.

But while recognizing the importance of these manifestoes, they should not be exaggerated. They do not show that the trade-union movements of Quebec have shifted from a pro-capitalist to a pro-socialist position. The activists, including the top officers, perhaps have adopted that stance. But there is no evidence to indicate that the mass of workers have become so-cialists, nor that the trade unions were ready to become political parties as one observer has suggested.[29]

The trade unions remained trade unions, even to the extent of engaging, after the manifestoes, in some of the most intense in-fighting between the two main trade-union centrals over juris-dictional disputes. Even though the socialists have been urging for some time the establishment of a workers' party through the trade unions, nothing along these lines has happened and it is the PQ that has been the main beneficiary of the radicalism of Quebec labor.

Certainly the changes in the labor movement, the growth of socialist ideology, and the militant struggles which flared up during the sixties, had their impact on the rise of the PQ, and are reflected in its economic and social platforms. Outside of the main plank, which is the establishment of Quebec as a separate state, the platform, manifestoes, publicity material, and speeches by its leading personalities, are similar to those of social demo-cratic parties of the British, Scandinavian, and Canadian models.

But while there are similarities between the PQ and other social democratic parties, there are important historical, pro-grammatic, and sociological differences. Social democracy arose in most industrial societies *after* the growth of liberalism and socialism and as a variant of the latter. The Parti Québécois emerged mainly out of the Liberal Party and has never pro-

---

* CSN—Confederation of National Trade Unions (CNTU – formerly the Catholic Syndicates); FTQ—Quebec Federation of Labour (QFL), part of the CLC; CEQ—Confederation of Quebec Teachers.

[28] For the English translations of these manifestoes, see Daniel Drache ed., *Quebec— Only the Beginning* (Toronto, 1972).

[29] See Daniel Drache, p. XIII.

claimed socialism as its goal. Because of the absence of a mass socialist or labor party, the PQ has addressed its appeal to the workers on the basis of left liberal-reformism.

Its radicalism, however, is expressed in its separatism, which is not just a reform but involves a major structural change which cannot be brought about merely by legislative fiat. But the merging of a social democratic outlook with what is essentially a question of "décolonisation" sets up contradictions and tensions which are bound to affect the PQ and its policies. Pierre Vallières in his explanation for joining the PQ called the "independence process, a revolutionary process in a society such as ours",[30] which involves a "profound transformation of structures and social relations".[31] But the PQ, which is to be the instrument for carrying through this "revolutionary process", is not a revolutionary party. Its leaders have become vague as to how they propose to carry through this change. At first they asserted that a majority vote for the PQ would be sufficient justification for legislation separating Quebec from the rest of Canada. Then they introduced the idea that a referendum would be undertaken. But they have no clear picture as to what would follow an affirmative vote, or for that matter what they would do in the event of a negative vote.

In its social composition and especially in its leading core, the PQ represents a technocratic élite in Quebec, which wants a larger share in the economic life of the society. This élite aims to accomplish that through greatly enlarging the role of the state in the economy and through national measures such as language status, to give it a dominant position. It is interested in a managerial "revolution" which will be nationalist in form, state capitalist in content.

Vallieres's book *Choose!* is essentially a debate with the Marxist revolutionary groups which, since the collapse of *Parti pris* and the FLQ, have proliferated in Quebec. In particular Vallières is arguing with his erstwhile colleague in the FLQ, Charles Gagnon, whose views were later summarized in a pamphlet *Pour le parti proletarien* (Montreal, October 1972). Gagnon's argument is a revival of the thesis of the old Marxist left that social democracy is the main enemy in the labor movement. Gagnon states this in his opening sentence:

---

[30] Pierre Vallières, *Choose!*, p. 29.

[31] *Ibid.*, p. 31.

Together with the social democrats, the petty bourgeois nationalists constitute today the most dangerous ideological current in the labour movement.[32]

In Gagnon's view the urgent need is a revolutionary proletarian party on the Chinese, Vietnamese, and Albanian models. In the absence of such a party, the main efforts of the Marxists ought to be the ideological and organizational tasks needed to bring such a party into being. A major part of this work must be a constant attack on the social democrats and nationalists, mainly the PQ. He rejects the idea that the trade unions can build such a party. This can be done only by a revolutionary vanguard, completely devoted to Marxist-Leninist theory and practice.

The rapid growth of socialist thought and action in Quebec since 1960 has been one of the most significant by-products of the Quiet Revolution. A well-known Quebec political scientist in a study of Quebec politics said that "taken together, nationalism and socialism are now the major themes of the Quebec political culture".[33] An important feature of this development has been the volume and high quality of material written by socialists about Quebec society. Much of this material constitutes new approaches to Quebec history, sociology, economics, and politics, the usefulness of which has been acknowledged by many non-socialists such as Léon Dion. The greatest impact in this regard was made by two studies jointly authored by Gilles Bourque and Nicole Laurin-Frenette on the class structure of Quebec and the nature of Quebec nationalism.[34] They posit three nationalisms that have dominated Quebec history, but analyse them from widely different criteria. The first two are the nationalism of sections of the petty-bourgeoisie as their needs changed.[35] The dominant nationalism up until 1960 was a conservative ideology which from 1760 to 1840 was based on the seigneurs and high clergy, and from 1840 to 1960 on a combination of the rural and urban petty-bourgeoisie, the latter satisfied to be a minor partici-

---

[32] Charles Gagnon, *Pour le parti proletarien* (Montreal, 1972), p. 9.

[33] Daniel Latouche, "Quebec", Bellamy, Pamett, Rowat eds., *The Provincial Political Systems* (Toronto, 1976), p. 28.

[34] "Classes sociales et idéologiques nationalistes au Québéc (1760-1970)", *Socialisme Québécois* No. 20, (1970) and "La Structure nationale québécoise" in Nos. 21-22, (1971).

[35] *Ibid.*, No. 20, pp. 34-35.

pant in the Canadian capitalist economy. The second nationalism which flourished between 1800 and 1840, and again since
1950, represents that section of the petty-bourgeoisie that wants
dominant control over the economy. But in dealing with the
third nationalism, the authors use a different methodology:

*. . . A nationalist ideology linking national liberation to the instal-
lation of a socialism controlled from below. This ideology promoted
by the activists in the workers' movement and the intellectuals,
attempts to translate the aspirations of the working class and to
formulate the conditions for its liberation.*[36]

The first two nationalisms are seen from the outside through
an objective analysis of the prevailing ideologies and of the
interests of the petty-bourgeoisie which they express. The third is
seen from the inside as the ideology formulated and promoted
by the "activists in the workers' movement and the intellectuals"
who have the responsibility for defining the links between "nationalism and national liberation" as well as the conditions for
working-class liberation.

These two studies are widely quoted for the new interpretation they make of Quebec society and in particular for their
original approach to the study of Quebec nationalism. They are
also used in the left to buttress the opposition of the revolutionary groups to the PQ. As a result, they repudiate the nationalism
of the socialists in the sixties as a non-class analysis which led to
support for petty-bourgeois liberalism and social democracy.
Most of the Marxist groups now share this repudiation of "petty-
bourgeois" nationalism in favor of a concept which expresses
what they consider to be the genuine interests of the working
class and which is aimed at bringing that class to the leadership
of the nation.

Yet even though they have a common theoretical framework
in the theories of Marx and Lenin, and a common hostility to
the PQ, they cannot agree on a strategy for Quebec socialists.
Their differences are often bitter and acrimonious. The main
reason for this hostility is that most of the Marxist groups in
Quebec (as in English Canada) now mirror the international
divisions in revolutionary socialism. There are several Maoist
parties, groups, and circles, two or three Trotskyist organizations,

---

[36] *Ibid.*, p. 35.

and the Communist Party based on the Soviet model. The Maoist and Trotskyist groups are made up mostly of Francophones and are growing. The CP remains largely Anglophone.

The Communist Party of Quebec has proposed "a mass federated party of the working people", which would consist of the CP and the NDP, the trade unions, and "other left groups" providing they are "genuine". The CP would have a special status "because this party is based on scientific socialism, which is the revolutionary generalization of the experience of the working class of the world".[37] On the other hand, Charles Gagnon has formulated the perspective of the Maoist groups which calls not for a mass working-class party but for a Leninist vanguard of revolutionary élites. It rejects the idea that the CP already fulfills that role. Whereas the CP in its statement proposes a working peoples' party on a broad common denominator and cautions against "an intense ideological struggle", those Trotskyists who support the proposal for a mass workers party criticize the CP's conception of it as "reformist" and insist on a more ideologically based party.

But the existence of a mass party such as the PQ, which is both nationalist and social democratic, makes the proposal for another mass party on the left problematical. Léon Dion puts it this way:

The Parti Québécois intends to be the place for integrating the diverse groups on the left, but between the social democracy which it proposes and Marxism-Leninism, no reconciliation appears possible, at least on the ideological level.[38]

Nevertheless, in spite of the ideological differences, the Marxist left and the PQ do interact. The existence of a strong and growing Marxist movement helps to radicalize the PQ, or at least keeps it from going too far and too fast to the right. Léon Dion has pointed out that the PQ emerged in large measure as a response to the activities and ideological work of the socialists.[39]

Socialism and social democracy are thus joint products of the Quiet Revolution, and have become firmly entrenched in the ideological spectrum of Quebec. They continue to grow, each in

---

[37] *For A Mass Federated Party of The Working People* issued by Samuel Walsh, President, Parti Communiste du Québec, (Montreal, November 1973), see p. 13.

[38] Dion, *Nationalismes et politique au Québec*, p. 110.

[39] *Ibid.*, p. 38.

its own way. The PQ has become in a short period the major electoral instrument for social change in Quebec. From 1967, when René Lévesque walked out of the Liberal Party convention taking with him 100 delegates, to the elections of 1976 when the PQ under his leadership became the government of the Province, this movement has served as the main measure of radical discontent in Quebec.

The Marxist groups, which have proliferated since 1970, do not constitute a mass movement in any sense, but they do represent an important development among the young intellectuals who have broken completely with liberal or social democratic values to embrace and propagate a Marxist view of capitalist society. In spite of fierce differences between these groups as to what this view is when applied to Quebec, the collective impact of their ideological and political work should not be underestimated. They are a significant part of the radicalization of Quebec. They already do perform to some extent the role which Marx and Engels prescribed for such movements in *The Communist Manifesto*, "that section which pushes forward all others".

But a major problem which confronts and confounds the Marxists is the delineation of their relationship to the PQ. The appeal of the editorial board of *Socialisme Québécois* in its first issue, April 1970, for a more constructive, though critical, attitude toward the PQ is still rejected by most of the Marxist groups. Their approaches range from the Maoist designation of the PQ as the main enemy, to the CP's call for a mass workers' party to by-pass and eventually destroy the PQ. But this prospect, always illusory, appears even more remote after the election of the PQ to the government of Quebec, with solid working-class support.

Since the differences between the Marxist groups are reflections of international divisions, they are not likely to be resolved in the near future. They undermine but do not eliminate the impact of Marxism in present-day Quebec.

The New Socialism in English Canada After 1960

The cold war which flourished during the fifties did considerable damage to the radical, socialist, and communist movements. The

Communist Party of Canada (then called the Labor-Progressive Party) lost heavily in membership, in electoral support, and in its positions in the trade-union movement. Its decline was aggravated and accelerated by the revelations of the Communist Party of the Soviet Union in 1956 and by the uprisings in Poland, Hungary, and East Germany which followed.

The CCF supported the major thrust of the cold war. In the bitter struggle it waged in the trade-union movement against the Communists, it did not hesitate to make abundant use of the anti-Communist prejudices of that period.

But the CCF found that the cold war, while mainly directed at Communism, also undermined support for socialism and social democracy. The federal elections of 1953, 1957, and 1958 resulted in the CCF getting their lowest votes since the war: 11%, 11%, and 9%, respectively. A history of the CCF says of this period that "the party had been slowly bleeding to death at the polls".[40]

The reaction of most of the CCF leadership to this decline was to move further to the right. According to Walter Young this shift began as early as 1950 when Frank Scott, then National Chairman, proposed at the CCF Convention the redrafting of the Regina Manifesto. The process proved to be a "lengthy one, involving six years, three national conventions, and a plethora of documents, minutes, drafts, and memoranda".[41] It culminated in the Winnipeg Declaration of 1956 which Young characterizes as follows:

The Winnipeg Declaration lacked the fire of the Regina Manifesto and was accepted only after long, and at times bitter debate. The members resented the change in policy despite their earlier acceptance of the need for change. The leaders of the CCF were attempting, in good faith, to provide the party with a central body of doctrine that had none of the revolutionary overtones of the Regina Manifesto and which would, they earnestly hoped, be more acceptable to the public and place their party in a more favourable light.[42]

Another historian declared of the Winnipeg Declaration that

---

[40] Walter D. Young, *The Anatomy of a Party: The National CCF 1932-61* (Toronto, 1969), p. 128.

[41] *Ibid.*, p. 126.

[42] *Ibid.*, p. 129.

"friends and foes of the CCF alike, unanimously agreed that it constituted a significant shift to the right".[43] He quoted Andrew Brewin, a CCF leader, who exulted in the Winnipeg Declaration with these words:

Let those of us who are active in the CCF make it clear to all who believe in the liberal tradition and in a living and vigorous democracy that the CCF is their party.[44]

Another compelling reason for adopting the Winnipeg Declaration was, according to Young, "the pending unification of the two major labour congresses in Canada . . . "[45] and the hope that the new unified trade-union center would adopt the CCF as its political arm. This had long been the aim of David Lewis in particular, and now at last it seemed on the verge of being realized. There is no doubt that the elimination of all references to socialism was thought necessary to win the support, or at least the neutrality, of those trade unions whose American executives were hostile to socialism of any kind. The Winnipeg Declaration eased the way for the Canadian Labour Congress to adopt a resolution at its April 1958 Convention which called for

. . . a broadly-based people's political movement which embraces the CCF, the Labour Movement, farm organizations, professional people and other liberally-minded persons.[46]

This resolution led to the joint creation by the CLC and CCF of a National Committee for a New Party, which crystallized in 1961 in the formal dissolution of the CCF and its replacement by the New Democratic Party, which was endorsed by the CLC. The main difference between the CCF and the NDP was structural: the NDP could affiliate trade unions *en bloc* with delegate rights at NDP conventions based on the membership of each affiliated union.

Certainly the shift to the right as typified by the Winnipeg Declaration was a step backward. It expressed a conservative mood in the country at the time. But there is some truth in Walter Young's observation that "it remains a fact of politics

---

[43] Leo Zakuta, *A Protest Movement Becalmed* (Toronto, 1964), p. 93.

[44] *Ibid.*, p. 97.

[45] Young, *The Anatomy of a Party*, p. 131.

[46] Quoted in Young, *The Anatomy of a Party*, p. 132.

that the programme does not change the popular image of the party, nor does it change the individuals who stand on it".[47]

The NDP came into existence at a time when the cold war was beginning to recede. Its federal and provincial votes climbed. Its connection with the CLC gave it a new and stronger image.

It was attracting some of the young people from the radical student movements that were flourishing at the time. It began to express some of the concerns of the new Canadian nationalism that was rising in response to the growing U.S. control of the Canadian economy. All of these developments culminated in the Waffle movement which burst out in the NDP in 1969 and which, for the next three years, made a major impact on Canadian socialist thought and action.

The group that drafted and signed the "Waffle Manifesto" was a cross section of the NDP: students and young academics, many of whom were relatively new in the party, elected members of various legislative bodies, trade unionists, and officers at all levels in the NDP organization. Its aim was to strengthen the NDP by "making it a truly socialist party", merging socialism and Canadian independence. The Manifesto was a sharp attack on U.S. "corporate capitalism", "characterized by militarism abroad and racism at home" and now "the dominant factor shaping Canadian society". Canada was fast becoming "an economic colony of the United States". There did not exist "an independent Canadian capitalism" capable of resisting this trend and therefore the fight for Canadian independence had to rely on the socialist forces in Canada, in which the key political role would be played by the NDP:

The struggle to build a democratic socialist Canada must proceed at all levels of Canadian society. The New Democratic Party is the organization suited to bringing these activities into a common focus. The New Democratic Party has grown out of a movement for democratic socialism that has deep roots in Canadian history. It is the core around which should be mobilized the social and political movement necessary for building an independent socialist Canada. The New Democratic Party must rise to that challenge or become irrelevant. Victory lies in joining the struggle.

There was no mention in the Manifesto of two issues which

---

[47] *Ibid.*, p. 134.

later became important to the Waffle supporters: women's liberation and the independence of the Canadian trade unions. On the Quebec question the Manifesto limited itself to the declaration that Canada consists of two nations, which was merely a restatement of the founding program of the NDP in 1961. In 1971 as part of the campaign of James Laxer for the leadership of the NDP, the Waffle went beyond that by proposing NDP support for the right of Quebec to self-determination up to and including separation, if desired by the Quebeckers.

The Waffle Manifesto and the subsequent literature of the Waffle groups remained within a social-democratic frame of reference, although always more militant and radical than the main body of the NDP. Even those that left the NDP in 1972 to form a new party conceived of their party as little more than a left-wing NDP. Two of the principal originators of the Waffle underlined their positive estimation of Canadian social democracy in an article published shortly after the formation of the Waffle:

The culture and traditions of the Canadian working class are the lifeline of the Canadian left. The great achievements of the Canadian left—the political affiliation of many of the trade unions and the strengths of social democracy—grow out of that culture and tradition... The NDP is the most important institutional expression of the Canadian left. More than any other organization, it embodies the cultural and political traditions of the Anglo-Canadian working class... The NDP brings together the essential constituencies—workers, farmers, students, intellectuals—that are necessary in building a mass socialist movement. [48]

To say that the Waffle was left-wing social democracy is not to belittle it, but to emphasize its importance and uniqueness. It attracted into the NDP many of the young people who had participated in the New Left activities and who became enthusiastic at the possibility of radicalizing the NDP. The debates that it sparked within the NDP and its periphery produced some important new studies of Canadian society, and stirred up a controversy on theoretical and ideological questions of a kind which had been absent from social democratic ranks since the foundation of the CCF in the thirties. Its impact went beyond

---

[48] Gerald L. Caplan and James R. Laxer, "Perspectives on Un-American Traditions in Canada", pp. 314-15.

the NDP and made a strong impression on the developing nationalist movement in English Canada. But it made that impact only so long as it was functioning as part of the NDP.

The key study that initiated this debate was the work of Kari Levitt, a McGill economist. Written in 1967, published in 1968 as a monograph in a Caribbean journal *New World*, it was expanded and published in 1970 under the title *Silent Surrender*. In his preface to the book, Mel Watkins reports that since its first appearance in mimeographed form it "has already had an active underground life".[49] Whatever Watkins implies by that phrase, it should not be taken literally. Desmond Morton reports that in December 1968, at the invitation of David Lewis, Kari Levitt presented her paper to the federal caucus of the NDP, hardly an underground experience![50] There is no doubt that by the time the Waffle Manifesto was drawn up, most of the signatories, and certainly all of the authors of that Manifesto, were fully acquainted with Levitt's study, and were enormously influenced by it. That is what Watkins probably had in mind when he wrote:

Professor Levitt has become one of the few Canadian academics to earn the respect of Canadian radicals. . . . [51]

Léon Dion believes that this book, when translated into French in 1972 (*La Capitulation tranquille*), had an equal if not greater impact on the socialist movement in Quebec:

The devastating thesis of Kari Levitt concerning the American domination of Canada, notably through the complex role of the multinational corporation, has greatly reinforced the convictions of the spokesmen of socialist and social-democratic nationalism on this question (it was the economic adviser of the PQ, Jacques Parizeau, who wrote the preface to the French edition of this work). [52]

But while most of the Waffle, and the radicals outside it, accepted Levitt's book without argument, a series of related questions surfaced around which there was no agreement: is

---

[49] Mel Watkins, Preface to Kari Levitt, *Silent Surrender* (1970), p. XVII.

[50] Desmond Morton, *NDP: The Dream of Power*, p. 91.

[51] Mel Watkins, Preface to *Silent Surrender*.

[52] Dion, *Nationalismes et politiques au Québec*, p. 100.

Canada a colony, a sovereign nation, a dependency, or a secondary imperialist power? Does the Canadian capitalist class rule Canada on its own, or in partnership with U.S. capitalists, or is it a comprador class consisting of nothing more than managers of a branch plant economy and a branch plant state? And under each of these possible analyses, what were the strategic implications for the left?

These and related questions were debated in public forums, conferences and conventions, in a large number of periodicals, and particularly in several books. Probably the most influential of these were: *Close The 49th Parallel* (Toronto, 1970), edited by Ian Lumsden; *Capitalism and The National Question in Canada* (Toronto, 1972), edited by Gary Teeple; *(Canada) Ltd. The Political Economy of Dependency* (Toronto, 1973), edited by R. M. Laxer; and *Imperialism and The National Question In Canada* (Toronto, 1975) by Steve Moore and Debi Wells.*

The first three asserted and defended the theory of Canadian dependency, whereas the Moore-Wells thesis refuted it. The essay which attracted most attention was R. T. Naylor's "The Rise and Fall of The Third Commercial Empire of The St. Lawrence" in Teeple's volume. In it Naylor postulates that the Canadian capitalist class has been "a mercantile one, accumulating wealth through circulation rather than production", which leads to an endemic "perpetuation of colonialism and underdevelopment".[53] Laxer in his book agrees with the main burden of Naylor's argument but adds that as a consequence of its role as a hinterland for U.S. industry, Canada is being "de-industrialized". He calls this "the most crucial aspect of the analysis presented in this volume", and says:

The drive to de-industrialize Canada is not only a strategic aim of U.S. government policy as it tries to solve the crisis of overproduction, now aggravated by its inter-imperialist rivalries with Japan and Western Europe. Such a policy to shift manufacturing and jobs to the U.S. has received official support from the top leadership of American labour.[54]

---

* The fact that publishing houses, including some of the old established firms, were not only willing but anxious to put out Marxist books was in itself an indication of the wide interest in such studies.

[53] R. T. Naylor, Teeple ed., *Capitalism and The National Question In Canada*, p. 1.

[54] R. M. Laxer, ed., *(Canada) Ltd.*, p. 9.

In their book Moore and Wells take issue with the de-industrialization thesis, which they call "a myth". They also reject the whole concept of Canadian colonialism which this thesis, in their words, is designed to support. They produce figures to support their argument that "de-industrialization" is a process going on in *all* advanced capitalist countries. The increasing role of technology creates a relative decline in the work force engaged in manufacturing, while at the same time producing a growth in the public and private service sectors.

There are some other studies which appear in these books, particularly those of Leo Johnson, S. B. Ryerson, Frenette and Bourque* (in the Teeple volume) and by Daniel Drache (in Lumsden), which provide new and original insights into Canadian class structure, French-Canadian nationalism, and Canadian ideologies. Johnson in his article makes the point that in the past most of the theoretical work on Canada done by Marxists has been polemical rather than analytical, which is true, although in making exceptions to this assertion, he ignores or misses some important studies which are referred to in Chapters 5 and 6 of this book. There is no doubt that the new Marxists are beginning to provide an intellectual input which was largely missing in the past. C. B. Macpherson, in his review of the Teeple book, stated that some of the new analyses that have been produced ought to lead to "rethinking among several parts of the Canadian left".[55]

There is a big gap, however, between the new analyses that were being made of Canadian society and the kind of political conclusions that were deduced from them. These point to a continuing problem that has confronted generations of Canadian socialists on the relationship between theory and practice. Daniel Drache after arguing persuasively that the Canadian bourgeoisie has never acquired a national consciousness, says, "analysis leads to strategy. Ideas require testing in practice".[56] Robert Laxer in his foreword to *(Canada) Ltd.* is more categoric:

A sound plan of action can arise only from a sound analysis and

---

* This was an abridged translation of the study which was published earlier in *Socialisme Québécois*.

[55] C. B. Macpherson, "Marxism In Canada: A New Beginning", *Canadian Dimension*, Vol. 9, No. 7-8, p. 72.

[56] Daniel Drache, "The Canadian Bourgeoisie and Its National Consciousness", I. Lumsden ed., *Close the 49th Parallel*, p. 22.

*cannot be logically separated from it. Conversely a political eco-
nomic analysis which has no strategic consequences makes no
contribution either to developing understanding or towards action.*[57]

The problem is reflected in the fact that from analyses that
are quite similar, the authors drew different tactical conclusions.
Moreover, in the case of the leading group in the Waffle, their
unchanging analysis led to a whole series of changing "strategic
consequences". As for the proposition that "ideas require testing
in practice", this seems to imply that if the practice does not
produce the results expected, the ideas themselves must be
changed. But this formula has rarely, if ever, been put to its own
test.

Drache proposed as his strategy the idea "that there should
be people's committees to investigate, document, then fight
American imperialism in Canada".[58] Those authors in *Capitalism and the National Question in Canada* who made political
proposals (Teeple, Scott, Howard, Naylor, Lipton) are much
more specific and detailed than that. Teeple summarizes these
proposals in the last three paragraphs of his introduction. All
existing parties, he claims, are unable or unwilling to stand up to
American domination: "the Liberals, and Conservatives, are
mainly American", "the NDP keeps the trade union movement
divided and weak"; "the Communist Party of Canada remains
hopelessly dogmatic . . . the Social Credit party hopelessly irrelevant", "the Parti Québécois is a wolf in lamb's wool. . . ." From
these postulates he draws two main immediate tasks: "the formation of a new political party" and "more immediate though is
the question of detaching the trade unions from American control and making them into 'schools of socialism', centres in
which *to begin* the conscious struggle of labour against foreign
and domestic capital".[59] Jack Scott and Roger Howard in their
detailed treatment of the U.S. control of Canadian trade unions,
make this last task even more immediate than Teeple does:

*It is clear that a total break, organizationally and
ideologically, with the internationals is the necessary first step toward building of a movement that will serve the real interests of Ca-*

---

[57] Robert Laxer, *(Canada) Ltd.*, p. 25.

[58] Daniel Drache, *op. cit.*

[59] Teeple, *Capitalism and the National Question in Canada*, p. XV

nadian workers.[60]

What these authors have done is compress into an organizational *first step* almost the entire historical process of politicizing the working class in Marxist terms. To win the workers to an "ideological break" with capitalist and imperialist ideas, and to turn the trade unions into "schools for socialism", can only be done, they say, by establishing Canadian unions.

The Waffle strategy went through a number of stages: first as part of the NDP, second outside of the NDP but as a movement not a party, third the formation of a party based on socialism and independence, and finally to proposals by the leading group to emphasize independence over socialism.[61]

The fact that these authors and groups are attempting to posit an alternative to the existing political system and parties is by itself an important development of the present period. In doing so, many of them, instead of "rethinking" those ideas of the old left which have not measured up to the test of practice, are repeating them.

This is particularly true of the Marxist attitude towards Canadian social democracy. Teeple, who called the Communist Party of Canada "hopelessly dogmatic", revives what undoubtedly must rank as a product of the CP's worst dogmatism: its analysis and approach to the CCF-NDP. In fact he quotes approvingly from the book *Socialism and the CCF*, which was published by the CPC in 1934 and which was based on Stalin's designation of social-democracy as "social-fascism". He paraphrases this and applies it to the NDP as well:

The belief in the principles of liberal democracy and social reformism has made the CCF-NDP a major buttress for the colonial, capitalist system in Canada.[62]

This passage implies that if there was no CCF-NDP the "colonial, capitalist system in Canada", would be considerably weaker than it is. This argues as though social democracy is something created by social democrats, whereas in all advanced

---

[60] Roger Howard and Jack Scott, "International Unions and the Ideology of Class Collaborations", Teeple, *op. cit.*, p. 80.

[61] See Virginia Hunter, "Why I Left the Waffle", *Canadian Forum*, March 1975.

[62] Teeple, p. 237

capitalist countries, social democracy has evolved out of the labor movement and sections of the petty-bourgeoisie and is the spontaneous expression of anti-capitalist consciousness of these classes and groups. It has followed a similar pattern in Canada, in spite of Naylor's completely unhistorical essay in which he claims that CCF-NDP in Western Canada has not evolved beyond the ideological framework of the Métis fur traders in their struggle with the Hudson's Bay Company in 1849![63]

The problem which the left confronts with respect to defining its relations with the NDP (and also with the PQ) was illustrated by the following passage, which is not at all untypical:

One can only conclude from this brief examination of the NDP that not only is it not a viable channel for radical politics, but it does not even answer the requirements of contemporary reform-minded left liberals. Too bad it is still there cluttering up the left of the political spectrum.[64]

One might pose the question: if the NDP "does not even answer the requirements of contemporary reform-minded left liberals", how come "it is still there, cluttering up the left of the political spectrum"? This question is not posed facetiously but to suggest that a proper analysis might start with this proposition, rather than conclude with it. If the NDP "is still there" in spite of the best efforts of the CPC to destroy it in the past, or of some contemporary Marxists to wish it away, it must indeed answer some of the requirements of left-moving Canadians. An analysis that sets out to answer that question might lead to very different conclusions of a practical nature than those which have been tried and failed in the past.

The debate in the left about Canada's status, the role and character of the Canadian bourgeoisie, and the form for working class political action, has been taken up systematically by a whole number of new Marxist groups that have emerged in this period. Many of their members have come out of the radical student movements and Waffle to join or form what they consider movements with precise and definite objectives and working within a tight ideological and theoretical framework. All of

---

[63] R. T. Naylor, "The Ideological Foundations of Social Democracy and Social Credit," Teeple, p. 256.

[64] Evelyn Dumas and Edward Smith, "The NDP Since Its Founding", D. Roussopoulos ed., *Canada and Radical Social Change*, (1973), p. 119.

them consider themselves Marxist-Leninists and most of them follow international models: Maoist, Trotskyist, and Soviet. The latter is represented by the CPC, and is the one Marxist party that is not a product of this period.

The Maoist movement is made up of a party, the Communist Party of Canada (Marxist-Leninist), and embryonic party La Ligue Communiste (Marxist-Leninist), and a number of groups around publications *En Lutte, Mobilization, Canadian Revolution*. The Trotskyist groups are the Revolutionary Marxist Group, the League for Socialist Action, the Socialist League, the Group Marxiste-Revolutionnaire and the International Socialists. The one group that is not identified easily with any international model is the Canadian Party of Labour, which is an emanation of the Students for a Democratic Society.

The Maoists, who probably account for the majority of the new Canadian Marxists of this period, are prompted by the model of a successful socialist revolution, as were the generation of socialists who followed the Lenin path after the Bolshevik Revolution of 1917. They see in the Chinese experience the model of a continuing revolution in which movements from below counter and defeat the tendency for bureaucracies to grow and become all-powerful. With the sharpening of the Sino-Soviet split, the propaganda of the Maoists in Canada reflects an ever-increasing hostility to the Soviet Union and to the Soviet-backed Canadian party whose leadership is termed "revisionist" and "social imperialist". All the Maoist groups have explicitly revived the role of Stalin, whose work they describe in terms reminiscent of the Soviet propaganda prior to 1956.

Their view of the path to socialism in Canada is direct and dogmatic. In an editorial entitled *Against the Bourgeois State*, one of these groups outlined the path for the dictatorship of the proletariat in one paragraph:

It is because the Marxist-Leninists and the class conscious workers understand the role of the State, that they fight against the trade union leaders, the reformists of the PQ and the NDP, the revisionists of the false "Communist" Party of Canada ... the sole solution to the crisis of capitalism is the proletarian revolution where under the direction of their Party, the workers and broad masses will completely destroy the bourgeois state, to build a new State, their state, the workers' state, the dictatorship of the proletariat.[65]

---

[65] *La Forge*, Montreal, January 29, 1976, p. 3.

With such an apocalyptic view, the Maoists are reluctant to engage in struggles around immediate demands. In their statement distributed at the CLC demonstration in Ottawa in March 1976, they warned the workers that they would be unable to improve their conditions or defeat wage controls unless "the capitalist system is overthrown".

The Maoist position on the status of Canada, in the words of one of their principal spokesmen, is that "Canada is a nation economically dominated by a single great power to an extent not experienced by any other single country, with the possible exception of some countries in the Russian sphere".[66] The Canadian bourgeoisie is completely "a comprador" class working on behalf of U.S. imperialism and therefore "the principal contradiction", to use Mao's phrase, is the conflict between the working class and U.S. imperialism and "its Canadian lackeys". This struggle must be fought under "centralized leadership" uniting French and English in one class struggle. The national question in Quebec is only a secondary contradiction and therefore must be subordinated to the principal contradiction.[67]

An interesting feature of this period is the resurgence of interest among radical youth in the life and works of Leon Trotsky. Several new Trotskyist groups have emerged alongside the existing Trotskyist movement, the League for Socialist Action. The attraction of Trotsky lies in the fact that he is historically identified with the struggle against the bureaucracy and dictatorship of Stalin and the deformation of the Soviet state.

The various Trotskyist groups are linked in several ways with the Fourth International which puts them in touch with various Trotskyist movements throughout the world, particularly in Portugal, Spain, France, Belgium, Sri Lanka, and Chile. Unlike the Third International, this one does not dictate to nor impose solutions for complex national problems of the various Trotsky organizations but does offer criticisms and suggestions to them. In 1973, for example, the Fourth International criticized one of the Canadian Trotskyist groups for giving unconditional and uncritical support to the NDP, and also for failing to support the demand for an independent Quebec. It also criticized another group for adopting a position on Canadian independence which it felt was a concession to "bourgeois nationalism". Canada, it

---

[66] Jack Scott, "Review of 'Imperialism and The National Question' ", *Canadian Revolution*, August/September 1975, p. 54.

[67] *En Lutte* (English Digest), February 1976, p. 2, 3.

declared, was an imperialist country in its own right and there-fore the main struggle should be against the Canadian ruling class.

This position is reflected in the analysis of Canada by the Revolutionary Marxist Group (RMG), "a sympathising mem-ber" of the Fourth International. The RMG supports the general conclusions of the Moore-Wells thesis, even though it is not their publication:

. . . national independence (in the Marxist-Leninist political under-standing of the term) is not on the agenda for Canada. This is not to ignore Canada's economic dependence but only to place it in the proper perspective of a dependent capitalist country that has al-ready obtained political independence, national unity, bourgeois democracy, and capitalist relations of production. . . . [68]

In this analysis, the RMG rejected the issue of national independence as part of revolutionary strategy. In its view the revolution that is on the agenda for Canada is a classical prole-tarian revolution directed at the Canadian ruling class.

The Communist Party of Canada remains the only "old" Marxist party in the sense that it has a history behind it. The CPC takes the attitude that because of this, it is the only genuine Communist party in Canada. The number of members of the new Marxist groups, however, now exceeds the number in the CPC.

The strength of the CPC as compared to that of the new groups resides chiefly in the positions which the CP still has in the trade unions as a result of its long tradition of trade-union involvement. Many of the debates that are currently agitating the new Marxist groups were debated first in the CP. The CP's program on the fight for Canadian independence set the tone, and made many of the points that have been subsequently taken up by nationalist and socialist-nationalist movements. Unlike all other Marxist groups, the CP's connections with an external model are more than ideological. They are organic and forbid any criticism whatever of the Soviet Union. This remains the major reason why the CP fails to attract those Canadians who are becoming revolutionary in their outlook, but who are not prepared to accept Soviet leadership.

---

[68] Steve Moore and Debi Wells, *Imperialism and The National Question in Canada* (Toronto, 1975), pp. 108-9.

One of the significant characteristics of the new left is in the kinds of issues it has raised. One of its major efforts has been on women's liberation, which all sections of the Marxist movement have emphasized. As a result, women play a much more important and conspicuous role in these groups than in any other field in Canadian society. The participation of women in the leadership of trade unions has also grown, and this is in large measure due to the efforts of the left. Another issue which the left has campaigned on is the situation of the native peoples and the racist discrimination against the new immigrants.

Most of the new Marxist groups consider their main weakness to be their isolation from the labor movement. They talk about an orientation to the working class which in practice means sending a few of their members into plants where they can become active in the trade union local and the central labour bodies. But wherever this has been tried, it has not produced the results anticipated in terms of winning working-class recruits into the Marxist movement or in transforming the unions into "schools for socialism". The new Marxist movement for the present remains intellectual and middle class.

This is not to condemn it or to take it lightly. It is a reflection of the present stage of socialist thought and action in Canada. Revolutionary socialism is not a mass movement in Canada. Its most effective role up until now has been a propagandist one, even though this is deprecated by some if not most Marxist activists. Yet the role they attempt, of competing with or replacing social democratic movements such as the NDP or PQ, is the least productive and the most frustrating.

The most conspicuous feature of the new phase of socialism in Canada, as has already been pointed out, is the way it reflects international models. But this too cannot be wished away. The widespread growth and success of different revolutionary movements abroad has been the prime factor in the increase in socialist thought in Canada, as it has in all capitalist countries. But a significant difference between this phase and the one that followed the Bolshevik revolution is that the new movements are not subordinate to their external model. This leads at least to the hope that the present generation of socialists will work out on its own the kind of socialist theory and practice that suits the Canadian reality.

CHAPTER EIGHT

CONCLUSIONS AND SUMMARY

The socialist idea began to take root in Canada at the turn of the century. In its original manifestations it was an imported idea or set of ideas, not just in the sense that immigrants, particularly those from Britain and America, played a big part in publicizing socialism in Canada. Many pioneers of the Canadian socialist movement have said that they came to Canada without any knowledge of socialism and that their first contact with socialist ideas came through imported socialist and radical literature which was being sold at their trade-union locals or councils. The most popular books were Robert Blatchford's *Merrie England*, Edward Bellamy's *Looking Backward*, Henry George's *Progress and Poverty*, Lawrence Gronlund's *The Co-Operative Common-wealth*, Jack London's *The Iron Heel*, and the works of Marx and Engels which had just become available through a North American publisher in Chicago.

The socialist idea arrived in Canada mainly as an emanation from Britain and the United States, where the socialist movements were already well established. It came here when the first great wave of industrialization in Canada was well under way, changing the social patterns of urban centers, and creating a proletariat in English Canada. Socialism gravitated towards the developing trade-union movement and made that its place of operations, not from any worked out strategy, but because both socialism and trade unionism appealed to the more class-conscious sections of the workers. The trade-union movement at that time was not a mass movement. It was very small and unrepresentative, but it embraced those workers who had begun to look at themselves from a class angle, and it was a relatively short distance for many of them to go from there to socialism. Craft unionism, when compared with the later industrial unionism, was conservative, but in Britain and Canada and to some extent in the United States, the craft unionists were the advanced guard of trade unionism, and the trade-union movement and the socialist organizations which grew up around it reflected largely the outlook and concerns of this group of workers during the formative years of the labor movement.

Socialism was not simply an ideology: it was a theory, and through the works of Marx and Engels it had become a rigorous theoretical system. It had also become an international movement, with millions of members and voters, and engaging some of the keenest intellectual minds. Its main social basis was among the workers, but it was the intellectuals who brought the theory to them, helped them understand it, refined it, and developed it into political platforms.

But this was not the case in Canada. No intellectuals took up socialism. It was not taught at the universities. No socialist spokesmen were allowed onto the campuses to give lectures on the subject. None of the socialist classics was included in social science courses. This reflected a number of things: an atmosphere of repression, a lack of intellectual vigour and curiosity, the extreme narrowness and élitism of the universities, and the role in the social sciences of British imperalist ideology, which, as Hobson pointed out, was much stronger among the bourgeoisie and intellectuals of the colonies than in the metropolitan centers. But however it is explained, the lack of intellectuals in the socialist movement affected its character for years to come.

The adaptation of socialism to the Canadian setting was left to the socialist workers. They had great difficulty with that task; they had neither the time nor the training for it. Working on the job, usually from fifty to sixty hours a week, they had only their limited leisure time in which to study Marxism and the related literature. They saw their task as spreading Marxist propaganda, but they had difficulty in determining the relationship of Marxist theory to political action.

Marxism, as they understood it, consisted mainly of political economy and their propaganda centered around expositions of the theory of capitalist exploitation. They spent little time on historical materialism and even less on attempting a class analysis of Canadian society. They felt that the formulation of immediate demands was not the function of socialist parties, although they supported such demands, nor did they consider it necessary to take a position on current Canadian political issues.

They were not members of the International Socialist Bureau and never attended the Congresses of the Second International. The Social Democratic Party, which was formed after a split in the Socialist Party of Canada, decided that this isolation was a serious handicap to the Canadians, and in 1914 decided to send their secretary to the Congress of the International in Vienna. But the war interrupted that trip and the socialist movement in Canada remained outside the International movement until the formation of the Communist International. The Canadian socialists were not completely isolated, however, as they did invite such speakers from the British and American socialist movements as Ramsay MacDonald, Keir Hardie, Tom Mann, Eugene Debs, Bill Haywood. The *Appeal to Reason*, the American socialist journal, was widely circulated in Canada. They also had access to the *International Socialist Review*, and certainly felt themselves part of a world movement.

But if any of the debates that took place in the International Congress and Bureau meetings got through to them it was not reflected in the Canadian socialist press. When they did take a stand on some international socialist issue, such as the admission of the British Labour Party to the International Socialist Congress, they were usually to the left of the main body of the world movement.

Almost from the beginning, socialist parties in Canada were based on Marxism as they understood it. Although there were elements of Fabianism and Christian Socialism in some of the earliest groups, particularly the Canadian Socialist League, by 1904 when the CSL merged with the Socialist Party of British Columbia, socialism in Canada was committed to what one of its leaders, G. Weston Wrigley, described as "probably the shortest and most uncompromising statement of the principles of revolutionary socialism that has ever been drafted in any country".[1]

---

[1] G. Weston Wrigley, *International Socialist Review*, Vol. 4, 1903-1904, p. 398.

By 1913, socialism in Canada was already developing to an extent that a well-known professor, O. D. Skelton, was prompted to write a warning to Canadian businessmen about the threat of socialism and to give them sage advice as to how to meet this threat. In an article in the *Monetary Times*, January 1913, he advocated policies of reforms and of concessions by the state and by the capitalists as the best way of dealing with the advance of socialism. Such reforms would be in his opinion "bulwarks against Socialism". Canadian socialism, although still very weak, had nevertheless grown so that what Skelton regarded four years previously as of little consequence in Canada, was now perceived by him as a significant movement. Thus, as in European nations, so now in Canada the growth of the socialist idea was acting on some bourgeois spokesmen as a stimulus for liberal democracy. "The hour of social as well as political democracy has come", Skelton concluded, and he became later one of the principal architects of liberal reformism.

It is interesting to note that Skelton confined his attention to socialism and the working class at a time when the movement of agrarian revolt was gathering strength. The expressions of radical criticism from farm organizations and the farmers' press were in some respects more militant and certainly more specific than those in the socialist and labor press.

But Skelton made two points about socialism which did not apply to agrarian radicalism. First, socialism was directed at the entire system, whereas agrarian radicalism, while attacking the centers of financial power, made it quite clear by its demands that it was neither attacking the system nor advocating revolutionary change. Second, socialism in Canada was part of a world movement, with its "growing millions of adherents", which were impressing "many people to shift their attitude about socialism from a conviction not of its justice or expedience but of its inevitability".

Yet agrarian radicalism was to make a significant contribution to the eventual form and character of Canadian socialism. It provided the first concrete analysis of the structure of Canadian capitalism and of its close relationship with the Canadian state. It made this a constant and predominant theme in the farmers' press and organizations. It was among the first in English Canada to actively oppose British imperialism. It associated with the currents in Canadian political thought which were agitating for Canadian autonomy. It complemented the social demands of the organized labor movement with its own. Altogether its attention to specific Canadian questions contrasted with the abstract character of much of the propaganda of the early socialist movements.

In Western Canada agrarian radicalism helped influence the ministers of the Social Gospel movement, who later served as a vital link between labor and the farmers. Above all, it was a major element in making the main body of Canadian socialism social democratic in character, because of the farmers' opposition to revolutionary change.

J. A. Hobson, the eminent British economist, had foreseen in 1905 the conditions existing in Canada for a farmer-labor alliance, and he saw in this the only hope for a successful political alternative to capitalism:

At any rate it is evident that Canada is going through a long era of protection, moulded in the usual fashion by industrial greed and political cowardice. Whether the tillers of the soil and the workers in the mills, mines, stores, and on railroads, who form the immense majority of the population, will have the intelligence and the power to rescue themselves from the coils of this Protective serpent, is a great question for the future. It arouses little interest at present. When the workers of Canada wake up they will find that Protection is only one among several economic fangs fastened in their "corpus vile" by the little group of railroad men, barbers, lumber men, and manufacturing monopolists who own their country.[2]

The turning point in the farmers' movement was the defeat of Reciprocity in 1911. After that their literature of protest became more radical and militant, and began to express the need for independent political action. At the very time that Skelton published his article on the drift towards socialism among the workers, *The Grain Growers' Guide* blazoned this manifesto on the front cover of its issue of January 15, 1913:

The princes of the house of privilege in Canada, who control our railway, banking, and manufacturing system, are levying tribute upon every citizen of Canada to a greater extent than was done by the feudal barons when knighthood was in flower. These Canadian princes of privilege levy their tributes under the protection of the law, which is made to suit them. Thus they stand upon the topmost pinnacle of respectability and are regarded as the "pillars" of society. When it is considered that the wealth these princes are accu-

---

[2] J. A. Hobson, *Canada Today* (London, 1960), pp. 46-7.

mulating has not been earned by them but is filched from the pockets of the common people by the aid of barbarian laws, it would seem that these powers would be better described as the "cater-pillars" of society.

The main themes in that manifesto became the constant themes of radical farm groups. Besides putting out their own literature, mainly in the farmers' press, they supported and distributed the works of writers of other countries, who attacked society along the same general lines. However different the conclusion that these critics advocated, if they were against monopolies, the bankers, the railroad magnates, or the monetary system, they were popular with the farmers. This was particularly true of Henry George, Edward Porritt, Gustavus Myers, and Major C. H. Douglas. They did not publicize Marxist works, except indirectly through Myers, whose Marxism was implicit rather than overt.

The socialist movement was attacking capitalist society in general through propagating the works of Marx, Engels, and their followers. The farm movement was attacking Canadian capitalist society through expository literature rather than theoretical. The socialists were addressing their propaganda efforts mainly to the organized labor movement. Yet the twin attacks on Canadian capitalism were in fact converging. These attacks mounted during the war, particularly in the latter period. The workers and farmers found common ground in exposing war profiteering, corrupt politics, restrictions on civil liberties, and conscription.

The increased radicalism that accompanied this agitation brought to the fore in a much sharper way the question of political action by these groups. The socialists and the labor movement began moving in the direction of a labor party, the farmers towards a "non-partisan" farmers' party. Woodsworth advocated "a people's party" joining labor and farmer. But this proposal was premature for a number of reasons.

The idea of a Canadian Labour Party, which had been endorsed by the TLC in 1917, was now under attack from many in the Marxist left, who preferred a party along the Bolshevik lines. The Russian Revolution in fact had produced two opposite reactions. Among the Marxists, it had the effect of strengthening the revolutionary spirit of the three socialist parties, although this was not shared by all members. On the other hand, the upsurge in revolutionary socialism repelled a good many radical farmers, who, while still as militant in their denunciations of

Canadian capitalist politics as before, were not prepared to join forces with revolutionists. While the labor movement had grown rapidly during the war, it was still weak as an independent political force, and the divisions within its ranks over a Labour Party made it even weaker in that respect. Moreover, the radicalism of these years gave a strong impetus to liberal reformism, and under the leadership of Mackenzie King a determined effort was launched to win dissident workers and farmers to the reform liberal banners.

The twenties were decisive in reshaping Canadian politics. The Progressive Party, which flared up out of agrarian discontent, succumbed as a party to blandishments of King, but a significant section of it broke with the two-party system and helped found the CCF in 1932. The Communist Party failed to rally and rebuild the Marxist movement on the basis of revolutionary socialism and Leninism. It was during this period that social democracy emerged as the main ideology of anti-capitalist and anti-imperialist opinion in English Canada. The Communists attacked the social democrats as betrayers of the revolution, but in fact the growth of social democracy was the result, not the cause, of the ebb in revolutionary prospects. Social democracy develops in those capitalist societies where the opportunity still exists for reforms of a major character. At the same time the fact that social democracy exists alongside liberal democracy shows that with all its concessions and reforms, liberal democracy does not and cannot eliminate or replace social democracy.

Socialism, in whatever form, is basically an alternative to capitalism, the only real alternative to emerge in this century. In its earlier years socialism and radicalism in Canada concentrated their attention on attacking the exploitative essence of capitalism, and the close relationships between capital and political power. The lack of attention given by socialists to immediate demands is often criticized retrospectively, but it is important to understand that this served to emphasize that they did not regard socialism as simply the improvement of the economic and social welfare of the workers. It is true that they underestimated the capacity of capitalism to produce consumer goods in abundance and diminish inequities in their distribution. But even if they had correctly gauged this capacity of capitalism, it would not have answered their criticism of the system. A popular socialist slogan "human rights before property rights" expressed the basic nature of their critique of capitalism. Every major evil in Canadian society—poverty, war, imperialism, repression—was linked to capitalism and to its most basic characteristic: the private owner-ship of social property. Political power was sought not simply to ameliorate the living conditions of the people, but as a means of recasting the entire structure of society, or, as expressed in the Re-gina Manifesto, "to eradicate capitalism". However much these aims have been muted in current social democratic thought, in the public perception, the NDP, inheriting the legacy and image of the CCF, is still regarded as the socialist alternative to the main-stream political culture of Canada. It is because of its place in the Canadian ideological spectrum that the CCF−NDP has remained the genuine third party in Canadian politics.

Nevertheless, the relative emphasis given to immediate re-forms and to fundamental criticism of capitalism has caused, and continues to cause, considerable tension and difficulty within so-cialist organizations. It has been the source of all schisms and fac-tional struggles within the CCF and NDP. It has un-doubtedly been a major source of difficulty for the Communist Party, and it is currently the subject of great debates in the various Marxist groups that have sprung up since the sixties.

The Communist Party of Canada represented the acceptance of Leninism by a section of the Canadian socialist movement, out of a conviction that Lenin's strategy and tactics for the socialist revolution, having proved successful in Russia, would be successful in Canada as well. The key to this success was to be the creation of a truly revolutionary party on the Bolshevik model, closely linked with similar parties through the Commun-ist International. The Communist International was to be not just a federation of like-minded parties, as was the Second Interna-tional, but in fact an international party. It was to be monolithic in structure and ideology on a world scale and made up of individual national units that would be subordinate to the higher interna-tional committees.

The Communist Party of Canada began in a great burst of enthusiasm, determination, and cohesiveness, at a time when the rest of the socialist movement seemed confused and disunited. This enthusiasm was based on a conviction that the revolution-ary wave that had followed the war was still in its upswing, and that revolutionary strategy and tactics were needed to meet that situation. Yet as this wave began to recede, the CPC was faced with the problem, which it was never able to solve, of defining a role for a revolutionary party without immediate or even longer-term revolutionary prospects. The frequent and sudden oscilla-tions in policy reflect this uncertainty. The long and extensive debates that went on in the party press and at Central Committee meetings and conventions over the constantly changing perceptions of party work, show confusion and doubt, masked by self-confident assertions that every change was a correct one.

Basically the CPC settled for advocating reforms, more militant in many cases than the CCF, but essentially taking up the same issues that the CCF was concerned about. The CPC consequently saw itself as being in competition with the CCF, fighting it, denouncing it, running candidates against CCFers, and seeking at other times to unite or even merge with it. The failure of the CPC to adjust itself to the CCF was in many ways its central failure, but this derived from the fundamental dilemma that confronted communism in Canada. Engels's judgement on Hyndman and the British Social Democratic Federation seems to apply in some measure to the CPC:

It has ossified Marxism into a dogma, and, by rejecting every labor movement which is not orthodox Marxism (and that a Marxism which contains much that is erroneous), that is, by pursuing the exact opposite of the policy recommended in the Manifesto, *it renders itself incapable of ever becoming anything else but a sect.*[3]

In spite of Communist attacks on the CCF which were reciprocated in full by the CCF, the Communists and the CCF interacted with each other to their mutual benefit. The CPC by its militant activities, particularly in the Depression, and by pioneering work in organizing industrial unions, influenced directly and indirectly the parliamentary and trade union activity of the CCF. The CPC, on the other hand, made use of the CCF and LSR's analysis of Canadian society and took up many demands which were initiated by them, and before them by the labor-farm group in Parliament. In these ways revolutionary socialism and social democracy complemented each other, and jointly contributed to implanting the socialist idea in Canada.

The main contribution which the CPC made to Canadian political thought throughout these years was in keeping the Marxist critique of capitalism alive. In this respect it continued the tradition of the early socialist parties in Canada. Its efforts to combine this with attention to immediate demands and thus correct a weakness in these parties was not as successful, primarily

---

[3] Engels to K. Kautsky, August 12, 1892, in Marx and Engels, *On Britain*, p. 594.

because social democracy, being reformist in philosophy as well as in practice, could do it better.

The Marxism which the CPC propagated was greatly influenced by Stalin's theoretical formulations, which were simplistic, dogmatic, and utilitarian in the sense of subordinating theory to constantly changing tactics. While the CPC has half-heartedly come to terms with Stalin's brutal dictatorship, it has failed to come to terms with his theoretical leadership. One of the gravest errors he made was in his analysis of social democracy as "social fascism" and his postulation that social democracy was the last social basis of capitalism and therefore the main enemy for the Communists to combat. While the CPC is now trying to correct some of the consequences of that theory without attacking the theory itself, some of the new Marxist groups are borrowing the theory and using it as their own.

The sixties could be considered a third stage in the genesis of the socialist idea in Canada. The first was from the early beginnings up to the Russian Revolution, when the main socialist parties were based on Marxism; the second after 1917 when the historic split between revolutionary socialism and social democracy opened up and developed in Canada. The third stage saw the strengthening of both trends, but the distinguishing feature at this time was the proliferation of the New Left and a resurgence of Marxism, particularly among the youth, outside the Communist Party.

This development was inspired initially by international events, the colonial liberation movements, the revolutions in Cuba, Algeria, China, the uprising of the blacks and the growth of anti-war struggles in the United States. These events merged with the Quiet Revolution in Quebec, and the rise of nationalist feelings in English Canada directed at U.S. domination. Thus the new socialist currents took on a nationalist flavor, in which Canadian strivings for independence were equated to the anti-imperialist colonial struggles in the Third World.

This merging of socialism with nationalism had a bigger impact in Quebec than in English Canada for obvious reasons. The nationalist sentiment had always been strong in Quebec and became stronger during the Quiet Revolution. Thus the first indigenous socialist movement in Quebec which came into being as part of the Quiet Revolution, was stamped with Quebec nationalism, as were subsequent movements in the sixties. With the appearance of a strong social democratic party which upholds the idea of separation, many of the Marxist groups in Quebec have begun to reject this nationalism as petty bourgeois.

The merging of socialism and nationalism in English Canada resulted in the appearance and spectacular growth of the Waffle as an organized caucus inside the NDP. When the Waffle activists tried to move both the socialism and nationalism beyond the limits of the NDP, they ran into immediate difficulty both with the NDP leadership and eventually with their own members and supporters. Many of them joined or founded new Marxist groups to answer their need for a more fundamental critique of Canadian society. Some of them rejected nationalism while others accepted it but gave it a more revolutionary connotation.

Both in English Canada and in Quebec the old barriers against teaching Marxism in the universities have been let down. There is a constant expansion in the number of courses being offered in Marxism, and an increase in students taking such courses. Many of these students and academics are connected with the Marxist political movement and are contributing original and significant new approaches to Canadian society from the viewpoint of Marxism and thus adding to Canadian political and intellectual thought.

Socialism came to Canada as an imported idea, but as a result of three quarters of a century of political development, including periods of sharp and bitter conflict, it has become a viable and distinctive element in Canadian political thought. Firmly implanted by previous generations it is now undergoing a new growth as a result of the complex of international and national factors.

Canadian socialism has always been closely associated with the labor movement. It remains so today. It has also been closely associated with the farmers, but that is less so now as the small producers, the basis for earlier agrarian radicalism, have virtually disappeared. Part of the urban middle classes have moved towards the NDP and it is this element that is now greatly influencing the direction of social democratic thought and action. On the other hand, a small but growing section of the intellectuals are turning to Marxism not just as an academic exercise, but with the aim of influencing the direction of socialist thought along revolutionary lines. So far they have made little contact with the class-conscious workers who support the NDP. Nevertheless, as in the past, the activities of the Marxist left merge with those of the social democratic forces to strengthen the overall socialist presence in Canada.

BIBLIOGRAPHY

In an effort to keep footnotes from getting too unwieldy, I have tried to indicate in the body of the book, dates and sources where primary documents were used, leaving footnotes to the books and periodicals which are relatively current and accessible. For the student who is interested in doing further research, I list here all the sources which I have used, and on which I base my exposition.

N.P.

A. Primary Sources

1. ARCHIVAL COLLECTIONS

Public Archives of Canada, Ottawa

W. C. Good Papers
Agnes Macphail Papers
R.C.M.P. Files
Winnipeg General Strike Papers
J. S. Woodsworth Papers

University of Toronto. John P. Robarts Research Library

James Mavor Papers
University Curriculum Records
J. S. Woodsworth Papers

University of British Columbia Library. Special Collections

Angus MacInnis Papers

Province of Ontario Archives

Attorney General's Department, Record Group. Communist
Party Documents

2. PRIVATE COLLECTIONS

W. W. Lefeaux Papers. Files, notes, correspondence in the
possession of his widow, Mrs. E. Lefeaux, Vancouver, British
Columbia

3. INTERVIEWS

Interview with Jacob Penner conducted by Roland Penner.
Transcript at Glendon College.
Interview with W. A. Pritchard conducted by Norman Penner.
Tape at Glendon College.
Interview with Stewart Smith—conducted by S. R. Penner. *York
Oral Labour History*. ed. I. M. Abella.
Interview with Stewart Smith conducted by J. Starobin. *Ibid*.
Interviews with Socialist Pioneers. Transcript of Paul Fox, CBC,
1961.

4. DOCUMENTS

Early Socialist Movements

Ontario Socialist League. *Platform*. St. Thomas: 1902.
Social-Democratic Party of Canada. *Constitution, By-Laws,
Platform*. Berlin, Ont.: May 31, 1912.
Socialist Party of Canada. *Federal Election Manifesto*. 1921.
Socialist Party of Canada. *Platform*. Vancouver: 1903.
Socialist Party of North America. *Declaration of Principles*.
Toronto: 1918.

Labor Parties

Canadian Labour Party. *Platform. Vancouver Civic Elections*.
December 10, 1924.
Federated Labor Party of British Columbia. *Manifesto and
Platform*. 1918.

Independent Labor Party (B.C.). *Federal Election Manifesto and Platform*. July 28, 1930.
Independent Labor Party (B.C.). *Platform and Manifesto*. 1926.
Independent Labor Party (B.C.). *Provincial Election Manifesto*. July 18, 1928.
Independent Labor Party of Manitoba. *Manifesto*. 1921.
Independent Labor Party (Socialist) of B.C. *Platform and Manifesto*. 1931.

Co-operative Commonwealth Federation

Co-operative Commonwealth Federation. *Declaration of Principles*. Winnipeg: 1956.
Co-operative Commonwealth Federation. *Federal Election Manifesto*. Adopted at the Eighth National Convention, Montreal: November 29, 30 and December 1, 1944.
Co-operative Commonwealth Federation. *Programme of the Quebec CCF*. Montreal: n.d.
Co-operative Commonwealth Federation. *Programme* (Regina Manifesto). Adopted at the First Annual Convention, Regina: July 1933.
Co-operative Commonwealth Federation. *Study Outline on Socialism Today*. Ottawa: CCF National Office, 1952.
Co-operative Commonwealth Federation. *The Unions and the CCF*. Vancouver: Trade Union Committee, 1944.
Woodsworth, J. S. *President's Address to the First Annual Convention, CCF*. Regina: July 1933.

Workers' Party of Canada, Communist Party of Canada and Labor-Progressive Party

Central Committee, CPC. *Report of Proceedings*. January 1930.
Central Committee, CPC. *Toward a People's Front*. Proceedings of the Ninth Plenum, November 1935.
Communist Party of Canada. *Federal Election Manifesto, 1940*.
Communist Party of Canada. *Report*. Sixth National Convention, May 31.
Communist Party of Canada. *Resolution*. Enlarged Plenum, February 1931.
Communist Party of Canada. *Resolutions*. Eighth Dominion Convention, October 8-12, 1937.
Communist Party of Canada. *The Road to Socialism in Canada*. Program adopted at the 21st National Convention, November 27-29, 1971.

Communist Party of Canada. *Soviet Canada is the Only Way Out for the Laboring People*. Manifesto of the Seventh National Convention, July 23-28, 1934.

Communist Party of Canada. *Synopsis and Proceedings*. Enlarged Executive Meeting, October 1928.

Communist Party of Canada. *Trade Union Thesis*. March 1929.

Court of Appeal, Province of Ontario. *The King Versus Buck and Others*. Report of Judgement, 1932.

Degras, Jane, ed. *The Communist International Documents*. Vols. I, II, III. London: Frank Cass and Company, 1971.

Dominion Committee, CPC. *Toward Democratic Unity in Canada*. Submission to the Royal Commission on Dominion-Provincial Relations, 1938.

Labor-Progressive Party. *Canada's Future*. Submission to the Royal Commission on Canada's Economic Prospects, January 1956.

Labor-Progressive Party. *Canadian Independence and A People's Parliament*. Program adopted at the Fifth National Convention, March 28, 1954.

Labor-Progressive Party. *Canadian Independence and People's Democracy*. Adopted by the National Committee, February 1952.

Labor-Progressive Party. *Programme*. 1943.

Labor-Progressive Party. *Speeches and Main Resolutions*. National Convention, June 1-5, 1946.

Workers' Party of Canada. *Programme*. Adopted at the First National Convention, Toronto: February 1922.

Workers' Party of Canada. *Secretary's Report*. Third National Convention, Toronto: 1924.

General

House of Commons. *Debates*.

5. BOOKS AND PAMPHLETS

Bland, Salem. *The New Christianity (1920)*. Toronto: University of Toronto Press, 1973.

Buck, Tim. *Canada: The Communist Viewpoint*. Toronto: Progress Books, 1948.

————. *Canada and the Russian Revolution*. Toronto: Progress Books, 1967.

————. *Canada Needs a Party of Communists*. Toronto: 1943.

————. *Europe's Rebirth*. Toronto: Progress Books, 1947.

————. *Keep Canada Independent*. Toronto: Labor-Progressive Party, 1948.

————. *Lenin: A Man for All Time*. Toronto: Progress Books, 1969.

————. *Lenin and Canada*. Toronto: Progress Books, 1970.

————. *New Horizons for Young Canada*. Toronto: National Committee, Labor-Progressive Party, 1948.

————. *Our Fight for Canada*. Toronto: Progress Books, 1959.

————. *The People vs Monopoly*. Toronto: New Era Publishing Ltd., 1937.

————. *Put Monopoly Under Control*. Toronto: Progress Books, 1964.

————. *Steps to Power*. Toronto: 1925.

————. *Thirty Years 1922-1952*. Toronto: Progress Books, 1952.

Coldwell, M. J. *Left Turn, Canada*. London: Victor Gollancz Ltd., 1945.

————. *What Does the C.C.F. Stand For?* Ottawa: Co-operative Commonwealth Federation, 1943.

Gagnon, Charles. *Pour le parti prolétarien*. Montreal: L'Equipe du Journal, 1972.

Good, W. C. *Is Democracy Doomed?* Toronto: The Ryerson Press, 1933.

Irvine, William. *The Farmers in Politics*. Toronto: McClelland and Stewart Ltd., 1920.

————. *Co-operative Government*. Ottawa: Mutual Press, 1930.

Ivens, William. *Revolutionary Russia Versus Evolutionary England*. Winnipeg: Central Labor Church, 1924.

League for Social Reconstruction. *Social Planning for Canada*. Toronto: Thomas Nelson and Sons, 1935.

Lewis, David. *For A People's Victory*. Ottawa: Co-operative Commonwealth Federation, 1943.

————. "Socialism Across the Border—Canada's C.C.F." *The Antioch Review*, 1943.

————, and Frank Scott. *Make This Your Canada*. Toronto: 1943.

McCollum, Watt Hugh. *Who Owns Canada?* Regina: The Saskatchewan C.C.F. Research Bureau, 1935.

McEwen, Tom. *The Forge Glows Red*. Toronto: Progress Books, 1974.

MacInnis, Angus. *Labor, Servant or Partner?* Vancouver: CCF Economic Relations Committee, 1942.

McKean, M. Fergus. *Communism Versus Opportunism.* Vancouver: The Organizing Committee, 1946.

Morris, Leslie. *Look on Canada, Now.* Toronto: Progress Books, 1970.

_____. *The Story of Tim Buck's Party 1922-1939.* Toronto: New Era Publishers, 1939.

National Students Committee, Labor-Progressive Party. *Crisis on the Canadian Campus.* Toronto: 1949.

O'Brien, C. M. *The Proletarian in Politics.* Socialist Party of Canada, 1910.

Pierce, G. "Comments on the CCF Program." Reprint from *The Worker*, July 29, 1933.

_____. *Socialism and the C.C.F.* Montreal: Contemporary Publishing Association, 1934.

Pilkington, J. *Wage Worker and Farmer.* Dominion Executive Committee, Socialist Party of Canada, 1914.

Place, Jack. *Record of J. D. Hawthornthwaite, Member for Nanaimo City in the B.C. Legislature.* Socialist Party of Canada, 1910.

Planning for Freedom. Toronto: Ontario CCF, 1944.

Power of the People, Le Pouvoir du Peuple. History Outline of the Communist Party of Canada 1921-1971. Central Executive Committee, Communist Party of Canada, 1971.

Questions for Today. Toronto: Communist Party of Canada, 1964.

Ryerson, Stanley B. *1837, The Birth of Canadian Democracy.* Toronto: Francis White Publishers Limited, 1938.

_____. *French Canada.* Toronto: Progress Books, 1943.

_____. *Two Peoples: One Land, One Future.* Toronto: Labor-Progressive Party, 1944.

Scott, F. R. *Le CCF et la centralisation.* Ottawa: Le Bureau National du CCF, 1949.

Smith, Rev. A. E. *All My Life.* Toronto: Progress Books, 1949.

Steeves, Dorothy G. *Builders and Rebels, A Short History of the CCF in British Columbia 1932-1961.* Vancouver: B.C. Committee for the New Democratic Party, 1961.

Unity is the Workers' Lifeline. Report by Thomas A. Ewen at the Third Dominion Convention of the W.U.L., November 9, 1935.

Woodsworth, J. S. *Following the Gleam.* Ottawa: 1926.

_____. *My Neighbor (1911).* Toronto: University of Toronto Press, 1972

————. *Strangers Within our Gates (1909)*. Toronto: University of Toronto Press, 1972.

6. NEWSPAPERS AND PERIODICALS

B.C. Federationist, 1912-1920.
Canadian Dimension, 1969-1976.
The Canadian Forum, 1920-1935.
Canadian Forward, 1914-1918.
Canadian Labor Monthly, 1928-1929.
Canadian Magazine, 1890-1898.
Canadian Tribune, 1940-1976.
Cotton's Weekly, 1910-1914.
Daily Clarion, 1936-1939.
Farmers' Sun, 1900-1930.
The Grain Growers' Guide, 1913-1920.
The Indicator, 1919.
Industrial Banner, 1912-1919.
International Socialist Review, 1901-1918.
The Last Post, 1970-1976.
The Marxian Socialist, 1918.
Monetary Times, 1900-1915.
National Affairs Monthly, 1946-1957.
Our Generation, 1970-1976.
Parti pris, 1963-1968.
Red Flag, 1919.
Saskatchewan CCF Research Bureau, 1934-1935.
The Searchlight, 1919-1920.
The Social Democrat, 1918-1920.
Socialisme, 1964-1969.
Socialisme Québécois, 1970-1974.
University of Toronto Monthly, 1910-1918.
Western Clarion, 1905-1928.
Western Labour News, 1918-1923.
The Worker, 1922-1936.

B. Secondary Sources

1. BOOKS AND ARTICLES

Abella, Irving Martin. *Nationalism, Communism and Canadian Labour*. Toronto: University of Toronto Press, 1973.

d'Allemagne, André. *Le RIN et les débuts du mouvement indépendantiste*. Montreal: Les Editions de l'Etincelle, 1974.

Allen, Richard. *The Social Passion*. Toronto: University of Toronto Press, 1971.

Avakumovic, Ivan. *The Communist Party in Canada*. Toronto: McClelland and Stewart Ltd., 1975.

Aveling, Edward, and Eleanor Marx. *The Working Class Movement in America*. New York: Arno Press and the New York Times Co., 1969.

Bax, Ernest Belfort. *The Ethics of Socialism*. London: Swan Sonnenschein & Co., 1893.

Beer, M. *A History of British Socialism*. Vols. I and II. London: George Allen and Unwin, 1953.

Bellamy, Edward. *Looking Backward*. Vancouver: The Totem Press, 1934.

Bernstein, Edward. *Evolutionary Socialism*. New York: Schocken Books Inc., 1967.

Birney, Earl. *Down the Long Table*. Toronto: McClelland and Stewart Ltd., 1974.

Blatchford, Robert. *Merrie England*. Chicago: Charles H. Kerr and Company, n.d.

Borkenau, Franz. *World Communism*. Ann Arbor: The University of Michigan Press, 1963.

Caplan, Gerald L. *The Dilemma of Canadian Socialism*. Toronto: McClelland and Stewart Ltd., 1973.

Clark, S. D. *Movements of Political Protest in Canada 1640-1840*. Toronto: University of Toronto Press, 1968.

Coldwell, M. J. *Left Turn Canada*. Toronto: Victor Gollancz Ltd., 1973.

Cole, G. D. H. *Socialist Thought—The Forerunners*. London: Macmillan Publishing Co., 1959.

———. *Socialist Thought—Marxism and Anarchism*. London: Macmillan Publishing Co., 1959.

———. *Socialist Thought—The Second International*. London: Macmillan Publishing Co., 1960.

Cole, Margaret. *The Story of Fabian Socialism*. New York: John Wiley and Sons Inc., 1960.

Collins, Henry, and C. Abramsky. *Karl Marx and the British Labour Movement*. London: Macmillan Publishing Co., 1965.

Cook, Ramsay. *The Politics of John W. Dafoe and "The Free Press"*. Toronto: University of Toronto Press, 1971.

Cox, Carolyn. "Bialystock—McGill—Oxford—Ottawa." *Saturday Night*. April 3, 1943.

———. "How Tim Buck Got That Way." *Saturday Night*, June 19, 1943.

Crysdale, Stewart. *The Industrial Struggle and Protestant Ethics in Canada*. Toronto: The Ryerson Press, 1961.

DeLeon, Daniel. *Flashlights of the Amsterdam Congress*. New York: New York Labor News Co., 1929.

Dick, William M. *Labor and Socialism In America*. Port Washington: National University Publications, 1972.

Dion, Gerard. *Le Communisme dans la province de Québec*. Québec: Service Exterieur d'Education Sociale, 1949.

Dion, Leon. *Nationalismes et Politique au Québec*. Montréal: Hurtubise—HMH, 1975.

Donnelly, M. S. "The Political Ideas of J. W. Dafoe." *The Political Process in Canada*, ed. J. H. Aitchison. Toronto: University of Toronto Press, 1963.

Drache, Daniel, ed. *Quebec—Only The Beginning*. Toronto: New Press, 1972.

Draper, Theodore. *The Roots of American Communism*. New York: Viking Press Inc., 1966.

Ewart, J. S. *The Kingdom Papers*. Ottawa: 1912.

Ferns, H. S. and B. Ostry. *The Age of Mackenzie King*. Toronto: James Lorimer and Company, 1976.

Foster, William Z. *History of the Communist Party of the United States*. New York: International Publishers, 1952.

———. *History of the Three Internationals*. New York: Greenwood Press Inc. 1968.

———. *Pages from a Worker's Life*. New York: International Publishers, 1970.

Fox, Paul W. "Early Socialism in Canada." *The Political Process in Canada*, ed. J. H. Aitchison. Toronto: University of Toronto Press, 1963.

Fox, Ralph. *The Class Struggle in Britain*. London: Martin Lawrence, n.d.

Fried, Albert. *Socialism in America*. New York: Doubleday & Co. Inc., 1970.

Gélinas, Pierre. *Les Vivants, les morts et les autres*. Ottawa: Cercle du Livre de France Ltée., 1959.

George, Henry. *Progress and Poverty*. New York: The Modern Library, n.d.

Godfrey, Dave, and Mel Watkins. *Gordon to Watkins to You*. Toronto: New Press, 1970.

Gompers, Samuel. *Seventy Years of Life and Labor*. New York: E. P. Dutton & Co., Inc., 1943.

Gray, J. H. *The Winter Years*. Toronto: Macmillan Publishing Co., 1973.

Gray, John. *A Lecture on Human Happiness*. London: Sherwood, Jones & Co., 1825.

Gronlund, Lawrence. *The Cooperative Commonwealth*. Cambridge: Harvard University Press, 1965.

Hardie, J. Keir. *Karl Marx: The Man and his Message*. Manchester: National Labour Press Limited, 1910.

Harrington, Michael. *Socialism*. New York: Saturday Review Press, 1972.

Heaps, Leon. *The Rebel in the House*. London: Niccolo Publishing Company, 1970.

Hillquit, Morris. *History of Socialism in the United States*. New York: Funk and Wagnalls Co., 1906.

Hoar, Victor, ed. *The Great Depression*. Toronto: The Copp Clark Publishing Company, 1969.

Hoar, Victor. *The Mackenzie—Papineau Battalion*. Toronto: The Copp Clark Publishing Company, 1969.

————. *The On To Ottawa Trek*. Toronto: The Copp Clark Publishing Company, 1970.

Hobson, J. A. *Canada To-Day*. London: T. Fisher Unwin, 1906.

————. *Imperialism: A Study*. London: George Allen and Unwin, 1968.

Horn, Michiel, ed. *The Dirty Thirties*. Toronto: The Copp Clark Publishing Company, 1972.

Horowitz, Gad. *Canadian Labour In Politics*. Toronto: University of Toronto Press, 1968.

Hutchison, Bruce. *The Incredible Canadian*. New York: Longmans, Green, 1953.

Hyndman, Henry Mayers. *The Record of an Adventurous Life*. London: Macmillan Publishing Co., 1911.

Innis, H. A., ed. *Labour in Canadian-American Relations*. Toronto: The Ryerson Press, 1937.

Jamieson, Stuart Marshall. *Times of Trouble: Labour Unrest and Industrial Conflict in Canada, 1900-66*. Ottawa: Information Canada Publishing Branch, 1968.

King, Mackenzie W. L. *Industry and Humanity*. Toronto:

Macmillan Publishing Co., 1947.

Laxer, Robert. *Canada's Unions*. Toronto: James Lorimer and Company, 1976.

―――, ed. *(Canada) Ltd.* Toronto: McClelland and Stewart Ltd., 1973.

Lefeaux, Wallis Walter. *Winnipeg—London—Moscow*. Winnipeg: Canadian Workers' Defense League, 1921.

Lenin, V. I. *British Labour and British Imperialism*. London: Lawrence & Wishart, Ltd., 1969.

―――. *Selected Works*. 12 volumes. New York: International Publishers, 1943.

Levitt, Kari. *Silent Surrender*. Toronto: Macmillan Publishing Co., 1970.

Logan, H. A. *Trade Unions in Canada*. Toronto: Macmillan Publishing Co., 1948.

Lumsden, Ian, ed. *Close the 49th Parallel etc.* Toronto: University of Toronto Press, 1970.

McCormack, A. R. "The Emergence of the Socialist Movement in British Columbia." *B.C. Studies*, No. 21, Spring 1974.

MacDonald, J. Ramsay. *Socialism and Society*. London: Independent Labour Party, 1906.

McEwen, Tom. *He Wrote For Us*. Vancouver: Tribune Publishing Company, 1951.

MacInnis, Grace. *J. S. Woodsworth: A Man to Remember*. Toronto: Macmillan Publishing Co., 1953.

MacIver, R. M. "Capital and Labour—The New Situation." *University of Toronto Monthly*, Vol. XVII, 1917-1918.

―――. *Labour in the Changing World*. Toronto: J. M. Dent & Sons, 1919.

McNaught, Kenneth. *A Prophet in Politics*. Toronto: University of Toronto Press, 1963.

Macpherson, C. B. *Democracy in Alberta*. Toronto: University of Toronto Press, 1962.

―――. "Marxism in Canada: A New Beginning." *Canadian Dimension*, Vol. 9, Number 7-8, 1974.

―――. *The Political Theory of Possessive Individualism*. Oxford: The Clarendon Press, 1962.

Marx, Karl. *Capital*. Vol. I. Chicago: Charles H. Kerr and Company, 1906.

―――. *Critique of the Gotha Programme*. Moscow: Foreign Language Publishing House, n.d.

―――, and Friedrich Engels. "The Communist Manifesto." *A Handbook of Marxism*, ed. Emile Burns. New York:

International Publishers, 1935.

———. *The German Ideology*. Moscow: Progress Publishers, 1968.

———. *The Holy Family*. Moscow: Foreign Languages Publishing House, 1956.

———. *On Britain*. Moscow: Foreign Languages Publishing House, 1962.

———. *Selected Correspondence 1846-1895*. New York: International Publishers, 1936.

Masters, D. C. *The Winnipeg General Strike*. Toronto: University of Toronto Press, 1950.

Mills, Ivor J. *Stout Hearts Stand Tall*. Vancouver: Evergreen Press Limited, 1971.

Milner, Sheilagh Hodgins, and Henry Milner. *The Decolonization of Quebec*. Toronto: McClelland and Stewart Ltd., 1973.

Moore, Steve and Debi Wells. *Imperialism and the National Question in Canada*. Toronto: 1975.

Morgan, H. Wayne. *American Socialism, 1900-1960*. Englewood Cliffs: Prentice-Hall Inc., 1964.

———. *Eugene V. Debs Socialist for President*. Syracuse: Syracuse University Press, 1962.

Morris, William, and G. B. Shaw, et al. *Hand and Brain*. East Aurora, Ill.: 1907.

Myers, Gustavus. *History of Canadian Wealth*. Chicago: Charles H. Kerr and Company, 1914.

Not Guilty! Toronto: Canadian Labor Defence League, 1932.

Owen, Robert. *A New View of Society and Other Writings*. London: J. M. Dent & Sons Ltd., 1966.

Park, Libbie, and Frank. *Anatomy of Big Business*. Toronto: James Lewis and Samuel, 1973.

Pelling, Henry. *A Short History of the Labour Party*. London: Macmillan Publishing Co., 1962.

Penner, Norman, ed. *Winnipeg 1919*. Toronto: James Lewis and Samuel, 1973.

Phillips, Paul. *No Power Greater*. Vancouver: B.C. Federation of Labor, 1967.

Porritt, Edward. *The Revolt in Canada Against the New Feudalism*. London: Cassell and Company Ltd., 1911.

———. *Sixty Years of Protection in Canada*. London: Macmillan Publishing Co., 1908.

Quint, Howard H. *The Forging of American Socialism*. Columbia: University of South Carolina Press, 1953.

Robin, Martin. *Radical Politics and Canadian Labour*. Kingston: Queen's University Press, 1968.

Rodney, William. *Soldiers of the International*. Toronto: University of Toronto Press, 1968.

Rolph, William Kirby. *Henry Wise Wood of Alberta*. Toronto: University of Toronto Press, 1950.

Rotstein, Abraham, and Gary Lax. *Independence: The Canadian Challenge*. Toronto: Committee for an Independent Canada, 1972.

Roussopoulos, Dmitrios, ed. *Canada and Radical Social Change*. Montreal: Black Rose Books Ltd., 1973.

————. *The New Left in Canada*. Montreal: Black Rose Books, 1970.

Ryan, Oscar. *Tim Buck—A Conscience for Canada*. Toronto: Progress Books, 1975.

Ryerson, Stanley B. *The Founding of Canada*. Toronto: Progress Books, 1972.

————. *Unequal Union*. Toronto: Progress Books, 1968.

————. *A World to Win*. Toronto: Progress Books, 1950.

Saywell, John Tupper. "Labour and Socialism in British Columbia." *B.C. Historical Quarterly*, Vol. XV, No. 3 & 4, July—October 1951.

Scott, F. R. *Canada Today*. London: Oxford University Press, 1938.

Scott, Jack. *Sweat and Struggle*. Vancouver: New Star Books, 1974.

Sharp. P. F. *The Agrarian Revolt in Western Canada*. New York: Octagon Books, 1971.

Shaw, George Bernard, ed. *The Fabian Essays on Socialism*. Boston: The Ball Publishing Co., 1909.

Skelton, O. D. *Socialism: A Critical Analysis*. New York: Houghton Mifflin Co., 1911.

Stalin, Joseph. *Works*. 13 volumes. Moscow: Foreign Languages Publishing House, 1952.

Starobin, Joseph R. *American Communism in Crisis, 1943-1957*. Cambridge: Harvard University Press, 1972.

Teeple, Gary, ed. *Capitalism and the National Question in Canada*. Toronto: University of Toronto Press, 1972.

Thompson, E. P. *The Making of the English Working Class*. London: Victor Gollancz Ltd., 1963.

Thompson, Phillips. *The Politics of Labor*. New York: Belford, Clark & Co., 1887.

Trotsky, Leon. *Marxism in the United States*. New York:

Workers' Party Publications, 1947.

Warshaw, Leo. "The Economic Forces Leading to a Centralized Federalism in Canada." *Essays in Political Economy*, ed. H. A. Innis. Toronto: University of Toronto Press, 1938.

Webb, Sidney. *Socialism in England*. New York: Charles Scribner's Sons, 1893.

Wolfe, Bertram David. *Marx and America*. New York: John Day Co, 1934.

Young, Walter D. *The Anatomy of a Party: The National CCF 1932-61*. Toronto: University of Toronto Press, 1971.

Zakuta, Leo. *A Protest Movement Becalmed*. Toronto: University of Toronto Press, 1964.

2. THESES AND UNPUBLISHED MANUSCRIPTS

Acheson, T. W. "The Social Origins of Canadian Industrialism: A Study in the Structure of Canadian Entrepreneurship, 1879-1911." Ph.D. Thesis, University of Guelph, 1972.

Armstrong, Myrtle May. "The Development of Trade Union Political Activity in the C.C.F." M.A. Thesis, University of Toronto, 1959.

Chisick, Ernie. "The Early Marxist Socialist Movement in Manitoba, 1901-1926." Honours History Essay, University of Winnipeg, 1968.

Connor, James McArthur. "The Labor and Socialist Movement in Canada." Unpublished manuscript in the Woodsworth Collection, University of Toronto, John P. Robarts Library, n.d.

Fournier, Marcel. "Histoire et Idéologie du groupe Canadien-français du Parti Communiste, 1925-1945." M.A. Thesis, Université de Montréal, 1969.

Grantham, R. G. "Some Aspects of the Socialist Movement in British Columbia, 1898-1933." M.A. Thesis, University of British Columbia, 1943.

Grimson, C. D. "The Communist Party of Canada, 1922-1946." M.A. Thesis, McGill University, 1966.

Hart, John Edward. "William Irvine and Radical Politics in Canada." Ph.D. Thesis, University of Guelph, 1972.

Horn, Michiel Steven Daniel. "The League for Social Reconstruction: Socialism and Nationalism in Canada, 1931-1945." Ph.D. Thesis, University of Toronto, 1969.

Irving, Joe. "Marxism and the Western Canadian Working

Class." Undergraduate Essay, Simon Fraser University, 1970.

Loosemore, T. R. "The British Columbia Labour Movement and Political Action, 1879-1906." M.A. Thesis, University of British Columbia, 1954.

McCormack, Andrew Ross. "The Origins and Extent of Western Labour Radicalism." Ph.D. Thesis, University of Western Ontario, 1973.

McIvor, William John. "Revolutionary Socialism." M.A. Thesis, University of Manitoba, 1912.

McKillop, Alexander Brian. "Citizen and Socialist: The Ethos of Political Winnipeg, 1919-1935." M. A. Thesis, University of Manitoba, 1970.

O'Brien, Gary. "Maurice Spector and the Origins of Canadian Trotskyism." M.A. Thesis, Carleton University, 1974.

————. "Towards the Roots of Canadian Radicalism: An Analysis of the Social-Democratic Party of Canada." Essay, Carleton University, 1973.

Pentland, H. C. "Labour and the Development of Industrial Capitalism in Canada." Ph.D. Thesis, University of Toronto, 1960.

Pratt, Rev. Douglas Frederick. "William Ivens, M.A., B.D., and the Winnipeg Labor Church." B.D. Thesis, St. Andrew's College, Saskatoon, 1962.

Rainboth, Mabel. "Socialism and Its Trend in Canada." M.A. Thesis, University of Ottawa, 1938.

Rhodes, D. Berkeley. "The Toronto Star and the New Radicalism, 1917-1926." M.A. Thesis, University of Toronto, 1955.

Rowland, Douglas Charles. "Canadian Communism: The Post-Stalinist Phase." M.A. Thesis, University of Manitoba, 1964.

Stuart, Richard Grey. "The Early Political Career of Angus MacInnis." M.A. Thesis, University of British Columbia, 1970.

Troop, G. R. F. "Socialism in Canada." M.A. Thesis, McGill University, 1922.

Van Loon, Richard J. "The Political Thought of the United Farmers of Ontario." M.A. Thesis, Carleton University, 1965.

Watt, Frank William. "Radicalism in English-Canadian Literature since Confederation." Ph.D. Thesis, University of Toronto, 1957.

INDEX